RACECRAFT

KAREN E. FIELDS is Distinguished Visiting Scholar at the Center for African and African American Research at Duke University. Her books include a translation of Emile Durkheim's *Elementary Forms of Religious Life*. She is at work on *Racism in the Academy: A Traveler's Guide* and *Bordeaux's Africa*.

BARBARA J. FIELDS is Professor of History at Columbia University. Her books include the prize-winning *Slavery and Freedom on the Middle Ground: Maryland During the Nineteenth Century*; *The Destruction of Slavery* (coauthored with the Freedmen and Southern Society Project); and *Free at Last: A Documentary History of Slavery, Freedom, and the Civil War*.

RACECRAFT

The Soul of Inequality in American Life

KAREN E. FIELDS AND BARBARA J. FIELDS

VERSO
London • New York

This paperback edition published by Verso 2022
First published by Verso 2012
© Barbara J. Fields and Karen E. Fields 2012, 2014, 2022

1 3 5 7 9 10 8 6 4 2

Verso
UK: 6 Meard Street, London W1F 0EG
US: 20 Jay Street, Suite 1010, Brooklyn, NY 11201
www.versobooks.com

Verso is the imprint of New Left Books

ISBN-13: 978-1-83976-564-3 (PBK)
eISBN-13: 978-1-84467-995-9 (US)
eISBN-13: 978-1-78168-438-2 (UK)

British Library Cataloguing in Publication Data
A catalogue record for this book is available from the British Library

Library of Congress Cataloging-in-Publication Data
A catalog record for this book is available from the Library of Congress

Typeset in Fournier by MJ Gavan, Truro, Cornwall
Printed and bound by CPI Group (UK) Ltd, Croydon, CR0 4YY

As teachers ourselves, we dedicate this book to our teachers, who gave us the tools for the task we here set ourselves and who helped us refine our techniques for using them:

Egon Bittner, 1921–2011
C. Vann Woodward, 1908–1999

Contents

Authors' Note

Some readers may be puzzled to see the expression *Afro-American* used frequently in these pages, *African-American* being more common these days. We do not take a dogmatic view on such terminological questions, preferring the approach of our grandmother, who used all but two of the terms that prevailed in her day (she died in 1987, just short of ninety-nine): Colored, Negro, Afro-American, and black. She used the term *nigger* and its close South Carolina cognate *nigra* only when quoting others with disapproval. Although we leave our fellow citizens to their own choice, we prefer *Afro-American*. We prefer it because it is time-honored, having deep roots in the literary life of American English. Moreover, it leaves room for useful distinctions. Karen's husband Moussa Bagate, a naturalized American citizen born in Ivory Coast, is an African-American. Barack Obama, the child of a Kenyan father and a Euro-American mother, is an African-American. Karen and I, like Michelle Obama, are Afro-Americans. Like the Obamas' daughters, Karen's daughter Maïmouna is the child of an African-American and an Afro-American. She may choose whichever term she likes.

The Introduction, Chapters 1, 2, and the Conclusion are published here for the first time. Chapters 3 through 8 are republished with minor changes. Details of original publication are given in notes at the beginning of each chapter.

Introduction

In the beginning was the deed.

Ludwig Wittgenstein quoting Goethe
misquoting John the Apostle

The Idols of the Tribe have their foundation in human nature itself, and in the tribe or race of men.

Francis Bacon

"Race" is the witchcraft of our time.

M. F. Ashley Montagu

During the 2008 presidential election campaign, hardly a week passed without a reference to America's "post-racial" society, which the election of Barack Obama supposedly would establish. If anyone really was imagining such a thing as a post-racial America, what that might be was hard to pin down. Right through the campaign, references to "race" and the "race card" kept jostling the "post" in "post-racial." When insinuations about Obama's supposed foreignness cropped up, one journalist called that "the *new* race card."[1] In fact, it is among the oldest and most durable. Pronouncing native-born Americans of African descent to be aliens goes as far back as Thomas Jefferson and the other founders. More than a century later, D. W. Griffith's *Birth of a Nation* launched American cinema with

---

1   Peter Beinart, "Is He American Enough?" *Time*, October 20, 2008, 56.

the same pronouncement in its opening sequence.² And, a few days after the 2008 vote, suits filed in Pennsylvania and New Jersey to overturn President Obama's election denied his American birth in order to deny his citizenship. Far from holding mere playing cards in their hands, those who brought suit had historical bedrock under their feet, and a ready-made place in national discourse.³ How and why a handful of racist notions have gained permanent sustenance in American life is the subject of this book.

Other supposedly new notions are just as old and as deeply embedded. Today's talk of "biracial" or "multiracial" people rehabilitates *mulatto, quadroon, octoroon*, and the like—yesterday's terms for mixed ancestry.⁴ Although they now reemerge in the costume of post-racial progressiveness, not to say a move toward "an ideal future of racelessness,"⁵ their origins are racist. *Mulatto* made its first appearance on the US census in 1850, after two theorists, Josiah Nott, a physician, and James De Bow, a political economist, decided to classify and count individuals with one parent of African and one of European descent.⁶ Today's lobby-

2   In the same vein, a 2002 sociological study counts the intermarriage of Caribbean immigrants with white Americans, but not with black Americans, as evidence of assimilation. See Chapter 3, below.

3   Howard Fineman, "Playing With Fire," *Newsweek online*, July 28, 2009; *Richmond Times-Dispatch*, AP, "Suit Questioning Obama's Eligibility Rejected," December 9, 2008. A Georgia native of the president's age told an interviewer that "if you had real change it would involve all the members of Obama's church being deported." Quoted in Jesse Washington, "Race Crimes Around the Country Spurred by Obama's Win," www.huffingtonpost.com, November 16, 2008.

4   United States Bureau of the Census, *The Census: A Social History* (Washington, DC: USBC, 2002), 11.

5   Quoted in Kim M. Williams, *Mark One or More: Civil Rights in Multiracial America* (Ann Arbor, MI: University of Michigan Press, 2006), 1.

6   Nott's medical practice included slaves. De Bow held the chair of political economy at the University of Louisiana at New Orleans. See Williams, *Mark One or More*, 23; Reginald Horsman, *Josiah Nott of Mobile: Southerner, Physician, and Racial Theorist* (Baton Rouge, LA: Louisiana State University Press, 1987).

ing for a new census classification, called *multiracial*, defines it the same way, "someone with two monoracial parents."[7] Does it matter that these citizen rejuvenators of obsolete racist categories cannot reasonably share the agenda of their predecessors—to validate the folk theory that mixed offspring are degenerate in mind and body?[8] Today, some parents passionately seek a state-sponsored classification as a means of protecting their own children from feelings that enter all American children's minds via toxic drip. "Self-esteem is directly tied to accurate racial identity," said one mother.[9] Whatever she thought she was saying about mixed ancestry and mental health, the very phrase *accurate racial identity* ought to set off sirens. Dangerous lies do not always dress the part.

Where but in recycled racist fiction are "monoracial" parents to be found to serve as guarantors of "accurate racial identity"? The least one can say is that the fiction misrepresents the American experience. According to an estimate derived from decades of census reports, some 24 percent of Americans listed in 1970 as "white" probably had African ancestors, while more than 80 percent of those listed as "black" had non-African ones, which implies that there were nearly twice as many white as black Americans of African descent.[10] Thomas Jefferson's descendants fit both descriptions.[11]

---

7   Williams, *Mark One or More*, 44.

8   This speculation, retailed as science, advanced the career of Dr. Nott, who wrote De Bow that "my nigger hallucinations have given me more notoriety than I had any idea of." De Bow once asked his friend to "do a lecture for me on niggerology." Horsman, *Josiah Nott of Mobile*, 101, 109. In *Types of Mankind* (1854), Nott inferred degeneration from his definition of black and white Americans as separately evolved biological species (ibid., 102, 170, 270). On American theories of "mongrelization," see Edwin Black, *War Against the Weak: Eugenics and America's Campaign to Create a Master Race* (New York: Thunder's Mouth Press, 2003), 159–82.

9   Susan Graham, national director of Project RACE, quoted in Williams, *Mark One or More*, 43.

10   Stephan Palmié, "Genomics, Divination, 'Racecraft'," *American Ethnologist* 34:2 (May 2007), 206.

11   In 1873, Madison Hemings, the son of Sally Hemings and Thomas

But misrepresentation is not all. While redacting America's real history, the fiction revives an old fallacy: the move, by definition, from the concept "mixture" to the false inference that unmixed components exist, which cannot be disproved by observation and experience because it does not arise from them.[12] In the twentieth century, that logic had hideous real-world consequences. In the comparative innocence of the nineteenth, the same logic aligned itself with a zeal for measurement, and percentages of mixture between (theoretically) unmixed individuals beckoned as avenues of further investigation. In due course, the Census Bureau experimented with the classifications *quadroon* and *octoroon* (respectively, an individual with a black grandparent or a black great-grandparent). Some states enacted laws to prevent people with African ancestry from "passing" as white, and set up genealogical research procedures to detect violators.[13] In sum, restoring notions of race mixture to center stage recommits us, willy-nilly, to the discredited idea of racial purity, the basic premise of bio-racism.

The latter, meanwhile, is neither gone nor forgotten. "Bio-racism" is a more precise appellation for the nineteenth-century research just sketched than the more usual term, "race science." For all the measuring and experimenting that research inspired, it failed as science.[14] Modern genetics began afresh, and on a basis so

Jefferson, told an interviewer that his brother Beverly "went to Washington as a white man." John W. Blassingame, ed., *Slave Testimony* (Baton Rouge, LA: University of Louisiana Press, 1977), 474–80. See also Annette Gordon-Reed, *Thomas Jefferson and Sally Hemings* (Charlottesville, VA: University of Virginia Press, 1997), and *The Hemingses of Monticello: An American Family* (New York: Norton, 2008).

12   We take instruction from A. J. Ayer, *Language, Truth, and Logic* (New York: Dover, 1946 [1956], 78–9.

13   Black, *War Against the Weak*, 163–6. Findings by John H. Burma, "The Measurement of Negro Passing," *American Journal of Sociology* 52:1 (July 1946), 18–22, raised a stir when they appeared in *Collier's* magazine, and were followed by E. W. Eckhard's "How Many Negroes 'Pass'?" in the same journal, 52:6 (May 1947), 498–500.

14   Foundational work toward something new includes Julian Huxley and

different as, perhaps, to deserve labeling *non-racial*. *Race* in today's biology is not a traditionally named group of people but a statistically defined population: "the difference in frequency of alleles between populations (contiguous and interbreeding groups) of the same species."[15] Unlike the units of bio-racism, these populations are not held to be visible to the naked eye, or knowable in advance of disciplined investigation. So the news is not good when scientists studying the human genome—adept in some of the twenty-first century's most sophisticated research techniques—hark back to the old notion, yoking those techniques to a system of classifying people that is steeped in folk thought.[16] They have a choice in the matter. Today's probabilistic methods and molecular-biological evidence by no means compel resort to the folk system. Indeed, they would seem to be incompatible with it.[17] Therefore, if the scientific logic is indeed non-racial, the folk classification ought to wither under its influence. To adhere to both old and new is to pick up and put down modern science with shameless promiscuity.

However, such picking up and putting down has its defenders, sometimes offering defenses so remarkable as to justify this book's new coinage, "racecraft." That term highlights the ability of pre- or

A. C. Haddon, *We Europeans* (1936), M. F. Ashley Montagu, *Man's Most Dangerous Myth: The Fallacy of Race* (1942), William C. Boyd, *Genetics and the Races of Man* (1950), and Frank B. Livingstone, "On the Non-existence of Human Races" (1962).

15 Anthony Griffiths et al., *Introduction to Genetics, Ninth Edition* (New York: W. H. Freeman and Co., 2008), 206.

16 See Troy Duster, "Buried Alive: The Concept of Race in Science," in Alan H. Goodman, Deborah Heath, and M. Susan Lindee, eds., *Genetic Nature/Culture: Anthropology and Science Beyond the Two-Culture Divide* (Berkeley, CA: University of California Press, 2003), 258–77.

17 Troy Duster writes that when scientists are asked to do their work with already categorized samples, they "are necessarily 'buying in' to a taxonomic system that has little to do with a molecular geneticist's professional training or expertise…" In "Lessons from History: Why Race and Ethnicity Have Played a Major Role in Biomedical Research," *The Journal of Law, Medicine & Ethics* 34:3 (Fall 2006), 487–96, esp. 488.

non-scientific modes of thought to hijack the minds of the scientifically literate. Here, an anthropologist defends the traditional folk
classification: "After all, genetics has added very little to what scientists, or indeed any observant people, have known for centuries
about human groups ... Modern genetics can be a bit more techni-
cally specific, *but the basic truths are not new.*"[18] The anthropologist
proceeds to justify, on grounds of data-processing convenience,
the routine use of "[subjects'] 'race' as categorical (check-box)
variables in studies ... to identify epidemiological risk factors."[19]
Notice that, even where properly genetic risk factors exist, no part
of the procedure, as described, prevents the subject's "race" from
being taken, before the fact, to "explain" whatever is found after
the fact. A psychologist has noted the "garbage in/garbage out"
circularity of "elegant experimental designs and statistical analyses applied to biologically meaningless racial categories."[20] The
check-box method reduces "genetics" to a matter of querying, or
simply glancing at, the research subject. If "looks-like" genetics
and "says-so" genomics are respectable tools, what, indeed, could
modern science add to popular belief?

Fortunately, not all American scientists choose to yoke their
technological racehorse to the centuries-old oxcart. J. Craig
Venter, whose imagination accelerated to warp speed the race to
map the human genome, reflected on his work autobiographically
in *A Life Decoded.*[21] In his depiction, mapping the human genome
revealed nature's real world of irremediably diverse individuality
—Venter's own (the first genome ever to be posted online) as
well as everyone else's.[22] Nature's world of diverse individuality

18   Kenneth Weiss, "On Babies and Bathwater," *American Ethnologist* 34:2
(May 2007), 242. Our italics.

19   Ibid., 243.

20   Jefferson M. Fish, "Mixed Blood: An Analytical Look at Methods of
Classifying Race," *Psychology Today*, November 1, 1995.

21   J. Craig Venter, *A Life Decoded: My Genome, My Life* (New York:
Viking, 2001).

22   Thus, in contrast to the anti-individualism of "racial medicine" that

is precisely *not* one that "observant people have known about" for centuries. Rather, that world stands open to fresh discoveries about nature in the make-up of human beings. Venter links his own susceptibility to asthma to probable genetic determinants that he shares with various statistical populations of Americans. Presented in a series of insets, his own particulars disclose enormous complexity. *Not* "known for centuries," for instance, is the family of enzymes glutathione S-transferase (GST), variants of which, found on chromosomes 1 and 11, are believed to affect individuals' allergic response to diesel exhaust particles. Other sites also seem to be involved; Venter's own combination may be "read," and the "reading" suggests why he must reach for an inhaler on a foggy San Francisco day.[23]

Venter's way of introducing new science to a lay public seems more in accord with the ingrained individualism that so impressed early visitors to America, like Alexis de Tocqueville in the 1830s, than with the ingrained anti-individualism that the very word "gene" evokes for many today.[24] Venter makes few concessions to that anti-individualism, whatever phase of his work or life he is recounting; and race has no entry in his book's index. When questions arose about his decision to take his private[25] Human Genome Project's five samples from individuals who differed by what Americans call race, he replied that the point was to "help

---

captured headlines a few years ago (when the Food and Drug Administration allowed two old drugs to be re-patented together as supposedly "race-specific" Bidil), some research geneticists are now pursuing the ultimate individualism in their search for the cause of disease: sequencing the individual patient's genome. Nicholas Wade, "Disease Cause Is Pinpointed With Genome," *New York Times*, March 11, 2010, A1.

23   Venter, *A Life Decoded*, 79.

24   Alexis de Tocqueville, *Democracy in America, Vols. 1&2*, trans. Henry Reeve, with an Introduction by Joseph Epstein (New York: Bantam, 2000), 383–440.

25   Venter left the public Human Genome Project, at the National Institutes of Health, to create a private one at the Celera Corporation.

illustrate that the concept of race has no genetic or scientific basis; and that there is no way to tell one ethnicity from another in the five Celera genomes"[26]—surely a caution against the widespread habit of treating "race" and "genetics" as though they were interchangeable terms. Later, he told a BBC interviewer that "skin colour as a surrogate for race is a social concept, not a scientific one."[27]

Venter was surely mistaken, however, when he suggested that "greater scientific literacy" might help combat (altogether predictable) discrimination in the use of genomics.[28] That bit of naive catechism glares amid the sophistication of the book as a whole. Few can claim greater scientific literacy than James D. Watson, a Nobel laureate for his work on DNA and founding director of the public Human Genome Project. Yet remarks he made to interviewers during his 2007 book-promotion trip to London owed less to that scientific literacy than to the racist certainties in which many Chicagoans of his generation were reared.[29] Pronouncing himself "inherently gloomy about the prospects of Africa," Watson said that "all our social policies are based on the fact that their intelligence is the same as ours—whereas testing says not really." Indeed, in his view, reason is not properly regarded as "some universal heritage of humanity." For evidence, however, the man of science resorted to personal impressions, haphazardly collected: "People who have to deal with black employees find this is not true." From his digest of anecdotes, he went on to prophesy that genetic evidence for black people's lesser intelligence would emerge within a decade.[30]

---

26 Venter, *Life Decoded*, 317.
27 BBC News, "Lab Suspends Pioneer Watson," October 19, 2007, http://news.bbc.co.uk.
28 Venter, *Life Decoded*, 317.
29 Born April 6, 1928, he belonged to the same generation as Martin Luther King, Jr. (born January 15, 1929). Both were in their late thirties when, on August 5, 1966, Chicago residents attacked King and other marchers with such violence that the SCLC abandoned its campaign against segregation in the North.
30 Helen Nugent, "Black People 'Less Intelligent' Scientist Claims,"

But a statement does not acquire validity because a duly ordained scientist utters it. The sirens went off immediately. Certain of Watson's fellow molecular biologists took the floor with a scientifically correct formulation: It was "not possible to draw such conclusions from the work that has been done on DNA." Dr. Venter, who happened to be traveling in the United Kingdom at the same time, said, "There is no basis in scientific fact or in the human genetic code for the notion that skin colour will be predictive of intelligence."[31] For his part, Watson did not defend himself by citing his own scientific work to date or anyone else's. Reporters later observed that he at first denied what he had said, and seemed stunned. Perhaps a pre-scientific layer of his mind had taken over momentarily.[32]

Not all who piled onto Dr. Watson can claim to differ fundamentally from him. Shortly after he published his own genome online, scientists at Iceland's deCode Genetics startled the world with a revelation. Watson had "16 times more genes of black origin than the average white European—16 percent rather than the 1 percent that most of his origin" would have. "This level is what you would expect in someone who had a great-grandparent who was African."[33] In other words, Dr. Watson is someone whom

www.timesonline.co.uk, October 17, 2010. As quoted in the *Independent* (October 17, 2007), Watson's book affirmed that "there is no reason to anticipate that the intellectual capacities of peoples geographically separated in their evolution should prove to have evolved identically. Our wanting to reserve equal powers of reason as some universal heritage of humanity will not be enough to make it so." He is apparently a twenty-first-century adherent of the American theory of "polygenism," promoted in the nineteenth century by Josiah Nott and Harvard's Louis Agassiz.

31 BBC News, "Lab Suspends Pioneer Watson."

32 By contrast, while Venter's individual intelligence lights his book, he offers no generalities about it; and, like race, intelligence does not appear in his index, thereby imposing the complexity of the whole book upon simplifying and selective readers.

33 Robert Verkaik, "Revealed: Scientist Who Sparked Racism Row has Black Genes," *Independent*, December 10, 2007.

nineteenth-century census takers would have classified as an *octoroon* if they had been able to see behind appearance. In those days, a technology able to expose "genes of black" origin (expressed in percentages, no less) would have appealed to people who yearned for a sure-fire way to know an octoroon when you could not know by looking. Watson's comeuppance, so deliciously prompt upon the sin, occasioned so much laughter that it is easy to miss the unhappy fact that deCode Genetics' researchers themselves yoked the new technology to the uses of yore.[34]

As if all that were not enough, now comes a techno-fad that purports to determine the so-called tribal origins of Afro-Americans with the help of Personal Genetic Histories (PGHs).[35] The same method and logic might equally have revealed Dr. Watson's African tribal origins to the world.[36] Anyone who is committed to thinking of tribes as objectively occurring biological phenomena cannot think differently about bio-racists' races.[37] What an irony, then, if the World War II defeat of the Nazis did indeed discredit race science, only to have the yearning for "identity" and the jaw swabs of Afro-American bio-genealogists abet its revival. Whatever the "post" may mean in "post-racial," it cannot mean that racism belongs to the past. Post-racial turns out to be—simply—racial; which is to say, racist.

34 William Faulkner's *Light in August* (Norwalk, CT: Easton Press, 1992 [1932], 344, 346, 350) circles the troubled terrain of those uses of yore. The ambiguity of Joe Christmas, the "white nigger that did that killing up at Jefferson last week," maddens the townspeople. "He dont look no more like a nigger than I do," one declares. And another: "He never acted like either a nigger or a white man ... That was what made the folks so mad ... It was like he never even knew he was a murderer, let alone a nigger, too."

35 Stephan Palmié provides an astute analysis in "Genomics, Divination, 'Racecraft,'" 207.

36 The late Jack Temple Kirby wrote a dead-serious yet uproarious account of his own tribal genealogical investigations, based on historical documents, in "ANCESTRYdotBOMB: Genealogy, Genomics, Mischief, Mystery, and Southern Family Stories," *Journal of Southern History* 76 (February 2010), 3–38.

37 Palmié, "Genomics, Divination, 'Racecraft,'" 206.

Something is afoot that is the business of every citizen who thought that the racist concepts of a century ago were gone—and good riddance!—as a result of the Civil Rights Movement. The continued vitality of those concepts stands as a reminder that, however important a historical watershed the election of an African-American president may be, America's post-racial era has not been born. Perhaps it can be made if America lets those concepts go. But if they are hard to let go, why is that? What are they made of? How do they work? And what work do they do? Those are our subjects in the coming chapters. For now, we sketch our answers briefly and bluntly, so as not to preempt the essays to come. One general point must be made at the outset, however, and with an important caveat: Racist concepts do considerable work in political and economic life; *but*, if they were merely an appendage of politics and economics, without intimate roots in other phases of life, their persuasiveness would accordingly diminish.

From very early on, Americans wove racist concepts into a public language about inequality that made "black" the virtual equivalent of "poor" and "lower class," thus creating a distinctive idiom that has no parallel in other Western democracies. The French Revolution assigned universal validity to the slogan *Liberté! Egalité! Fraternité!* By contrast, America's rendering of the same sentiments added asterisks, for it had to make sense of an anomalous reality: the presence of native-born people who were "foreign," hardworking people who were not free. When Tocqueville sought to convey to French readers the racist prejudice he found in the United States, North and South—a signal exception to the enthusiasm for equality that he duly noted—he wrote that he could draw no direct comparison from French experience. Instead he proposed as an "analogy" the gut-level physical repugnance aristocrats felt toward their equally white, but unequally born, compatriots.[38] In that tiny vignette of white-on-white struggles in France lay the

38 Tocqueville, *Democracy in America*, 414.

kernel of a legitimate public language to come, in which the French might tackle class inequality in straightforward terms. In America, straightforward talk about class inequality is all but impossible, indeed taboo. Political appeals to the economic self-interest of ordinary voters, as distinct from their wealthy compatriots, court instant branding and disfigurement in the press as divisive "economic populism" or even "class warfare."[39] On the other hand, divisive political appeals composed in a different register, sometimes called "cultural populism," enlist voters' self-concept in place of their self-interest; appealing, in other words, to who they are and are not, rather than to what they require and why. Thus, the policies of the 1980s radically redistributed income upward. Then, with "economic populism" shooed from the public arena, "cultural populism" fielded something akin to a marching band. It had a simple melody about the need to enrich the "investing" classes (said to "create jobs"), and an encoded percussion: "culture wars"; "welfare mothers"; "underclass"; "race-and-IQ"; "black-on-black crime"; "criminal gene"; on and on.[40] Halfway through the decade, as the band played on, a huge economic revolution from above had got well under way. The poorest 40 percent of American families were sharing 15.5 percent of household income, while the share of the richest 20 percent of families had risen to a record 43.7 percent, and the trend appeared to be (and has turned out to be) more and more of the same.[41]

39   Howell Raines, "Winning the Populism PR War," *Washington Post*, online edition, July 27, 2004. On the salience of this theme in 2011, see Paul Krugman, "Panic of the Plutocrats," *New York Times*, October 10, 2011, A23.

40   Its predecessor in the 1890s, the so-called Gilded Age, marched with two varieties of racism, one directed against Afro-Americans, and the other against immigrants from eastern and southern Europe. Aiming to eliminate "the unfit," bio-racism supported both varieties, and, besides, a eugenics program against the white poor. See Black, *War Against the Weak*, 413–19.

41   Derrick Bell, "After We're Gone: Prudent Speculations on America in a Post-Racial Epoch," *St. Louis University Law Journal* 34 (1990), reprint, 6. The US census first tracked such figures in 1947. Today's figures, according to David

The late Derrick Bell seems to have coined the phrase "post-racial." In his 1990 essay, "After We're Gone: Prudent Speculations on America in a Post-Racial Epoch," he intended not to gesture at a vague future state, but to examine the relationship between two developments of the 1980s: the need to manage politically the radical redistribution of income toward the well-to-do and the suffocation of public sentiment favorable to civil rights.[42] Bell used allegory. Space Traders arrive with a proposal for America's deciders. They will sell America a proven technology for producing unlimited wealth and will buy in return every living Afro-American. Their deal poses constitutional and moral problems, obviously, but also a practical one. The practical problem is not whether to accept the deal (which is inevitable) but how to couch, stage-manage, and spin it. Bell portrays the ensuing National Conversation with hilarious fidelity to its real-world models. In taking the deal, however, the deciders overlook a fundamental problem. The traditional political language will become obsolete the instant the ships lift off. What then? The curtain falls, and bits and pieces are heard as post-racial America confronts—straightforwardly, for the first time—the problem of who gets what part of the nation's wealth, and why.

Strange though it may seem, *The Bell Curve: Intelligence and Class Structure in American Life* (1994) by Richard Herrnstein and Charles Murray, provided a coda to Bell's article "After We're Gone" (1990). Contrary to its strenuously promoted race-and-IQ public identity, *The Bell Curve* is far more centrally a class-and-IQ book, a story about a society that no longer rewards hard work by the "not very smart." Furthermore, the authors, like Bell, not only cite the top-heavy income distribution; they also begin where he does, with many white Americans faring badly. Where Bell sees

---

Johnson ("Income Gap: Is It Widening?" The Official Blog of the US Census Bureau, September 15, 2011) are 11.8 and 50.2 percent, respectively.

42   Ellis Cose recorded the testimony of accomplished Afro-Americans about the closing of doors, in *The Rage of a Privileged Class: Why Do Prosperous Blacks Still Have the Blues?* (New York: HarperCollins, 1993).

"politics," however, they see "nature," with born winners and losers, not tilted playing fields or policies with intended outcomes. They conclude, therefore, from the same statistics as Bell's, that a "*cognitive* elite has pulled away from the rest of the population economically, becoming more prosperous even as real wages in the rest of the economy stagnated or fell."[43] If smart people are gaining ground by virtue of their IQ, hardworking others are losing ground by virtue of theirs. Who now remembers this principal story of *The Bell Curve?* In the time it takes to say "racecraft," growing class inequality, the shared theme of their work and Bell's, became inaudible, despite its prominence in a very long book.

Furthermore, if the main story went unheard, the reason is not that the authors spoke softly. A year before publication, Charles Murray contributed a raise-the-alarm piece to the *Wall Street Journal* about "the coming white underclass." Burdened with unemployment, illegitimacy, jail—in short, telltale exudations of class in America, not race—Murray's white underclass was identical to its black counterpart.[44] What is more, Murray and Herrnstein made no bones about their scientifico-ideological agenda, to counteract the "perversions of the egalitarian ideal that beg[a]n with the French Revolution."[45] Indeed, *The Bell Curve* opens with a quotation by Edmund Burke, a fierce detractor of that revolution, who made no bones about upholding the very same "natural" distinctions that Tocqueville the aristocrat deployed as an analogy to American racism. Imagine the fallout if the media had aired then, in a National Conversation about Class, the truly controversial views of these two authors. Indeed, what might happen today if neoconservatives addressed hardworking, moral, marrying (and,

43 Richard Herrnstein and Charles Murray, *The Bell Curve: Intelligence and Class Structure in American Life* (New York: Free Press, 1994), 538 (our emphasis).

44 Charles Murray, "The Coming White Underclass," *Wall Street Journal*, October 29, 1993. His new book continues in this vein. See *Coming Apart: The State of White America, 1960–2010* (New York: Crown Forum, 2012).

45 Herrnstein and Murray, *Bell Curve*, 534.

until recently, respectably employed) Americans with the authors' lodestar belief? The good society promotes "contentment," say they, simply by having "a place for everyone," even for those who "aren't very smart"—indeed, "a valued place." To explain what that place might be, they offer a "pragmatic definition" at once serene and ruthless: "*You occupy a valued place* (their italics) *if other people would miss you when you were gone.*"[46] In their version of America's future, the raised voices that Bell imagined are to hold their peace.

Perhaps the economic turmoil that lent resonance to Barack Obama's call for change may itself provide an opening toward better things than that. The debacle of the bankers rubbed the gloss from the justifications for inequality that prevailed in the 1980s. Americans of all colors now have good evidence that "genetic" testing back then for the "criminal gene" missed a bet by taking samples only among the incarcerated, while ignoring well-heeled virtuosos of thievery. Besides, Americans have taken a good look at incompetence rewarded with outsize pay and perks, while ordinary workers' day in, day out competence has failed even to protect their jobs. The image of CEOs gliding into Washington in silver jets, hands outstretched for taxpayers' money, has disrupted the old icons. The "welfare mother" can no longer stand for what is not right with America.

The authors have been living through recent events as Afro-Americans of Southern origin and as American citizens. But it is in another capacity—as teachers whose students are of all colors and origins—that we present these chapters. They begin with a guided tour of racecraft, followed by a joint essay in which we highlight common metaphors, such as the so-called racial divide, that becloud and misdirect thought. Three chapters examine America's past while testing the lenses (sometimes poorly ground) through which historians today try to "see" what happened in the

46   Ibid., 535.

past and understand why and with what lasting consequences. Another revisits a classic by the great anthropologist E. E. Evans-Pritchard, who showed how witch beliefs could be held by rational people. The last is an imaginary conversation between two great sociologists, Emile Durkheim and W. E. B. Du Bois, whose different national histories, French and American, confronted them with similar predicaments. The conclusion synthesizes what the preceding essays show about the intimate interaction between racecraft and inequality in American life. Throughout, we strive to think rigorously about the world of experience that Americans designate by the shorthand, *race*.

That very shorthand is our abiding target because it confuses three different things: race, racism, and racecraft. The term *race* stands for the conception or the doctrine that nature produced humankind in distinct groups, each defined by inborn traits that its members share and that differentiate them from the members of other distinct groups of the same kind but of unequal rank.[47] For example, *The Races of Europe*, published in 1899 to wide acclaim and lasting influence, set out to establish scientifically the distinctness of the "Teutonic," "Alpine," and "Mediterranean" races. After compiling tens of thousands of published measurements (of stature, shape of head and nose, coloring of skin, hair, and eyes, and more), the author, William Z. Ripley, had more than enough quantitative evidence to work with—indeed, far too much. A "taxonomic nightmare"[48] loomed up and forced on him a certain flexibility of method: shifting criteria as needed, ignoring unruly instances, and employing ad hoc helpers like the "Index of Nigrescence" (to handle the variable coloring of persons indigenous to the British Isles). Fitting actual humans to any such grid inevitably calls forth the busy repertoire of strange maneuvering

---

47 K. Anthony Appiah, *In My Father's House: Africa in the Philosophy of Culture* (New York: Oxford University Press, 1992), 13.

48 The fine phrase and analysis are drawn from Nell Irvin Painter, *The History of White People* (New York: Norton, 2010), 212–27.

that is part of what we call *racecraft*. The nineteenth-century bio-racists' ultimately vain search for traits with which to demarcate human groups regularly exhibited such maneuvering.[49] *Race* is the principal unit and core concept of *racism*.

Racism refers to the theory and the practice of applying a social, civic, or legal double standard based on ancestry, and to the ideology surrounding such a double standard. That may be what the economist Glenn Loury intends when he identifies "a withholding of the presumption of equal humanity."[50] *Racism* is not an emotion or state of mind, such as intolerance, bigotry, hatred, or malevolence. If it were that, it would easily be overwhelmed; most people mean well, most of the time, and in any case are usually busy pursuing other purposes. *Racism* is first and foremost a social practice, which means that it is an action and a rationale for action, or both at once. *Racism* always takes for granted the objective reality of *race*, as just defined, so it is important to register their distinctness. The shorthand transforms *racism*, something an aggressor *does*, into *race*, something the target *is*, in a sleight of hand that is easy to miss. Consider the statement "black Southerners were segregated because of their skin color"—a perfectly natural sentence to the ears of most Americans, who tend to overlook its weird causality. But in that sentence, segregation disappears as the doing of segregationists, and then, in a puff of smoke—*paff*—reappears as a trait of only one part of the segregated whole. In similar fashion, enslavers disappear only to reappear, disguised, in stories that append physical traits defined as slave-like to those enslaved.[51]

---

49   That maneuvering, as applied to intelligence, is nowhere dissected better, or with greater concision and elegance of expression, than in Stephen Jay Gould's *The Mismeasure of Man* (New York: Norton, 1981), 62–175.

50   Glenn Loury, *The Anatomy of Racial Inequality* (Cambridge, MA: Harvard University Press, 2002), 88.

51   Thus, in 1962, the Harvard anthropologist Carlton S. Coon found in the skulls of Afro-Americans a supposedly child-like trait: the "bulbous forehead," a trait formerly held to bespeak superiority. Gould, *Mismeasure of Man*, 132–35, 149–51.

Jefferson became so entangled in the reversals as to declare that the very people white Americans had lived with for over 160 years as slaves would be, after emancipation, too different for white people to live with any longer. He proposed that slaves be freed and promptly deported, their lost labor to be supplied through the importation of white laborers.[52] His catalogue of differences went from skin color (they do not blush) and internal organs ("They secrete less by the kidnies"), to intellect ("In imagination, they are dull, tasteless, and anomalous") and even emotion ("Their griefs are transient," he asserted without irony). Even so, as a man of science, Jefferson qualified: "I advance it therefore as a suspicion only that the blacks, whether originally a distinct race, or made distinct by time and circumstances, are inferior to the whites in the endowments both of body and mind."[53] He thus recognized the oddity of his position—even if intermittently, through the off-and-on blinking of racecraft.[54]

Distinct from *race* and *racism*, *racecraft* does not refer to groups or to ideas about groups' traits, however odd both may appear in close-up. It refers instead to mental terrain and to pervasive belief. Like physical terrain, racecraft exists objectively; it has topographical features that Americans regularly navigate, and we cannot readily stop traversing it. Unlike physical terrain, racecraft originates not in nature but in human action and imagination; it can exist in no other way.[55] The action and imagining are collective

52   Thomas Jefferson, *Notes on the State of Virginia*, in *Writings* (New York: Library of America, 1984 [orig. ed. 1787]), 264–5.

53   Jefferson, *Notes*, 270.

54   He contradicted himself four queries after the one he was answering when he laid out the differences that supposedly required deportation (see Chapter 3, below, and Jefferson, *Writings*, Query 18, 162–3). Answering a critic who had disputed his arguments, he admitted that, even if the Negroes' inferiority could be proved, it would not justify their enslavement. Thomas Jefferson to Henri Grégoire, February 25, 1809, in ibid., 1202.

55   Such artifacts are independent of subjective belief. See Karen E. Fields, "Political Contingencies of Witchcraft," *Canadian Journal of African Studies*

yet individual, day-to-day yet historical, and consequential even though nested in mundane routine. The action and imagining emerge as part of moment-to-moment practicality, that is, thinking about and executing every purpose under the sun. Do not look for racecraft, therefore, only where it might be said to "belong."[56] Finally, *racecraft* is not a euphemistic substitute for *racism*. It is a kind of fingerprint evidence that *racism* has been on the scene.

Our term racecraft invokes witchcraft, though not for the reason that may come first to mind. We regard neither witchcraft nor racecraft as "just mischievous superstition, nothing more," a position Loury has rightly dismissed as of little interest.[57] Far from denying the rationality of those who have accepted either belief as truth about the world, we assume it. We are interested in the processes of reasoning that manage to make both plausible. Witchcraft and racecraft are imagined, acted upon, and re-imagined, the action and imagining inextricably intertwined.[58] The outcome is a belief that "presents itself to the mind and imagination as a vivid truth." So wrote W. E. H. Lecky, a British scholar of Europe's past who, looking back from the nineteenth century, tried to understand how very smart people managed for a very long time to believe in witchcraft. He warned that it takes "a strong effort of the imagination ... [to] realise the position of the defenders of the belief."[59] To

---

16:3 (December 1992), 567–93, esp. 586.

56 For an ethnographer's exploration in a particular milieu, see Karen E. Fields, *Racecraft in the American Academy*, in progress.

57 Loury, *Anatomy of Racial Inequality*, 21–2.

58 Some readers may recall Benedict Anderson's *Imagined Communities* (London: Verso, 1991), about the invention of new nations. In our view, all human communities are imagined, not excluding those thought of as "natural"— like the Biblical families that reckon descent through men only. See Nancy Jay, *Throughout Your Generations Forever: Sacrifice, Religion, and Paternity* (Chicago: University of Chicago Press, 1992), esp. 17–40.

59 W. E. H. Lecky, *History of the Rise and Influence of the Spirit of Rationalism in Europe*, with an Introduction by C. Wright Mills (New York: George Braziller, 1955 [1982]), 38.

"realise," in his sense, is to picture a bygone real world of normally
constituted people who accepted, as obviously true, notions that
the real world of one's own present dismisses as obviously false.
What if we Americans applied that "strong effort" to our present?
Only if we imagined racecraft as a thing in itself worth scrutiny
might we imagine ourselves outside or beyond the belief. It is
impossible to understand what "post-racial" might be without first
understanding more profoundly than we do at present just what
"racial" is.

Of course, it is easier to see the movement between imagining and
doing, re-imagining and redoing, when it is they who are doing it
rather than ourselves. Distance can magnify. The "they" in Europe
who believed in witchcraft includes great reformers like Martin
Luther, whose wit and logic against the superstition he abhorred
crackle on the page.[60] Yet Luther not only made witchcraft accusations but also repeatedly emerged, physically exhausted, from his
own wrestling with spirits.[61] It could not be otherwise. He grew up
hearing folk notions about witches and their doings, taking them in
with mother's milk and his native tongue. In adulthood, he asserted
that a person could steal milk by thinking of a cow and that his
mother had contracted asthma via a neighbor's evil eye.[62] As he lay

60   See "The Pagan Servitude of the Church," in *Martin Luther: Selections
from his Writings Edited and with an Introduction by John Dillenberger* (New York:
Anchor, 1961), 249–359.

61   Erik H. Erikson, *Young Man Luther: A Study of Psychoanalysis and
History* (New York: Norton, 1962), 26, 243–50, and Roland H. Bainton, *Here I
Stand: A Life of Martin Luther* (New York: Abingdon Press, 1959), 44, 65. These
two authors work hard to express the idea that obvious features of everyday
life in Luther's time did not depend on constant leaps to belief against all
evidence. It is interesting to see the rhetorical tongs they devise to deal with
Luther's reports about farting to undo a demon, the devil's "mooning" outside
his bedroom window, and such like. When *race* demands longer tongs than the
now-conventional quotation marks, well, that will be the Day.

62   Susan C. Karant-Nunn and Mary E. Wiesner-Hanks, *Luther On Women:
A Sourcebook* (Cambridge: Cambridge University Press, 2003), 234; and Richard
Marius, *Martin Luther: The Christian between God and Death* (Cambridge, MA:

dying, he saw a demon.[63] Such reports conveyed nothing improbable to him or to his hearers. Their understandings about the world took for granted the existence of an active, well-populated invisible realm that manifested itself in the realm of the seen, as real things, events, and persons. Everyday experience reinforced those understandings, which in turn had bearing on everyday behavior and in the recounting of events.[64]

Thus Luther recounts, in a single thought, his mother's chronic asthma *and* her stated belief that a neighbor's evil eye caused it *and* her own explanation, that the woman had repeatedly rebuffed her friendly overtures. Today, the incompleteness of this "explanation" jumps off the page, for our everyday understanding denies power to the gaze (for example, in the common phrase "if looks could kill"). For Luther and his hearers, however, physical explanation has disappeared into a thicket of circumstances on the surface of life and visible to all. Local lore and a twice-told tale about neighbors thereafter conceal the gap between the illness and the gaze. Thus, for everyday intents and purposes, the gap does not come into view, and the question of ordinary cause and effect does not arise. In that light, consider again the weird incompleteness of the explanatory formula "because of skin color." How might an American account for the causal mechanism at work in that phrase?

Luther's story about the milk-less cow exposes another facet of suspended causality. As before, he begins with a mundane predicament, but rather than ignore the question "How?" he answers explicitly. Reminding his flock that witches "do many accursed things while they remain undiscovered," he gives them a (to us) show-stopping causal sequence: "Thinking about some cow, they

Harvard University Press, 1999), 27.

63   Erikson, *Young Man Luther*, 59.

64   On concepts that are intelligible in one time and place but not in another, consult the inimitable Alasdair MacIntyre, "Is Understanding Religion Compatible with Believing?" in Bryan R. Wilson, *Rationality* (New York: Harper & Row, 1970), esp. 72.

can say one good word or another and get milk from a towel, a
table, or a handle." Everyone present knows the ordinary sequence
(creeping into someone else's barn, scurrying away with a sloshing
pail), but the preacher has made it plain that the thievery is not of
that order; it is invisible thievery ("they remain undiscovered").
Then and there, cause and effect disappear into the smoky notion
of "witches"—by definition, people who can "do accursed things"
that, by definition, are the things witches can do. Like pure races
a while ago, Luther's witches enter the world, and come to matter
therein, not by observation and experience but by circular reasoning. Neither "witch" nor "pure race" has a material existence.
Both are products of thought, and of language. Having no material
existence, they cannot have material causation. Strictly speaking,
Luther's explanation omitted nothing essential.

   Witchcraft has no moving parts of its own, and needs none. It
acquires perfectly adequate moving parts when a person acts upon
the reality of the imagined thing; the real action creates evidence
for the imagined thing. By that route, belief of that sort constantly
dumps factitious evidence for itself into the real world. In Luther's
day, learned jurists and ecclesiastics produced mountains of such
evidence. The specialized language of the proceedings generated
evidence by shaping routine modes of narrating invisible (nay,
impossible) events. The very pageantry of witchcraft trials yielded
more evidence, and drastic executions of "accursed" people still
more of it, a kind of material proof that bad things happen to bad
people. Lecky concluded: "If we considered witchcraft probable,
a hundredth part of the evidence we possess would have placed
it beyond the region of doubt."[65] Correspondingly, if Ripley's
readers had considered racecraft improbable, his classification
would have trapped him well within the region of doubt. In both
instances, there was vast and varied evidence, but of what?

   Of products of imagining, "realised" in everyday practice. Here,
paraphrased, is an exchange between an unbelieving interviewer

65   Lecky, *Rise of Rationalism*, 39.

with the American children or grandchildren of European immigrants who believed in the evil eye: Q: How does the evil eye work? A: Some people are known to have it. Q: How do you know that? A: I have seen X's remedy work. Q: Is it always effective? A: I know for a fact that it worked for So-and-so.[66] Today, as in the sixteenth century, logical hopscotch of that kind is the warp and woof of banal sociability. The talkers respond to, but ignore, the interviewer's question about the *mechanism* of the evil eye. It exists, period. The interviewer does not press, and does not need to. Those present do not query assumptions, the nature of available evidence, or the coherence of their reasoning from that evidence. What they know they know intimately, but not well. Such is the stuff that racecraft is made of. It occupies a middle ground between science and superstition, an invisible realm of collective understandings, a half-lit zone of the mind's eye.

Dr. Watson was operating within it when he prophesied breakthroughs in genetics to account for things that happen when white people like him "have to deal with black employees." That a scientist of his stature slipped into that half-light demonstrates the ease with which scientific and non-scientific thinking conflate in the minds of individuals. Had he been chatting over his back fence with a like-minded (or risk-averse) neighbor, rather than to a battalion of journalists, there would have been no uproar. And the world would have missed a sober lesson: Science is forever dogged by those seductive cousins and ancient antagonists which Francis Bacon named "Idols of the Tribe."[67] In their grip, Luther, a powerful dialectician, held both a workaday notion of cause and effect and a phantasmic folk belief that contradicted it, and so, too, did his learned contemporaries. Lecky again: "The acutest lawyers

---

66 Derived from Louis C. Jones, "The Evil Eye among European-Americans," in Alan Dundes, ed., *The Evil Eye: A Folklore Casebook* (New York: Garland, 1981), 150–68.

67 Francis Bacon, *The New Organon and Related Writings, Aphorisms—Book One* XLI, Fulton H. Anderson, ed. (New York: Liberal Arts Press, 1960), 48.

and ecclesiastics confronted evidence that extends to tens of thousands of cases, in almost every country of Europe." For them, as for less well-educated people, there was little to impose the idea of absurdity or of improbability on stories about "old women riding on broomsticks."[68]

What about here and now? Americans acquire in childhood all it takes to doubt stories of witchcraft, but little in our childhood leads us to doubt racecraft. For us, as for bygone believers in witches, daily life produces an immense accumulation of supporting evidence for the belief. Think no further than the media-borne miscellany of things tabulated "by race"—from hardy perennials like teenage pregnancy to novelties like "under-representation" among blood donors[69] and "disproportionate representation" on Twitter,[70] constantly churning out factitious evidence for an ever-expanding American immensity, the so-called racial divide. A recent instance, carried out under the sign of sociological theory, includes familiar features: for example, mapping genomic data onto "census" (that is, folk) racial categories and assuming a genetic origin for social conduct, with the absent supporting evidence expected any day now.[71] Lecky's subjects had authoritative sources in the science and law of the day. So do we. For them, but no less for us, it often is (or seems) "impossible for so much evidence to accumulate around a conception which has no basis in fact."[72] To them, witchcraft was obvious, not odd. Turn now to a tour of racecraft. Will its features seem familiar or strange, obvious or odd?

68   Lecky, *Rise of Rationalism*, 34.

69   Beth H. Shaz, James C. Zimring, Derrick G. Demmons, and Christopher D. Hillyer, "Blood Donation and Blood Transfusion: Special Considerations for African Americans," *Transfusion Medicine Review* 22:3 (July 2008), 202.

70   See http://gawker.com/5802772/why-so-many-black-people-are-on-twitter.

71   Jiannbin Lee Shiao, Thomas Bode, Amber Beyer, and Daniel Selvig, "The Genomic Challenge to the Social Construction of Race," *Sociological Theory*, 30:2 (June 2012), 67–88. These sociologists propose a deployment of genomic science different from the approach of J. Craig Venter, one of the first scientists to sequence the human genome. See pp. 6–9.

72   Lecky, *Rise of Rationalism*, 39.

1   A Tour of Racecraft

The ideas of racecraft are pieced together in the ordinary course of everyday doing. Along the way, they intertwine with ideas that shape other aspects of American social life. Those of racecraft govern what goes with what and whom (sumptuary codes), how different people must deal with each other (rituals of deference and dominance), where human kinship begins and ends (blood), and how Americans look at themselves and each other (the gaze). These ideas do not exist purely in the mind, or in only one mind. They are social facts—like six o'clock, both an idea and a reality.[1] Because racecraft exists in this way, its constant remaking constantly retreats from view. This "now you see it, now you don't" quality is what makes racism—the practice of a double standard based on ancestry—possible.

To eliminate racecraft from the fabric of our lives, we must first unravel the threads from which it is woven. Thus, the current guided tour. Its three sections— "From Racism to Race," "Blood Works," and "How Americans Look"—are not linear. The sections circuit and overlap, like the social facts of everyday life that they chronicle.

From Racism to Race

Begin with a story about travel in Mississippi circa 1964, a time and place when racecraft daily performed its conjuror's trick of

---

1   Maïmouna F. Bagate deserves credit for suggesting "six o'clock" to illustrate social facts as simultaneously idea and reality.

transforming racism into race, leaving black persons in view while removing white persons from the stage. To spectators deceived by the trick, segregation seemed to be a property of black people, not something white people imposed on them. But Robert S. McNamara, in his memoir of service during the administration of Lyndon B. Johnson, recounts an incident that set all parties on the stage.[2] While addressing business and labor leaders whom he had summoned to the White House to demand their help in passing the Civil Rights Bill, Johnson told his story of the day he and Lady Bird lived Jim Crow. Johnson was speeding along a road in Mississippi with his wife and their black longtime cook, Zephyr, when Lady Bird turned to him and said, "Would you please stop at the next gas station [restroom]?" They stopped. Not long thereafter, Zephyr said, "Mr. President, would you mind stopping by the side of the road?" The President replied with his well-known earthiness, "Why the hell didn't you do it when Bird and I did?" Zephyr answered, "Cause they wouldn't let me." (Notice Zephyr's "they.")

At that point in the story, "LBJ pounded on the table and in a bitter voice said, 'Gentlemen, is that the kind of country you want? It's not the kind *I* want.'" For a brief moment, Johnson had lived Jim Crow as Zephyr did. Ordinarily, white Southerners experienced Jim Crow as law and order, not as the ever-present disorder it was for black Southerners. So white Southerners did not notice, or need to notice, their own presence on the Jim Crow stage. McNamara's anecdote recaptures a moment when Jim Crow inconvenienced the President of the United States.

The disorder engendered by racecraft did not end with Jim Crow. What better typifies it than being killed by mistake, as happened not long ago to an Afro-American police officer? While pursuing a car thief, the officer was shot to death by a white brother

---

2   Robert S. McNamara, *In Retrospect: The Tragedy and Lessons of Vietnam* (New York: Random House, 1995), 199–200.

officer, who took him for a criminal.[3] The instant, inevitable —but, upon examination, bizarre—diagnosis of many people is that black officers in such situations have been "killed because of their skin color." But has their skin color killed them? If so, why does the skin color of white officers not kill them in the same way? Why do black officers not mistake white officers for criminals and blaze away, even when the white officers are dressed to look like street toughs? Everyone has skin color, but not everyone's skin color counts as race, let alone as evidence of criminal conduct. The missing step between someone's physical appearance and an invidious outcome is the practice of a double standard: in a word, racism. It was his fellow officer, not his skin color, that caused the black officer's death. Even so, the fellow officer was devastated by his error and its fatal consequence. His grief and that of other white officers visibly weighed down the sad procession in blue that conducted the dead policeman toward his final rest. Racism did not require a racist. It required only that, in the split second before firing the fatal shot, the white officer entered the twilight zone of America's racecraft.

"Minority" ranks alongside "the color of their skin" as a verbal prop for the mental trick that turns racism into race. The word slips its literal meaning as well as its core definition, which is quantitative.

3 Serge F. Kovaleski, "Two Officers' Paths to a Fatal Encounter on a Street in Harlem," *New York Times*, May 30, 2009, A1; Michael Powell, "On Diverse Force, Blacks Still Face Special Peril," *New York Times*, May 31, 2009, A1; Nina Bernstein, "Coping With Police Shooting, and Working to Avoid a Repeat," *New York Times*, June 1, 2009, A16; Christine Hauser and Karen Zraick, "Paying Respects, With Mementos and Calls for Change," *New York Times*, June 2, 2009, A19; Christine Hauser, "Police Drills in Bronx Seek to Prevent Mistaken-Identity Shootings," *New York Times*, June 3, 2009, A23; Karen Zraick, "Hundreds Mourn Slain Officer in Brooklyn," *New York Times*, June 3, 2009, A23; Al Baker and William K. Rashbaum, "Preliminary Report Offers New Details on Fatal Shooting of Police Officer," *New York Times*, June 4, 2009, A21; N. R. Kleinfield, "Amid a Sea of Blue, Bidding a Slain Police Officer His Final Farewell," *New York Times*, June 5, 2009, A17.

Vice President Spiro Agnew once demonstrated the trick uncon-
sciously. Responding to a question about American policy toward
the white supremacist regime in what was then Rhodesia, he said
it was no business of the United States how other countries dealt
with their "minorities," by which he meant the country's black
majority. The quantitative meaning slips again in the paradoxical
formula "majority minority," referring to the projected numerical
predominance of non-white persons in the United States in the not-
so-distant future. If the logic were harmless, it would be hilarious.

But "minority" is not harmless. Zigzagging between quantitative
and invidious meanings, it justified a dragnet in September 1992 in
which officers rounded up all the black and Hispanic men and some
women in Oneonta, New York. Police deployed the dragnet after
an elderly white woman, victim of an attempted armed robbery,
described her assailant as a black male, possibly young and with an
injured wrist. Is it imaginable that police would round up, detain,
question, and search every white person in a town because an
elderly victim of attempted armed robbery described her assailant
as a white male, possibly young and possibly with an injured wrist?
Would they, furthermore, obtain lists of all white students on the
local campus of the State University of New York, question them,
and check their arms for signs of injury; detain white men found
arriving in or leaving the town by bus; pull over cars carrying white
persons; and even stop a white female admissions officer en route
to visit her ailing grandmother? When a group of students posed
that hypothetical question to a police official, he answered that it
would not have been "practical."[4] *Practical* hid the qualitative and

---

4   Diana Jean Schemo, "College Town in Uproar Over 'Black List' Search,"
New York Times, September 27, 1992, 1, 33; Lynne Duke, "When Race is Equated
With Crime; Manhunts for Black Suspects Raise Questions About Skin Color as a
Clue," *Washington Post*, October 21, 1992, A3; New York Civil Liberties Union,
Brown v. City of Oneonta, http://www.nyclu.org; Michael Cooper, "Judge Sides
With Woman in Oneonta Profiling Case," *New York Times*, October 29, 2005,
B3. Rebuffed by the federal courts, the male targets of the Oneonta dragnet are
pursuing a civil action against the state of New York.

invidious meaning of "minority" inside the quantitative one. It would not have been practical to arrest and search every white man in town over a vague suspicion attaching to one; neither would it have passed muster as legitimate police work.

Next on the tour, consider a habit so fundamental that, without it, there can be no racecraft: the will to classification. Writing in the *New York Times*, a social work consultant describes his intervention to stop a young woman from slapping her young child on the subway.[5] Ordering her to stop, he threatens to call the police. Of about thirty persons in the car, only a woman in her fifties seated near the young woman takes a hand, quietly suggesting ways to handle the child without slapping. A stranger from Mars (if suitably briefed about New York subways) might have considered intervention by two out of about thirty people a high percentage, whoever the interveners were. Observing through the smoke of racecraft, however, the New Yorker immediately shuffles the protagonists into categories: He, "a 54-year-old white Jewish guy"; the child-slapper, "a young African-American kid with a kid"; the quiet counselor, "an African-American woman in her fifties"; and two white men who congratulated him for intervening, after the fact and at a safe distance. His first impression, that the silent onlookers from whom he "wished [he] had received more support" were "mainly black," gave way upon later reflection to the realization that, actually, "there were many more whites."

Recounting the story to a friend, the consultant again classifies. His friend, a "30-something Arab-Canadian," says, "I don't get the white and black in this. Why would you want the black people to jump in and give you support? Are the black people her people and the white people yours?" The consultant regards his friend's response as "a post-racial analysis." Not so fast. The "Arab-Canadian" is the nearest equivalent to a stranger from Mars: a person raised outside the force field of American racism, whose

---

5 Spence Halperin, "Taking a Public Stand, Nearly Alone," *New York Times*, July 12, 2009, Metropolitan, 3.

view therefore is not distorted by the haze of expectations (in other words, racecraft) through which the American-bred consultant filters what he sees. The Canadian is the outsider who attributes a drought, a crop failure, or an illness to ordinary cause and effect; the American is the insider on the alert for witchcraft.

That imprint of American rearing is not limited to white Americans, nor does travel abroad automatically disable its mental apparatus. Thus: A black American woman professor, recently arrived in France, staggers into a sixteenth-century church to escape the hot sun of Bordeaux in August. Looking straight ahead from the entrance, her vision zooms toward an image at the very center of the stained-glass window behind the altar: a black slave, kneeling and in chains. She asks Bordeaux residents the why and wherefore of it. They are astonished to learn that such an image exists in that well-known old church. Some openly doubt the report: "*Where?!*" And: "What makes you think it is a slave?" One Saturday afternoon, the parish priest arrives to prepare for a wedding, just as the American visitor from Mars is leading a tour for University of Bordeaux students. The priest is as amazed as the students.[6] By rights, the window had other claimants to attention. A Crusader in his red-cross tunic stood prominently on the slave's right; above him, a huge Mary rose toward heaven; yet the eyes of the American went straight to the man in chains.

Black people everywhere do not "see" alike. Persons from Africa and the Caribbean may not see what Afro-Americans see. Visualize the Afro-American professor again, this time in Washington, DC, en route to Union Station, on a rainy fall afternoon in 2008, flagging down a taxi. She is safely on board when the African driver spots a soaked white traveler, loaded with baggage. He glances at her through the rearview mirror to ask if it will be all right to pick

---

6   The American visitor is footnoted in a local tour book as the "discoverer" of this monument to black people's past presence in the city. See Danielle Pétrissans-Cavaillès, *Sur les traces de la traite des noirs à Bordeaux* (Paris: L'Harmattan, 2004), 64.

up the other traveler as well. Why, of course! He pulls to the curb and proposes. The traveler jumps, his face the very portrait of fear. "No, thank you. No, no. Thank you." Getting under way again, the driver again glances in the mirror. "What was wrong with him?" At the professor's explanation, "He saw a car full of black people," the driver exclaims, his face registering shocked understanding. Asked later where he is from, he says, "I am Egyptian." In not instantly seeing the reality that both the white and the black American did, the African cab driver qualifies as a Martian, too.

So do children before they have absorbed the classification system. In late June of 2009, sixty-five children aged six to twelve, most of them Afro-American or Hispanic, bounced out of their bus and ran toward the pool of the Valley Club, in Huntingdon Valley, Pennsylvania, near Philadelphia.[7] Their day camp, Creative Steps, had a contract with the club for swimming one afternoon each week. At first sight of the children, the club members at the pool rose and flew like startled birds.[8] "Made for the exits" and "pulled their children out of the pool" were phrases that appeared in reports of the ensuing uproar. What exactly did "pulling their children out" look like? How must a child have felt to be pulled out or to see others pulled out? What about the three white children whose parents let them stay? Most of all, how is it that grown-ups decided, all at once, to run from children?

On the following day, the club banned all the summer camps

---

7 See "Pa. Swim Club Faces Discrimination Lawsuit," AP, July 13, 2009, www.msnbc.com, http://news.yahoo.com/s/ap/20090713/ap_on_re_us/us_swim_club. See commentary by Stephen Krol, "The Valley Swim Club: No Blacks, No Minorities," July 8, 2009, with many comments, www.manolith.com/2009; and www.msnbc.com/id/31880916/ns/us_news_life/, "Swim Club President Changes the Complexion of His Story," *The Reid Report, News and Current Affairs*, July 11, 2009, http://blog.reidreport.com/tag/John-Duesler, with a videotaped interview watched 13 June 2009.

8 Ron Todt, AP, "Pa. Looking Into Swim Club Discrimination Claim," www.salon.com/wires/ap/us; "Suburban Philly Pool Faces Discrimination Suit," AP, July 13, 2009, http://yahoo.com/s/ap/20090713/ap_on_re_us.

that had contracted to use the pool, which prompted the Justice Department to file suit. Members began explaining their actions to themselves and to the press.[9] According to the club's president, "There was concern that a lot of kids would change the complexion ... and the atmosphere of the club." Encouraged to rephrase (one supposes), he later affirmed that the events had "nothing to do with race." There simply were "too many children in the pool," so the situation "went from a safe swim club to an unsafe swim club." The director of Creative Steps pointed out that the contract specified sixty-five children, and that "no one was misbehaving."

The campers overheard remarks, prompting a seven-year-old to ask if she was "too dark" to go swimming.[10] Her white counterparts almost certainly made guesses of their own, but none were reported, as though only the black children had experienced and would remember those moments. To the contrary, interviews hint at discussions that almost certainly occurred within and among the families. One man, who seems to speak for others, tells CNN that, "as general members, we were not told that they were coming. If we knew we could decide not to come when the pool was crowded or come anyway. We could have had an option."[11] By contrast, the need for such an "option" does not seem to have crossed the mind of the club president or his wife, both white. He speaks with the personal burden of having negotiated the ill-starred contract. She recounts a birthday party for the camp director's son and his friends, held at the pool without incident the week before.

In an on-camera interview, the couple face the arrows alone: no other club members stand nearby. They identify themselves as Obama voters (to the sneers of some bloggers). The husband confesses to a "poor choice of words" and disavows the sentiment;

9   See www.philly.com, posting of January 13, 2010.

10   "The Valley Swim Club: No Blacks, No Minorities," July 8, 2009, www.manolith.com.

11   Susan Candiotti and Jean Shin, "Swim Club President Denies Racism in Pool Controversy," CNN, July 10, 2009.

but, in the hubbub, his action (having negotiated the contract) cannot speak louder than those words. The wife, in a how-could-this-happen torrent, blurts out that a little boy, "just eight years old," had "cried on CNN! *Cried on CNN!* He didn't deserve to feel those feelings." The viewer sees raw emotion on a mother's face; the interviewer seems not to and does not probe. Two hot seats have sprung up, one inside with club members, the other outside with sound-biting news hounds. By turns shocked and confused, furious and disillusioned, the couple seem to be good people, brutally waylaid in a white neighborhood they thought they knew well and once believed safe.

Whereas the children had not understood the classification system, the director and his wife had not grasped, until the moment came, that a sumptuary code was in effect. Sumptuary codes enforce social classification. They consist of rules, written or unwritten, that establish unequal rank and make it immediately visible. When there is no phenotypic difference, like the little girl's "too dark" skin, sumptuary rules do what nature leaves undone. In the pre-Revolutionary France to which Tocqueville referred,[12] sumptuary rules overcame visual similarity by defining who might (or must) wear or use what, where they must or must not go, and so on through limitless elaboration (Louis XIV weakened the nobility by compelling them to live opulently at Versailles). Even physical appearance, however, cannot speak inequality by itself. Sumptuary rules in slaveholding America reserved certain fabrics for slaves and might forbid certain colors. In that spirit, a group of Charlestonians demanded legislation to "prevent the slaves from wearing silks, satins, crapes, lace muslins, and such costly stuffs as are looked upon and considered the luxury of dress," because "every distinction should be created between the whites and the negroes, calculated to make the latter feel the superiority of the former."[13] An emancipated slave acted in the same spirit

---

12 See above, p. 11.

13 Quoted by Elizabeth Fox-Genovese, "Strategies and Forms of Resistance:

when she defined "freedom" as buying herself a blue dress with polka dots.[14]

In post-slavery America, Jim Crow presided over its own sumptuary code. A century ago, that code governed who might be received at the White House. In his remarkable concession speech on election night 2008, John McCain mentioned the national storm that buffeted the presidency of Theodore Roosevelt after he invited Booker T. Washington to dine at the White House, acknowledging and praising the enormous change since.[15] The story is more intricate than McCain had time for or, perhaps, even knew. Washington was the president of Tuskegee Institute and probably the best-known Afro-American at the time. Moreover, he was a political ally of Roosevelt's and the chief referee of federal patronage in the South during the administrations of Roosevelt and his successor, William H. Taft: the sort of person, in other words, that a president invites to dine at the White House. But not in 1907, at least not for publication in the South. "The worst enemy to his race of any white man who has ever occupied so high a place in this republic" was the verdict of the New Orleans *Daily Picayune* on Roosevelt's offense. Roosevelt complained "that he had appointed fewer Negroes and more white Democrats and showed more solicitude for Southern feelings than any previous Republican president, yet he had been rewarded with more hatred than any of them." Once Roosevelt had regained his popularity among white Southerners, public memory converted the dinner into a lunch, which, for reasons impenetrable today, did not carry the same taboo.[16]

Focus on Slave Women in the United States," in Gary Y. Okihiro, ed., *In Resistance: Studies in African, Caribbean, and Afro-American History* (Amherst, MA: University of Massachusetts Press, 1986), 157.

14   Thavolia Glymph, *Out of the House of Bondage: The Transformation of the Plantation Household* (Cambridge: Cambridge University Press, 2008), 204.

15   "John McCain's Concession Speech," *New York Times*, November 5, 2008.

16   C. Vann Woodward, *Origins of the New South: 1877–1913* (Baton Rouge, LA: Louisiana State University Press, 1951), 464–5; Louis R. Harlan, *The Wizard of Tuskegee, 1901–1915* (New York: Oxford University Press, 1983), 3–5.

Rules designed to promote feelings of inferiority and superiority travel in tandem with expectations of deference and with rituals that simultaneously create and express the requisite feelings. In the South just after the Civil War (and, depending on the place, for many years thereafter), a black person was required to step off the sidewalk when a white person approached and, if male, to uncover his head. Obedience usually concealed the intrinsic violence of the rule and kept black people visibly in their place. This etiquette was not unique to the United States. In *The Interpretation of Dreams*, Freud recorded his feelings when his father described the same ritual, as performed in the Moravian town of Freiburg. Well dressed and wearing a new fur cap, Freud senior was walking along one day, when "a Christian came up to me and with a single blow knocked my cap into the mud, shouting, 'Jew! Get off the pavement!'" The younger Freud then asked his father, "And what did you do?"[17] Freud senior said quietly: "I went into the roadway and picked up my cap." Thus did the ritual pass from a bygone real world into the dream life of a new generation.

Freud's sidewalk could as well be a highway. On May 24, 2009, just after 1:00 p.m., an ambulance owned by the Creek Nation Tribal Authority and an Oklahoma State Police cruiser are winding along the hilly road between Paden and Prague, one behind the other. What happened next, captured on a cell phone, traveled the world via YouTube. One blog yelled the headline: Cop pulls over EMT [Emergency Medical Technician] and gives him the CHOKE HOLD. Yikes! Holy crap!" Next came the news in brief. "It was a jarring scene, if only for its incongruity, a highway patrolman trying to arrest an EMT. All the while there was a woman in the ambulance on the way to the hospital."[18]

Because the man being choked was black and the trooper was white, the incident at first looked like an extreme case of "driving

---

17 Sigmund Freud, *The Interpretation of Dreams* (New York: Avon, 1998 [1899]), 230.

18 See http://forum.prisonplanet.com/index.php?topic=108257.0.

while black." It was not. When the driver of the Creek Nation ambulance at last agreed to a TV interview, he turned out to be, to all appearance, a white man. At length (and under enormous pressure), the authorities released a video of the whole encounter, recorded second by second by the cruiser's dashboard camera.[19] Loudly and with vulgarisms, the trooper chews out the ambulance driver for failing to yield to an emergency vehicle (though he, too, was driving one) and for having allegedly "flipped a bird" out the window: "I don't have to put up with this *shit* ... this *disrespect*." The paramedic, who to all appearance is black, and who, until then, has been in the back of the ambulance (treating the patient?), emerges through the back door of the ambulance, steps down, and, his back to the camera, walks slowly toward the trooper. "I am in charge of this unit," he says. He gives his name, presents his card, and suggests that the cruiser follow the ambulance to the hospital; there is a patient. "I don't want to talk to you," says the trooper, "Go back in the ambulance ... get your *ass* back in that ambulance." He is determined to deal only with the apparently white driver. Freud asked his father, "And what did you do?" The paramedic's question to himself must have been "What shall I do?"[20]

In response to the trooper's repeated order that he get back in the ambulance, the paramedic makes no move to obey, but keeps intoning words like "patient," "duty," "interfering," "emergency vehicle," and "sworn to protect." The patrolman moves to arrest him. A scuffle breaks out. The scuffle jolts the ambulance. The patient starts screaming. Newcomers enter the frame. Someone calls the police. The white trooper is heard screaming at the driver of the Creek Nation ambulance, "Tell *your manager*" and "Your *supervisor ... jail!*" A second trooper arrives. A new scuffle ensues

---

19   The cell-phone video created a stir that defeated the initial decision of the State Police to sequester the video taken by the cruiser's dashboard camera.

20   Dave Statter, "Creek Nation Paramedic Maurice White, Jr. Sues OHP Trooper Daniel Martin Over Traffic Stop, Claims Unreasonable Force," http://Statter911.com.

when the original trooper tries again to handcuff the paramedic. Though held in a chokehold, the paramedic never stops talking, always in low volume. The second trooper, who can also be heard talking in low volume, gradually calms the situation.

An observer from the blogosphere thought that the paramedic should have deferred to the trooper and that he "needed to be taken down a peg or two."[21] Uppity, was he, talking about his duty to his patient? And did the patient need taking down as well? No matter. The choices are not open to observers' remaking after the fact and at a safe distance. The point to notice is that, in the paramedic's encounter, as in the elder Freud's, violence crackles like electricity. Both encounters show that the everyday routines that organize racism do not always, but always can, explode.

Those routines do not require a large stage. They are just as powerful in small events, such as the children's expulsion from the swimming club, as they are in a duel between adults about deference and respect. Every one of the children present, black or not, participated in a routine of racism that might have ended in violence. (Imagine, for example, that just one of the campers' mothers had been present to overhear.) On the spot, unwritten rules that had been keeping black children out became explicit. When children who looked wrong to club members materialized at the pool, all but three parents (Heroines of the Republic!) did the same thing at the same time, as if a fire alarm had sounded.

Sumptuary rules produce a regular supply of circumstantial evidence about what the world is made of and who belongs where within it. Not only can rules endowed with that power shape action in advance, they can also shape opinions of which the holders may be unaware until the moment they come into play. Such rules shaped the campaign-era mocking of Candidate Obama's taste for arugula, the elegant tailoring of his suits, and, especially, his habit of speaking in complete, grammatically correct English sentences.

---

21 Ibid.

Counterparts of the rules under which pundits mocked Obama's speech daily materialize in inner-city schools whenever children learn to mock the use of Standard English as "trying to be white," and to enforce use of "Black English" through bullying. The present authors were teased good-naturedly for "talking all proper" as elementary-school children newly arrived in Washington, DC, and for speaking Standard English with Pittsburgh accents. Daily enforcement of such rules among peer groups of children both creates and polices racial distinctness.

Turn now to a familiar scene in which the sumptuary code in effect, from beginning to end, would doubtless escape a foreigner. Shoppers are scrutinizing the cart of a black woman holding food stamps, judging the appropriateness of her selections. Are food-stamp sirloins to be carried away in a welfare Cadillac? Turn the scene around. Now a black woman is under scrutiny for a large order, paid for at the last minute by credit card. Do the racecraft exercise yourself, and then do it again with a black man buying a large grocery order with cash. Now contemplate a double whammy: You are a black woman stepping into a shabby little store in upstate New York. Is it safe? How far away is help? (Far.) And look at that line of white people ahead of you buying their groceries with food stamps! Whoa! On top of being a black person surrounded by white people in the deep North, here comes the jaw-dropping (but why jaw-dropping?) spectacle of the white woman in front of you. She's coming out of her jeans pocket with a wad of food stamps in her fist!

Reason suggests that a racecraft short-circuit made the black woman's jaw drop at a sight that should have looked normal. It certainly looked normal to the white people in line with their food stamps. If white people are a majority in the area, then most poor people there are white, just as most rich people are. Turn the scene around again. What would have happened if the black woman, in turn, had pulled out a wad of food stamps? And which would race-craft single out for condemnation: an uppity Negro paying with

cash or an undeserving Negro paying with food stamps? Along
that way, the sumptuary code shades into the peculiar American
predicament of having multiple class resentments but no legitimate
language for talking about class. In that setup, the question "Why
food stamps?" has two stock answers, depending on the ancestry
of the person using them: on the one hand, fecklessness; on the
other, bad luck, plant-closing, and the like.[22]

Now try a final twist. The food-stamp program underwent
rebaptism in 2008 as SNAP (Supplemental Nutrition Assistance
Program). Sleek plastic cards replaced the old food-stamp vouch-
ers.[23] What else has probably changed?

What does not change is that racecraft generates a unique language, opaque to outsiders. The phrase "social equality" was once
widely understood by everyone, and especially everyone living in
the Jim Crow South. It denoted a precipice that might claim the
liberty, or even the life, of any Afro-American who ventured too
near (like the 14-year-old Emmett Till, pistol-whipped, shot, and
his mutilated body dumped into the Tallahatchie River in 1955,
because he allegedly said "bye, baby" to a white woman;[24] or the
young man whose misfortune is recounted below in Chapter 2).
Social equality was the taboo that Theodore Roosevelt violated
by inviting Booker T. Washington to dine at the White House.
Today, "social equality" has become a sepia-tinted relic, familiar
only to scholars and antiquarians. By contrast, "race relations,"
which was coined in the same era, sounds ordinary, and to grasp
its weirdness requires historical probing. Invented in the late-
nineteenth-century heyday of the Jim Crow regime, the term "race
relations" finessed the abrogation of democracy and the bloody

---

22 See Conclusion, p. 282.

23 Jason DeParle and Robert Gebeloff, "Food Stamp Use Soars Across
U.S., and Stigma Fades," *New York Times*, November 29, 2009, 1, 26.

24 Charles M. Payne, *I've Got the Light of Freedom: The Organizing Tradition
and the Mississippi Freedom Struggle* (Berkeley, CA: University of California
Press, 1995), 53–4.

vigilantism that enforced it.[25] Unlike "social equality," "race relations" has outlasted the regime that gave birth to it and continues
in wide use. A college administrator, discussing friction between
black and white roommates, automatically placed it under the
rubric of race relations, even while aware that the friction involved
no more than the usual occasions for roommate disputes, from
noise to unauthorized use of each other's property. Then and
there, through the transforming power of racecraft, an individual becomes a race, roommates become an "interracial pairing,"
and the outcome, whether friction or friendship, becomes "race
relations."[26]

Sometimes the fog of racecraft rolls in at the last minute, as a
derailing non sequitur to an otherwise logical argument. A few
years ago, the *New York Times* reported that scientists who conducted an epidemiological study of asthma among schoolchildren
in South Bronx produced damning evidence about environmental pollution caused by heavy truck traffic. Their study identified
the particle emissions, cited the location of major highways, and,
through resourceful data collection, drew conclusions about
the children's exposure, in specific neighborhoods, at different
hours of the day, to "very high fine particle concentrations on a
fairly regular basis." The correlations emerged: "Symptoms, like
wheezing, doubled on days when pollution from truck traffic was
highest." It would seem as clear as noonday that class inequality
had imposed sickness on these American schoolchildren. Yet the
article's summary tails off into confused pseudo-genetics. To a list
of contributors to high asthma rates that includes heavy traffic,
dense population, poorly maintained housing, and lack of access
to medical care, the article adds "a large population of blacks and

25   Michael Rudolph West, *The Education of Booker T. Washington: American
Democracy and the Idea of Race Relations* (New York: Columbia University
Press, 2006). See also, below, Chapter 4, p. 111.

26   Tamar Lewin, "Interracial Roommates Can Reduce Campus Bias,
Studies Find," *New York Times*, July 9, 2009, A16.

Hispanics, two groups with high rates of asthma." Racecraft has permitted the consequence under investigation to masquerade among the causes.[27] Susceptibility to filthy air does not depend on the census category to which the asthma sufferer belongs. And even if that susceptibility is (to whatever degree) genetically determined, Dr. Venter's account of his own asthma stands as a reminder that "genetic" is not equivalent to "racial" or "ethnic."[28]

Some of the oddest racecraft moments come when scientists yoke modern genetics to folk notions. In the controversy over Dr. James D. Watson's remarks in London,[29] some of his defenders charged his critics with a "politically correct" retreat from science, insisting that good science requires a free marketplace of ideas. Researchers must be free, they implied, to salvage the old bio-racist ranking of superior and inferior races, regardless of the collapse as science of its core concept, race. But it is doubtful that those foes of political correctness would wish to rehabilitate that part of bio-racism that once identified inferior white races.

If they took their own position seriously, they would applaud the writings of such eminent American scientists of the late nineteenth century as Edward Drinker Cope and Nathaniel Southgate Shaler (dean of Harvard's Lawrence Scientific School during the 1890s) on the inequality of races, not simply their work on dinosaurs and the earth's history. Cope advocated both "the return of the African to Africa" and restrictions on immigration by "the half-civilized hordes of Europe." Shaler agreed, characterizing those hordes as inferior "by birthright," "essentially in the same state as the Southern Negro," and distinct from "the Aryan variety of

---

27 Manny Fernandez, "A Study Links Trucks' Exhaust to Bronx Schoolchildren's Asthma," *New York Times*, October 29, 2006, 31.

28 See above, p. 6. The evolutionary biologist Joseph L. Graves has clarified for a lay audience that "genetic" and "racial" are not synonymous, in *The Race Myth: Why We Pretend Race Exists in America* (New York: Plume Press, 2005), 103–136.

29 See above, p. 8.

mankind."[30] Popularizers hustled bio-racist "science" into public policy. Madison Grant, who advocated "Nordic" superiority in his 1916 best-seller, *The Passing of the Great Race: The Racial Basis of European History*, purported to map class inequality onto physical traits, such as height:

> The Nordic race is everywhere distinguished by great stature. Almost the tallest stature in the world is found among the pure Nordic populations of the Scottish and English borders, while the native British of Pre-Nordic brunet blood are, for the most part, relatively short; and no one can question the race value of stature who observes on the streets of London the contrast between the Piccadilly gentleman of Nordic race and the cockney costermonger [street vendor] of the old Neolithic type.[31]

In 1924, the lay and scientific streams of bio-racism converged in the Immigration Act of 1924 (which excluded European races deemed undesirable) and the Virginia Racial Integrity Act (which prohibited "miscegenation"). In the same year, Virginia adopted a law (upheld by the US Supreme Court three years later) providing for compulsory sterilization of persons held to be "defective and degenerate," a group that included "the shiftless, ignorant and worthless class of anti-social whites of the South."[32] The Nazis

30   Both quotations appear in William H. Tucker, *The Science and Politics of Racial Research* (Champaign, Ill: University of Illinois Press, 1994), 35. In a careful and closely documented analysis, Tucker shows how the racist ideas and goals current in a society can promote seeming "science" as an evidentiary platform for racist public policy.

31   Madison Grant, *The Passing of the Great Race: The Racial Basis of European History* (New York: Scribner's, 1916), 26. Even as he wrote, "great stature" began to fail as a marker of racial superiority when tall Nordics discovered taller peoples in Africa, such as the Luos, from whom President Obama descends on his father's side.

32   Tucker, *Science and Politics of Racial Research*, 100–1. Edwin Black, *War Against the Weak: Eugenics and America's Campaign to Create a Master Race* (New York: Thunder's Mouth Press, 2004), 169–81, 187–221.

followed these developments closely. When they decided to weed out the "unfit," they had American models of how to proceed, from administrative searching of family trees to sterilization. They became "the dark apotheosis of eugenics."[33]

In 1946, Leslie C. Dunn, a distinguished geneticist and part of a group intent on severing genetics from eugenics, wrote that the field "had developed ... out of the racial problems presented so vividly to the United States by the great immigration of the early part of the century."[34] Consistent application of the "free market-place of ideas" principle today would restore to bio-racism and eugenics the respectability they once enjoyed.[35] Instead, "inferior white races" vanished from the lexicon of bio-racism, to rematerialize outside its purview as "ethnic" groups. The "shiftless, ignorant, and worthless" white people vanished altogether.[36] No one attributes to political correctness the demise of bio-racism as applied to white persons. So, the free-marketplace-of-ideas apologia for Watson's bio-racism as applied to black persons turns out to be a familiar interloper, the practice of a double standard.

One of the present authors some years ago tested the limits of the free market in racist ideas. A crotchety yet likable right-wing colleague approached, looking disquieted and in need of moral support. He was "having trouble" with a certain black student in

33 Richard Coniff, "God and White Men at Yale," *Yale Alumni Magazine* (May/June 2012), 50.

34 In 1935, horrified by the Nazis' Nuremburg Blood Law, Dunn urged the Carnegie Institution to close down its eugenics enterprise at Cold Spring Harbor, Long Island. Black, *War Against the Weak*, 391, 413. Dunn spoke out again in 1960, when the old blood mystique had an American renaissance.

35 Congress repealed the immigration law of 1924 and passed the Voting Rights Act in 1965, a dual testament to Lyndon Johnson's part in the civil rights revolution. See "Remarks at the Signing of the Immigration Bill," October 3, 1965, The Lyndon Baynes Johnson Library, online archive.

36 Katya Gibel Mevorach, "Race, Racism, and Academic Complicity," *American Ethnologist* 34:2 (May 2007), 238–41. See also Matthew Frye Jacobson, *Whiteness of a Different Color: European Immigrants and the Alchemy of Race* (Cambridge, MA: Harvard University Press, 1998).

his bio-psychology class. What was wrong, he wondered, with saying that "black people may, or (mind you) *may not*, prove to be intellectually inferior to white people? In science, you frame a hypothesis, devise an experiment, find out." The student raised her hand and, when recognized, blasted him. "Do you know So-and-So (the student in question)?" asked the bio-psychologist. (The author did happen to know the student in question, an eighteen-year-old single mother of twins who was as bright as they come and not one to brook insult.) "Why can't she grasp that there's a scientific approach to things, blah, blah?" Finally, the author put a question. "If, as you say, there is no hypothesis that science excludes, why not try this assignment? Let your students pick any white ethnic group and any stereotype commonly applied to it, greedy, mendacious, dumb, drunken, gangsterish, and so on, then formulate a hypothesis, design the experiment, find out." The colleague's face froze.

Years later, an exotic predicament of ethnicity arose in the classroom. A young woman raised her hand, but fumbled for words when recognized: "Some of us want ... I mean, we think we need," then said, "I wish I had a race," and fell silent. After a wait, the black woman professor prompted, "What do you mean?" The student explained that her family had immigrated to the United States from Iran, then stopped again. Perhaps the rest seemed obvious to her. It was not obvious to the rest of the class or to the professor. When asked why she "wants" a race, she mumbled something about the census form. "To have to write 'Other' isn't, well, it isn't very nice." Understanding then lit faces all around the room. For that young woman, not to "have" a race is to be less than fully American. What can she do but take America's imprisoning social forms as she finds them?

In recombinant varieties they flourish in America's prisons, where not "having" a race is worse than "not nice"; it can be a life or death matter. David Arenberg, a Jewish inmate in an Illinois penitentiary, has written movingly about how he has survived a five-race classification that leaves no room for him. There are "woods," short for peckerwoods (Euro-Americans, distributed between Skinheads and Aryan Brothers), "kinfolk" (Afro-Americans), "chiefs" (Native Americans), "razas" (Americans of Mexican descent), and "paisas" (Mexican immigrants).[37] Strictly enforced segregation creates the races: inmates may play team sports together but not individual games like chess; may visit each other's cubicles but not sit on each other's beds; may attend the same church services but not pray together. The prison's segregated markets also set up monopolies, with their associated economic rents. For example, although the razas and paisas vend drugs considered better and cheaper, a "wood" may buy only from another "wood."[38]

The rule that different races may not break bread together is "inviolate," with penalties ranging from beating to execution. Arenberg's predicament is that he cannot "fit into the chow hall." He may not sit with the "woods," to whom Jews are "not white but imposters who don white skin and hide inside it for the purpose of polluting and taking over the white race." He may not sit with "the other races who don't understand the subtleties of my treachery and take me for just another wood."[39] Arenberg lives on the edge of survival. Finally, a "head" in the Aryan Brotherhood brokers a classic Jim Crow solution. Once a suitable quid pro quo has been worked out, the Jewish prisoner is authorized to "sit at certain white tables after all the whites have finished eating."[40] The Aryan Brother is in earnest. He is logical, practical, and inventive within the racist premises. There is grim American humor in the likelihood that he believes his own rationale even though, or perhaps because, it is absurd.

---

37 David Arenberg, "A Jew in Prison," *Intelligence Report*, The Southern Poverty Law Center, (Fall 2009), 39–40. Arenberg does not capitalize the names.

38 On segregation in the organization of markets, see Michael Banton, *Racial Theories*, Second Edition (Cambridge: Cambridge University Press, 1998).

39 See Chapter 2, below.

40 Arenberg, "A Jew in Prison," 40.

Both absurdity and grim humor, perhaps unintended, combined in an 1895 *New York Times* obituary of Frederick Douglass, the celebrated son of a slave and a slave master. The author of the obituary ruminated on the idiotic question that must have been percolating in many minds: Which race could justly claim this superlatively gifted individual?

> It might not be unreasonable, perhaps, to intimate that his white blood may have something to do with the remarkable energy he displayed and the superior intelligence he manifested. Indeed, it might not be altogether unreasonable to ask whether, with more white blood, he would not have been an even better and greater man than he was, and whether the fact that he had black blood may not have cost the world a genius, and be, in consequence, a cause for lamentation instead of a source of lyrical enthusiasm over African possibilities. It is always more or less foolish to credit or discredit a race with the doings, good or bad, of a particular member of that race, but if it must be done, plain justice should see to it that the right race gets the glory or the humiliation.[41]

If anyone seeks a monument to racecraft, gaze at that one.

In *The Ultimate Solution of the American Negro Problem* (1913), the historian Edward Eggleston erected another. He solved the Douglass conundrum by invoking (of all things!) racial purity: "His father was a pure Anglo-American."[42] Eggleston's research on the general problem took him to a "Negro school" (Hampton Institute), where he noticed the prevalence of light-skinned students. He interviewed a "very intelligent and reliable colored man," whom he described as "one-fourth Negro, one-fourth Amerind and the remaining half white man." The "reliable" interviewee

---

41   Tucker, *Science and Politics*, 30, quoting the *New York Times*, February 27, 1895, 4.

42   Edward Eggleston, *The Ultimate Solution of the Negro Problem* (Boston, MA: Gorham, 1913), 252.

"regards the pure Negro as far below the half-breed in intelligence, though the latter is generally more vicious and criminal,
consequent, in part at least, upon a realization of his hopeless position as an inferior, apart from his individual worth, and especially
because of his classification as a Negro." Then the interviewee
added a twist, which Eggleston transcribed without comment: "He
also regards the mulatto as mentally and physically inferior to the
pure-blooded white man, but holds that justice demands that they
may be recognized as occupying an intermediate position between
the two races."[43]

While the "white races" of the past became ethnic groups,
the opposite has happened to the census category "Hispanic."
Discussing the "mark one or more" option that appeared for the
first time on the 2000 census, a reporter dutifully explained that
"Hispanic" designates an ethnicity, not a race, and that "Hispanics
can be of any race."[44] Such, in any case, was said to be official thinking when the Nixon administration concocted the term *Hispanic*
for the 1970 census. (Be it remembered that Nixon's infamous
"Southern Strategy" required alertness to every political nuance
of racecraft, North and South.)[45] Whatever the official rationale claimed, a new "minority" was born. Census enumerators
in California were soon locking horns with "Hispanic" families who rejected the term *Hispanic*. Some preferred "to identify
with a specific country of origin or heritage."[46] Others insisted on
their Indian ethnicity. (After all, they had been invited to "self-
identify.") By 2003, the Census Bureau was reporting that
"Hispanics" had become the largest "minority group" in the

43   Ibid., 250.

44   Genaro C. Armas, "Census Profiles Young Multiracials," AP, July 3, 2001.

45   See Richard Rodriguez's sharp-witted dissection of this pseudo-race that
exists only in the United States: "How Richard Nixon Invented Hispanics," in
The Future Uncertain: Culture, Economics, Future(s), September 26, 2005, http://
futureuncertain.blogspot.com.

46   Bill Analysis of AB1281, Assembly Third Reading As Amended May 18,
2009, ftp://leginfo.public.ca.gov.

United States, still insisting in its press release that, unlike blacks and Asians, Hispanics are not a race.[47]

Blood-bank officials in Detroit evidently thought otherwise. When they set out in 1986 to search for rare blood types found "almost exclusively" among "minority" donors, they were determined to identify the donors by race. From that, it surely followed that "Hispanic" had its place alongside "black " and "white" in their reports.[48] The new census category thus hatched a new pseudo-genetic population. Once hatched, the new population, by definition, would have its own distinguishing blood and rare antigens—though not so distinguishing as to rule out grouping "Oriental, Hispanic, and native American" donors together in the search.

By 2007, "Hispanic" had taken another step toward becoming a race when enterprising researchers sought, and received, taxpayers' money for research on something called a "Hispanic" genome. A brief article on an inside page of the *Washington Times* disclosed that the researchers, having received money from the Veterans Affairs Department, "broke federal rules by crossing the US border to pay subjects in Mexico for blood samples." The researchers' travel invoice included "taking the government car into Juarez ... to see a subject for the Latino Genetics Study." Their work "involved testing to identify genetic tendencies in illnesses and disorders among Hispanics.[49] The researchers had established contact with twenty subjects, and paid $125 for two blood samples and an interview, when an anonymous whistleblower prompted an investigation. Eventually, the director of the New Mexico Veterans

47 Rodriguez, "How Richard Nixon Invented Hispanics."

48 K. M. Beattie and A. W. Shafer, "Broadening the Base of a Rare Donor Program by Targeting Minority Populations," *Transfusion* 26 (1986), 402–3.

49 The phrasing uncannily echoes an old race science treatise, originally commissioned in 1896 by the American Economic Association: Frank L. Hoffman, *Race Traits and Tendencies of the American Negro*, recently reissued with a new Introduction by Paul Finkelman (Clark, NJ: The Lawbook Exchange, 2004 [1896]).

Administration Health Care System announced that the research projects had been suspended.[50]

Does anyone doubt that, in the future, a purportedly "race-specific" new remedy (or re-patented new dosage of an old one) will spring forth from work like that attempted by the researchers in Juarez—say, for asthma among Hispanics? After all, the Food and Drug Administration set the precedent by approving Bidil, a fixed-dose combination of two old drugs, allowing it to be re-patented as a "new" and "race-specific" drug for "African American" heart patients. The clinical trials involved only self-identified "African American" patients; that is to say, no control groups and says-so genetics.[51] The patent applicants' short-cut science stirred further controversy because the cost of the combination far exceeded that of its two components. Michael Banton's points about segregation in market organization apply in this instance.[52] Although the civilian purveyors of prescription drugs work by crafty marketing, while the imprisoned purveyors of street drugs work by occasional violence, both take advantage of segregated markets to augment their profits.

In everyday doing, visible things like segregated markets come into view as things done and imagined, and yet are thought of as having natural causes. It is as though the rules and rituals of segregation are sufficient to make race visible, but not sufficient to make it real. Along that way, blood, though ordinarily invisible, takes on a peculiar role and script that calls for an extravagance of light.

The Detroit blood bankers of a while ago, who imagined

---

50   *Washington Times*, December 7, 2007, A3. The article suggested no reason for the project's suspension.

51   Howard Brody, M.D., Ph. D. and Linda M. Hunt, Ph. D., "Bidil: Assessing a Race-Based Pharmaceutical," *Annals of Family Medicine* 4:5 (2006), 556–60.

52   Banton, *Racial Theories* (Cambridge: Cambridge University Press, 1998), 136–57. See also the research reviewed in Lee Herring, "What's Segregation Got to Do With the Nation's Subprime Mortgage Lending Fiasco?" *Footnotes*, Newsletter of the American Sociological Association (July/August 2009), A4.

extremely rare blood types as a racial characteristic, were strangely untroubled when nature had its say: Only fifty of the 7,706 black donors tested (fewer than 7 per thousand) carried the four rare antigens that they had sought "exclusively" among black donors.[53] For a time, however, they were troubled indeed by a widespread public mistrust and by "recalcitrant groups" opposed to labeling by race. So they had to prove not only that their program was worthy but also that its motives were trustworthy.[54] At a different level, the plot thickened over the practical question of how to determine an individual's race; the result had to be valid yet voluntary. It would not do simply to look at a would-be donor and then decide; or, just as bad, to look and then ask. In the end they devised an incantation: "Interviewers were instructed to ask, 'Which racial group should I record for you: black, white, Hispanic, American Indian, or other?' This has been accepted well." Talk of blood is as sticky and slippery as the substance itself.

Blood Works

Understood as kin and as kind, blood inhabits the profoundest layer of mystique that humanity has carried with it from time immemorial. As a natural substance, blood is far older than the mystique and entirely independent of it. When Karl Landsteiner described the A and B antigens in human blood (1900–1), he solved a puzzle: why transfusions helped some patients and killed others.[55] That decisive work, for which he was awarded the Nobel Prize in 1930, revealed natural blood's own profound layers and biochemical properties, moving parts that have nothing to do with human groups. "The scientifically established universal truth," declared the anthropologist Ashley Montagu, fuming over the Nazis' efforts

53 Beattie and Shafer, "Broadening the Base of a Rare Donor Program," 401.
54 Ibid., 402–3.
55 Unsigned Editorial, "Blood Transfusion and Race," *Journal of the National Medical Association* 52:4 (July 1960), 280.

to read the evidence otherwise, "is that all human beings, no matter of what creed or complexion they may be, are of one and the same blood."[56]

By contrast, metaphorical blood can dispense with the moving parts of natural blood and has always had everything to do with human groups. When nature made room for human society, human beings made room for nature in society.[57] And blood made in society by human beings has properties that nature knows nothing about. It can consecrate and purify; it can also profane and pollute. It can define a community and police the borders thereof. Natural blood never does that sort of thing: it only sustains biological functioning. If it is to perform metaphorical tasks, human beings must carry out those tasks on its behalf. This, Nazi scientists did in imagining blood type B (found somewhat more frequently among Eastern Europeans and Jews than among non-Jewish Germans) to be a "marker" of the "darker, Asiatic races."[58] Eventually, they claimed to have devised a blood test for "non-Aryanism."[59]

In 1946, as thoughtful observers drew lessons from World War II, Montagu dissected the popular belief that underpinned race: the belief that blood is equivalent to heredity, determining the quality of the person and his or her social as well as biological status. He numbered such ideas "among the oldest surviving from the earliest days of mankind."[60] Finding beliefs about blood implicated in the desolation of the recent war and genocide, Montagu reflected on the persistence of those beliefs in the twentieth century despite

---

56 M. F. Ashley Montagu, *Man's Most Dangerous Myth: The Fallacy of Race*, Third Edition (New York: Harper & Brothers, 1952), Montagu, 219.

57 Emile Durkheim, *The Elementary Forms of Religious Life*, trans. Karen E. Fields (New York: Free Press, 1995), 145.

58 Douglas Starr, *Blood: An Epic History of Medicine and Commerce* (New York: HarperCollins, 2002), 74–7.

59 Susan E. Lederer, *Flesh and Blood: Organ Transplantation and Blood Transfusion in Twentieth-Century America* (New York: Oxford University Press, 2008), 118.

60 Montagu, *Man's Most Dangerous Myth*, 214.

well-established scientific evidence of their falsity. He was not talking about the uneducated when he lamented that the thoughts of the great majority are controlled by "words, verbal habits," while only a minority of people "control their words by thoughts." Indeed, Montagu unwittingly illustrated the power of "verbal habits" by his own incomplete break with the folk notion of race.[61]

Blood in the form of words and verbal habits has proved to be an adroit stowaway. It crashed the celebration of Inauguration Day 2009. "We have our first bi-racial president," the website of Project RACE exulted, adding that "even if Obama identifies as an African American, he cannot deny DNA."[62] Turbulence is inevitable when the concepts of modern genetics fly in the wake of folk notions. What can it mean to "deny DNA"? If spelled out, the statement becomes unintelligible: "Even if Obama identifies as an African American, he cannot deny deoxyribonucleic acid." Substitute "blood," however, and notice that it is instantly intelligible: "Even if Obama identifies as an African American, he cannot deny blood." The scientific concept "DNA" has slid into a spurious synonymy with "blood," the ancient metaphor of kinship and descent.[63]

When equated to "DNA," "blood" resumes its prehistoric career. Only as metaphor may one speak of "black genes" and "white genes," or of "white" and "black" blood. But once invoked, the metaphor launches a logical program of its own: If "blood" is synonymous with "race," and "DNA" is synonymous with "blood," then "DNA" is synonymous with "race." Although spurious, that

---

61   Ibid., 210. See Anthony Q. Hazard, Jr., "A Racialized Deconstruction? Ashley Montagu and the 1950 UNESCO Statement on Race," *Transforming Anthropology* 19:2 (October 2011), 174–86.

62   Susan Graham, national executive director of Project RACE, January 1, 2009, www.projectrace.com.

63   Emile Durkheim recorded unforgettable images of blood symbolism in representations of kinship expressed as totems that join bounded groups of human beings to one another (but also to animals) and distinguished them from other human groups of the same kind. See Durkheim, *The Elementary Forms of Religious Life*, esp. 303–54.

synonymy engages a powerful logic in its turn. Invoke a race, and the notion of a distinguishing blood stands to reason. In the folk lexicon, that is precisely what *race* means. Invoke a disease, and a race-and-disease equation becomes plausible; as it did for the illicit research travelers to Juarez, mentioned earlier. If the race-and-disease equation does not work, a sub-program about disease process clicks on; as when researchers devised the infamous Tuskegee syphilis "experiment" to test the belief that syphilis killed black and white patients differently—though the test involved black subjects only.[64] If the sub-program about "race-specific" disease process stalls for want of data, the input of a drug defined as "race-specific" can easily restart it. The power of this ancient metaphor reveals itself fully when news articles identifying a genetic basis for this or that medical condition are read, and even written, as if "genetic" and "racial" were one and the same. At that point, "gene" is no longer a scientific notion. It is a folk notion traveling incognito.

The equation of *genetic* with *racial* slides into research, as reported in a 1990 *New York Times* article headlined "Uneasy Doctors Add Race-Consciousness to Diagnostic Tools":

One treatment for severe episodes of sickle cell disease, an inherited blood disorder that mainly affects blacks in this country, involves giving the patient blood transfusions. About one-third of these patients develop antibodies against foreign proteins in the donated blood, which makes it very difficult to find compatible blood for subsequent treatment ... Researchers determined that

64 For forty years (1932–72), the designers of the experiment tested the hypothesis by awaiting autopsy evidence from black subjects, withholding treatment in the meantime, and keeping their professional colleagues informed. Over the years and without moral qualms, they published the findings in the *American Journal of Public Health*, the *Journal of the American Medical Association*, and the *New England Journal of Medicine*. See James H. Jones, *Bad Blood: The Tuskegee Syphilis Experiment* (New York: Free Press, 1993), 27–8; and Alfred Yankauer, "The Neglected Lesson of the Tuskegee Study," *American Journal of Public Health* 88:9 (September 1998), 1406.

82 percent of the antibodies produced by sickle cell patients were against four proteins commonly found in blood donated by whites and suggested that the complication was partly a result of racial differences.[65]

Even a cursory examination of the evidence proves that what the researchers identified was not a racial characteristic. Among Afro-Americans, a minority exhibit sickle-cell trait. Of that minority, a further minority develops sickle-cell disease. Of that minority, one-third produced the antibodies in question. In other words, the antibodies occurred in a minority of a minority of a minority of Afro-Americans. Why call something a racial characteristic that is neither racial nor characteristic?[66]

And what of the researchers' sickle-cell patients, also black and also recipients of blood from white donors, who, when transfused with what the researchers call "racially unmatched blood, " did not produce the same reaction? By the reasoning at work, race retained its explanatory status as a "cause" even though it failed to account for the outcomes of two-thirds of the patients. Calling genetic *racial* simplifies analysis by cutting it off.

One might expect scientific investigators to discard and replace a so-called explanation that fails to account for two-thirds of their results; or, if not that, to make room for fresh questions about the

65   Warren E. Leary, "Uneasy Doctors Add Race-Consciousness to Diagnostic Tools," *New York Times*, September 25, 1990, C1. The news article was based on a paper that appeared in the *New England Journal of Medicine*, perhaps the most prestigious of American medical journals: Elliott P. Vichinski, MD, Ann Earles, PNP, Robert A. Johnson, MD, Silvija Hoag, MD, Amber Williams, MT, and Bertram Lubin, MD, "Alloimmunization in Sickle Cell Anemia and Transfusion of Racially Unmatched Blood," *New England Journal of Medicine* 322:23 (June 7, 1990), 1617–21.

66   In the footnotes to Chapter 3, "Of Rogues and Geldings," you will find a reference to the effort of Steven Pinker, a distinguished scientist, to rehabilitate the conception of biological race by referring both to sickle cell trait and to Tay-Sachs disease. He has committed the same error: confusing "genetic" with "racial."

ramifications of the disease itself; or at least to wonder whether doctors treating sickle-cell patients in Turkey, Italy, Greece, India, and elsewhere experience similar problems. After all, sickle-cell patients are not necessarily black Americans. The doctors who first described the sickle-shaped malformation of red blood cells were indeed treating a black patient (in Chicago in 1910). But by 1929, researchers had discovered it in white patients, documenting its existence in Southern Europe.[67] In 1946, researchers in Tarsus (Saint Paul's birthplace), finding sickle-cell sufferers with light hair and green eyes, remarked: "Negroid features ... were not observable in any of the patients."[68]

American folklore still calls sickle cell a "black" disease. In the 1950s, it figured in the vernacular of Southern campaigns to enact blood labeling by race into law.[69] And when Richard Nixon signed the Sickle Cell Control Act of 1972, he first characterized the disease correctly ("an inherited blood disorder, caused by a genetically determined change in the chemical constituents of hemoglobin, thus affecting the oxygen-carrying capacity of the blood") and in the next breath mischaracterized it as a disease that "strikes only blacks."[70] That mischaracterization enjoys a singular immunity to scientific disproof. During the fall of 2010, a hot exchange broke out at a respected medical school when a white woman doctor

---

67 Todd L. Savitt, "Tracking Down the First Recorded Sickle Cell Patient in Western Medicine," *Journal of the National Medical Association* 102:11 (November 2010), 981–92.

68 Musafer Aksoy, "Sickle Cell Anemia in South Turkey: A Study of Fifteen Cases in Twelve White Families," *Blood* 11 (1956), 463. See also William C. Boyd, "Detection of the Selective Advantages of the Heterozygotes in Man," *Physical Anthropology* 13:1 (March 1955), 37–52.

69 Lederer, *Flesh and Blood*, 130–2. Michael G. Kenny, "A Question of Blood, Race, and Politics," *Journal of the History of Medicine and Allied Sciences* 61:4 (2006), 474.

70 Richard Nixon, "Signing Statement for the Sickle Cell Anemia Control Act" (May 16, 1972), in John Woolley and Gerhard Peters, eds., American Presidency Project, www.presidency.ucsb.edu.

stood in a public lecture to contradict a distinguished speaker who had observed, in passing, that sickle cell was not a "black" disease.[71] Besides, the idea of blood exclusivity arouses emotion. Some Afro-Americans who do not even carry the trait embrace the disease as "racial identity"; Euro-Americans who do carry the trait and the disease have no public profile. As a disorder of the blood, sickle cell in America has become entangled in the folk notions surrounding the notion of blood-as-race.

A similar entanglement explains the contortions of a young woman, aspirant to a scientific career, as she lurches between scientific and folk conceptions.[72] "Thanks to knowledge of DNA," she allows, "race is not scientific." But, she goes on to insist that race may, nevertheless, be "meaningful" in medicine and has dreams of studying "genetic health risks in the multiracial population." To do that, she must ignore inheritance through parents (a proper subject for genetic study) and pursue instead the faux-genetics of "the multiracial population," a purely political concoction. From the initial false premise, she proceeds through a series of non sequiturs to elaborate her professional aspiration: to discover "genetic predictors that help identify whether multiracial people may have higher or lower efficacy in response to a drug." If she means "higher or lower" compared to (supposedly) unmixed persons, she has reinvented pure races, the core fiction of bioracist thought. And in identifying the offspring of mixed parents as a "multiracial population"—that is, literally sui generis, different from both parents—she has rediscovered a core fiction of folk-racism, unnatural neo-humans. It must bemuse any Martian who may be monitoring Earth from a distant outpost to find intelligent life studying nature, learning something about it, and then blithely discarding the results.

---

71   Personal communication by a witness (name withheld) to this exchange.
72   Kendall Baldwin, "The Mystery of Genetics in Multiracial Health Care," Teen Project RACE, www.projectrace.com.

Lay persons are not the only ones who, like that young woman, conjure with metaphorical blood. Most scientists learned to think within the metaphor long before they learned to think outside it, as scientists, about actual blood. Might not even a scientifically literate person, upon reading deCode Genetics' disclosure about Dr. James Watson's genome,[73] have offhanded something like, "To look at Jim [Watson] you'd never know he had black blood"? And of course you would not. Precisely the fear of not knowing has long amplified the dread of "miscegenation," a dread that even now, as President Obama has put it, evokes "a distant world of horsewhips and flames, dead magnolias and crumbling porticos."[74]

William Faulkner captured the dread, and the blood fixation behind it, in his novel *Light in August* (1932). When a mob castrated the "white nigger" Joe Christmas, "the pent black blood seemed ... to rush out of his pale body like the rush of sparks from a rising rocket; upon that black blast the man seemed to rise soaring into [the townspeople's] memories forever and ever." Black blood exists only as metaphor. Faulkner's genius was to convey the metaphor, not by inventing a further metaphor, but literally and realistically. The members of the mob saw and remembered physical evidence that seemed to corroborate what, in fact, they saw only with the mind's eye. Their own actions created evidence, not of Joe Christmas's ancestry (which they never ascertained), but for the blood-is-race equation:

> The black blood drove him first to the negro cabin. And then the white blood drove him out of there, as it was the black blood which snatched up the pistol and the white blood which would not let him fire it ... It was the black blood which swept him by his own desire beyond the aid of any man, swept him up into that ecstasy out of a black jungle where life has already ceased before the heart stops

73 See Introduction, p. 8.
74 Barack Obama, *Dreams From My Father: A Story of Race and Inheritance* (New York: Three Rivers Press, 1995), 11.

and death is desire and fulfillment. And then the black blood failed him again.[75]

This extraordinary metaphysics, which Faulkner ascribes to a Southern community circa 1932, animated the Frederick Douglass obituary of 1895 and updated itself in 2009, to kidnap a young woman's precious dreams of work worth doing.

A similar metaphysics led to a clash between natural and metaphorical blood under the Nazis' Nuremberg Blood Law of September 1935. The law forbade blood mixing but said nothing about transfusion.[76] An unsettling practical question rushed almost immediately into that silence. A Jewish doctor had used his own blood to give an Aryan patient an emergency transfusion. Having a compatible blood type, he saved the Aryan's life. The question was "Did the life-saving blood reclassify his Aryan patient?" On October 19, a certain Professor Leffler, highly placed in the racial-political bureau of the National Socialist Party, dismissed any such suggestion as "sheer nonsense," a product of "mental confusion due purely to the figurative use of the word 'blood' in the sense of heredity."[77]

But the law, which spoke of "defilement," that is, profanation, possessed not "confusion" but terrible ritual clarity.[78] By definition, a profanation alters something or someone instantly and absolutely; in the paradigm case, from life to death. As both a scientist and a Nazi official, Leffler had his boots in both natural and figurative blood. Therefore: The Jewish doctor's donation of natural blood saved an Aryan life, while his donation of figurative blood justified his being sent to a concentration

75   Faulkner, *Light in August* (Norwalk, CT: Easton Press, 1992 [1932]), 344, 449, 464–5.

76   "Law for the Protection of German Blood and German Honor (September 15, 1935)," Jewish Virtual Library, http://www.jewishvirtuallibrary.org.

77   Wireless to the *New York Times*, October 20, 1935, 28. Collection of the Boatwright Library, University of Richmond.

78   Durkheim, *Elementary Forms of Religious Life*, 303–13.

camp.[79] During the war, donors were compelled to prove their Aryan descent. To the real world models of Faulkner's Mississippians, such a regulation would have seemed entirely justified, never mind the likely cost in lives. In the words of a Louisiana politician of the succeeding generation, when his state's blood-segregation law came under attack: "I would see my family die and go to eternity before I would see them have a drop of nigger blood in them."[80]

The War Department appreciated the tenacity of such beliefs. In 1940, the United States, not yet in the war, was aiding Britain through the "Plasma for Britain" program, and calls went forth for blood donation to save victims of the Blitz. Despite the urgency, some questioned the propriety of sending "Negro blood" to the British wounded and even turned away black would-be donors. Their noise accompanied the work of Dr. Charles Drew, an Afro-American surgeon and expert on blood storage, who built and directed the program.[81] His close colleague was Dr. John Scudder, a professor at the Columbia University College of Medicine and Surgery who, two years earlier, had chaired his doctoral dissertation on blood storage. Drew had taken leave from his post at the Howard University College of Medicine and deferred his dream of training surgeons there. In New York, he worked with the racist drumbeat ever at his back. As the United States readied itself for war and the Red Cross Blood Bank's preparations became more urgent, the War Department silenced the drums. It ordered segregation of the blood supply for what it called "reasons not biologically convincing" but "commonly recognized [as] psychologically important in America."[82]

---

79   Wireless to the *New York Times*, October 20, 1935, 28.

80   Lederer, *Flesh and Blood*, 134.

81   Robyn Mahone-Lonesome, *Charles Drew* (New York: Chelsea House, 1990), 49, 62, 72–3.

82   Quoted in ibid., 77. Norman H. Davis, Chairman of the American Red Cross, answered a pointed question by Eleanor Roosevelt in almost identical language; quoted in Lederer, *Flesh and Blood*, 117.

"Indefensible from any point of view," declared Drew who, after returning to Howard University, took part in the fight against the exclusion of black people from donating blood.[83] If wartime sacrifice was every citizen's duty, then giving blood was every citizen's right. The campaigners won the point after a fashion, but the "victory" gave rise to blood labeling by race. The fight and its outcome soured Afro-Americans on blood donation for years thereafter.[84] Scudder, who took over after Drew's departure, presided over the logistics, sane and insane, of managing America's stored blood in the war emergency.[85] The insane logistics ranged from designating separate refrigerators (or labeled shelves therein) and separate days for black donors, to "do you mind?" queries addressed to transfusion patients.[86] (Landsteiner, settled in the United States since 1922, must have felt like an Extraterrestrial.) Not until 1950, the year in which Drew died tragically, did the Red Cross announce that it had stopped the practice of segregating blood.[87]

John Scudder added his own chapter to the ancient metaphysics of blood. At an annual convention of blood bankers in 1959, he and a Canadian colleague unveiled a "new philosophy" of racial blood that applied the blood-race equation to blood transfusion. Among other things, the new philosophy held that transfusion could be

83   Spencie Love, with a Foreword by John Hope Franklin, *One Blood: The Death and Resurrection of Charles R. Drew* (Chapel Hill, NC: University of North Carolina Press, 1997), 49.

84   The authors' father used to sniff with contempt when driving with them, as children, past the Red Cross headquarters near the Mall in Washington, D.C.

85   Psychologically speaking, blood was no different from a movie theater, a bank, a dry goods store, or a train, in that segregation had to be made practical. In consequence, the planning of public space for different purposes took on strange similarities. See Robert R. Weyeneth, "The Architecture of Racial Segregation: The Challenges of Preserving the Problematical Past," *Public Historian* 27:4 (Fall 2005), 11–44.

86   Lederer, *Flesh and Blood*, 122.

87   Ibid.

made safer by recruiting donors from the recipient's "own race."[88] By giving advance telephone interviews, Scudder promoted press attendance at the meeting and thereby stoked a national controversy.[89] A *New York Times* headline homed in on Scudder's key point: "Blood Expert Says Transfusion between Races May Be Perilous."[90] In the midst, and in the wake, of that controversy, some Southern states debated laws to require labeling or to prohibit transfusion between black and white persons.[91] Dr. W. Montague Cobb, Drew's colleague in the National Medical Association,[92] immediately invited Scudder to submit to the Association's journal "a concise statement of his premises and evidence" for review by scientific peers, a step Scudder had until then skipped.[93]

Scudder's argument, later reprised in a symposium in the *Journal of the National Medical Association*, rested principally on two cases.[94] In the first, testing the blood of a white veteran,

88   John C. Scudder and William Wigle, "Safer Transfusions Through Appreciation of Variants in Blood Group Antigens in Negro and White Blood Donors, Including Two Case Reports Showing Development of Anti- Jk^a; Jk^b; Anti-S and Anti-Fy^a Iso-Antibodies," *Journal of the National Medical Association* 52:2 (March 1960), 75–80. He later republished it in a eugenics journal. See Michael G. Kenny, "Toward a Racial Abyss: Eugenics, Wycliffe Draper, and the Origins of the Pioneer Fund," *Journal of the History of the Behavioral Sciences* 38:3 (Summer 2002), 259–83, 277.

89   Unsigned Editorial, "Blood Transfusion and Race," 281.

90   This *New York Times* article (November 7, 1959), A2, A3, by A. C. Wehrein, is quoted in Michael G. Kenny, "A Question of Blood, Race, and Politics," *Journal of the History of Medicine and Allied Sciences* 61:4 (2006), 457–91, 459.

91   Lederer, *Flesh and Blood*, 130–2. See also Kenny, "Toward a Racial Abyss," 277.

92   The association, founded in 1895, launched its journal in 1909. The American Medical Association opened to Afro-American doctors in 1969. Dr. W. Montague Cobb (see below, note 94) played a key role within the NMA and against the policies of the AMA. See Harriet A. Washington, "Apology Shines Light on Racial Schism in Medicine," *New York Times*, July 29, 2008, F5.

93   Unsigned Editorial, "Blood Transfusion and Race," 280.

94   Scudder and Wigle, "Safer Transfusions Through Appreciation of

who was being prepared for open-heart surgery, had revealed an "atypical" antibody. Scudder attributed it to the "Negro donor" who had given him blood during an exploratory procedure conducted earlier. In the second, a black Canadian woman with sickle cell anemia began to have severe reactions after sixteen years of transfusion and many units of blood. Scudder ascribed her difficulty to the likelihood that, in the city of Hamilton, Ontario, all of her donors were white. The symmetrical case studies, one white and one black, set up Scudder's slogan, "Unto each his own," his version of the Sunday-go-to-meeting, best-for-all-concerned formulation of Jim Crow.

Scudder's audience of scientists was riveted by the medical issue, safe transfusion, and thus by the moving parts of natural blood. In contrast, Scudder was addressing his other audiences as well. He freely intertwined his personal musings (about the superior rationality of arranged marriage under India's caste system and about the proper breeding of great racehorses) with his discussion of the blood factors implicated in the two incidents.[95] When focused on those incidents, Scudder argued that the danger of transfusion between black and white people arose because certain antigens occur in the two groups with different statistical frequency. But the particulars of the two incidents reveal a less tidy reality than Scudder envisaged.

The veteran in the first incident had been sensitized against an antigen that Scudder's table showed to be statistically more frequent among black people (93 percent) than white (77 percent). Drawing attention to that table, one commentator pointed out what would have been obvious to anyone not viewing the evidence through the haze of racecraft: that the white veteran might well have been

Variants in Blood Group Antigens in Negro and White Blood Donors," 75.

95   The unsigned editorial "Blood Transfusion and Race," 282 (probably by W. Montague Cobb, then editor of the *Journal of the National Medical Association*), doubted that "responsible Indian leaders would today defend the caste system and arranged marriage on biological grounds."

sensitized by a white donor's blood.[96] In the second incident, testing on the Canadian woman's blood revealed antibodies against an antigen statistically more common in white donors than black. But his own table revealed that she had about one chance in four of being sensitized by a black donor's blood. Furthermore, even then experts knew the risk of adverse reaction to be cumulative, and she had had a great many transfusions, over many years. One of the commentators, the president of the American Association of Blood Bankers, identified the key point: "Every individual has a complex arrangement of different blood factors, making his blood as unique as his own fingerprints."[97] In other words, the individual, not the group, is the appropriate unit of analysis. Guesswork rooted in statistical generalization is no substitute for individual testing to obtain the closest possible matching of blood.

End of story, it would seem. The ban on black blood donors ended before the war did. The commotion about blood segregation quieted in 1950, except in Deep South fastnesses, and is silent today. Leading American scientists refuted Scudder's "new philosophy." A new day seemed to dawn. Yet into that new light falls the shadow. The blood-race equation shambles from the grave in which Ashley Montagu's generation tried to bury it. As George Santayana (almost) said, those who do not learn from history will have no idea what they are repeating.

In August 2010, the Atlanta office of the American Red Cross mailed an appeal to black college students at the Atlanta University Center. "African-American donors," the letter explained, "provide the best chance of survival for patients of color with rare blood types or those who must have repeated transfusions for sickle cell anemia, heart disease, kidney disease, or trauma." There followed a tag line straight from John Scudder's "Unto Each His Own"

---

96   Leslie C. Dunn, "Comment," *Journal of the National Medical Association* 52:4 (July 1960), 293.

97   Dr. E. R. Jennings, "Statement," *Journal of the National Medical Association* 52:4 (July 1960), 295.

philosophy: "Blood from a donor with a similar ethnic background to that of the patient is less likely to be rejected or cause complications or illness."[98] A tireless time-traveler and agile shape-shifter, the blood-race equation is back, clothed in the good intentions of a Sickle Cell Awareness Month blood drive. Its generous message ("Come out and give blood") conceals a weird threat ("Because your loved one may not be able to accept white blood!").[99]

Was there new evidence to support the old claim? In response to an inquiry, the Red Cross forwarded two items. One was a 2008 article describing (among other things) a proposed "transfusion model" under which sickle-cell patients would be given blood "from only AA [that is, African-American] donors," on the rationale that an "E-negative, C-negative, Fy(a)-negative, K-negative, and Jk(b)-negative red blood cell product is 93 per cent likely from an AA donor and only 7% likely from a white donor."[100] But "AA" turns out to be a genetically meaningless category, for it includes persons who "identify with African American culture" or with "other cultural groups such as English-speaking Caribbean and African immigrants."[101]

That "English-speaking" and "identifying with African American culture" might be relevant to blood antigens came as news to the present authors. But most baffling was the inclusion of "African" in the catch-all "AA" category, since Africa's peoples

98 Regional Office, American Red Cross, [To Blood Donors in Atlanta], August 19, 2010, in authors' possession.

99 Personal communication from Jonathan Marks, February 12, 2011. Consider this excerpt from a 1990 letter by Gerald M. Bordin, MD, to the *New England Journal of Medicine*: some blood banks "permitted delays in the initiation of transfusion therapy because racially matched blood was not immediately available (although blood from a racially different donor was available)." *New England Journal of Medicine*, November 15, 1990, 1420.

100 Beth H. Shaz, James C. Zimring, Derrick G. Demmons, and Christopher C. Hillyer, "Blood Donation and Transfusion: Special Considerations for African Americans, *Transfusion Medicine Reviews* 22:3 (July 2008), 202–14, 202.

101 Ibid., 207.

are more diverse genetically than the rest of the world combined.[102] The working assumptions of the article seem to be that all sickle-cell patients are black, that all black people have similar assortments of antigens, and that a 93 percent likelihood of safety is an acceptable (because cost-saving) alternative to individual testing. The authors concede that "no clinical trials have been performed to show that such an approach would reduce the rate of alloimmunization." Still, a question arises whether an Ethical Review Board would approve research founded on what amounts to a bet that, when the trigger is pulled, the hammer will fall on an empty chamber 93 percent of the time and on a bullet in the other 7 percent. What would a consent form for participants in such a study look like?

The other item that the Red Cross offered was the study of sickle-cell patients discussed above, notable for its "partly" racial causality that proved irrelevant for two-thirds of the patients, and for the reappearance of "black blood" in modern camouflage. Equally notable is its talk of matching blood "by race or antigen," that is, by either a census category or a natural substance.[103] Another oddity is its junk comparison group: a small sample of "non-black" patients with miscellaneous anemias, drawn from a single hospital. The disinterment of that antiquated study prompted the present authors to read it along with the correspondence it provoked at the time. A group of doctors from Spain calculated the rate of mismatched red-cell antigens from data provided in the original article. They concluded that "racially mismatched blood would not be the cause of the high alloimmunization rate in patients with sickle cell anemia." A correspondent from Memphis wondered why the authors took for granted that the prevalence of antigens

---

102   Joel Achenbach, "Africans Have World's Highest Genetic Diversity, Study Finds," *Washington Post*, May 1, 2009, Met 2 Edition, A4, reporting on Sarah A. Tishkoff et al., "The Genetic Structure and History of Africans and African Americans, *Science* 324:5930 (May 22, 2009), 1035–1044.

103   Vichinski et al., "Alloimmunization in Sickle Cell Anemia," 1620.

would vary more between white and black populations than within those populations, when their own evidence showed the prevalence of the C antigen in the white American population, ranging from 68 percent to 83 percent.[104] The Red Cross offered no guidance on these questions to the lay recipients of its supporting "evidence."

And so the tour returns to its starting point, the mingling of peoples that goes back many generations in America. When, as mentioned above, Eggleston interviewed his "reliable colored man" at Hampton, he listed three sources of the man's genetic inheritance: "one-fourth Negro, one-fourth Amerind and the remaining half white man" (see above, p.46). Many Americans of long heritage in the United States do not owe their genetic constitution to any one of those tidily bounded quasi-genetic units called races. The phrase "to all appearance" deliberately qualified our description of the dark-skinned EMT in charge of the Creek Nation's ambulance as "black." Was he related to the Creek Nation? In fact, his surname, "White," appears on a genealogical list of "Black Creeks."[105] Nature need not follow the "one drop of blood" rule when passing along traits.[106]

The idea of a one-drop-of-blood rule for identifying black persons carries no trace of oddity for most native-born Americans. Outside that gravitational field, however, such language can be, literally, unintelligible. When one of the authors lectured at Keio University in Tokyo some years ago, that expression stumped a group of students, proficient in English, who were interpreting for their classmates. Although human beings do not actually have some of this blood and some of that, Americans typically do not

104   Arturo Pereira, Roberto Massara, and Ricardo Castillo; and Barbara J. Wilson-Relyea; Correspondence, *New England Journal of Medicine* 323:20 (November 15, 1990), 1421–2.

105   Googling out of curiosity turned up a book by Gary Zellar, *African Creeks: Estelvste and the Creek Nation* (Norman: University of Oklahoma Press, 2007), on a website devoted to "Mixed-Race Studies."

106   Virginia's "Racial Integrity Act of 1924" aimed for exhaustive enforcement of the "one-drop" rule. See Black, *War Against the Weak*, 167–81.

register the concept as metaphorical. Many non-Americans find it so bizarre as to defy translation. A Japanese colleague suggested that it smacked of the ghoulish, rather like speaking of someone's having a pound of this flesh and a pound of that.

"Ghoulish" fits the irruption of umbilical cord blood into politics, enlisting sensible efforts to "collect cord blood for public use and deposit in the national inventory" into a political project to create a racial classification. Umbilical cord blood, which holds the same promise for healing as embryonic stem cells, has no business in such company. Blood and state-sponsored racial classification form a political compound of known destructive power. But Project RACE has precisely that mission. Its motto is "Leading the movement for a multiracial classification." (RACE is an acronym for "Reclassify All Children Equally.") A 1996 bulletin urged participation in the bone marrow drive, proving that, if blood is the soul of racecraft and if the familiar recipe of politically concocted race calls for blood, then every phase of blood stands open to metaphorical application. To "ghoulish," therefore, we add "instructive."

Not all groups that might be thought akin to Project RACE, however, have traveled the same road, set the same goals, or reached the same conclusions. The logic to be examined now pertains to that organization and is not necessarily representative. Even Project RACE did not begin with blood. It launched itself with the claim that the new census classification would help to prevent mistaken diagnoses and thus "save lives."[107] In the early 1990s, a researcher repeatedly asked activists how a state-sponsored racial classification could possibly accomplish any such thing. No one proffered an answer. Indeed, no one seemed to have thought much, if at all, in terms of workaday cause and effect.[108] What seems to have mattered was the thought-structure of racecraft, which readily dispenses with material causality. Within it, the notion of

---

107   Kim M. Williams, *Mark One or More: Civil Rights in Multiracial America* (Ann Arbor, MI: University of Michigan Press, 2006), 44.

108   See Introduction, 21.

a race dovetails with the folk notion that different races of people have differently constituted bodies and correspondingly different susceptibilities to illness. Whereas Jefferson cited that notion as a rationale for deporting freed slaves,[109] its deployment today, with the rationale of "saving lives," lends a beneficent veneer to folk racism. Indeed, the will to beneficence may explain how the census classification "Hispanic" was "not a race" in 2003 but, by 2007, had become the object of the taxpayer-funded "Latino Genetics Study," which called for "testing to identify genetic tendencies in illnesses and disorders among Hispanics … ."[110]

By fall 1996, Project RACE believed in blood types called "ethnic" and "biracial/multiracial." Their efforts, in the national campaign to encourage Americans to register as bone marrow donors, appeared on a bulletin titled "Urgent Medical Concerns." Dr. Martin Luther King, Jr., at top right of the screen, speaks as he did in 1966, arguing for Medicaid: "Of all the forms of inequality, injustice in healthcare is the most shocking and inhuman."[111] Thirty years later, his memory and his words are annexed by a self-inventing new "minority" campaigning for the multiplication of racism rather than its uprooting, the antithesis of what King stood for. The bulletin warns the organization's members that "donors for multiracial people are RARE because of the need for racial and ethnic matching."[112] The truth is that matching is individual, tragically so when (as in about 70 percent of cases) close relatives and

109   See above, p. 18.
110   See above, p. 47. To complicate further, "the census figures for 'white' refer to those who are not of Hispanic ethnicity," while Hispanic, "for purposes of defining interracial marriages … is counted as a race." Hope Yen, "Multiracial People Become Fastest-Growing US Group," AP, May 28, 2009.
111   A 2009 video by Teen Project RACE, "Invisible PSA: Multiracial Americans Speak Up for Equality in Health Care," December 2009, www.projectrace.com.
112   "First National Effort to Reach Multiracial Bone Marrow Donors a Success," www.projectrace.com (extreme emphasis in the original).

even full siblings of the patient cannot provide a match.[113] The bulletin's blood-talk teeters on the edge of letting members imagine that they would be helping to prepare especially labeled supplies.

Pernicious falsehood seldom advertises its pedigree. Who would have thought, at this late date, that people would conceive a hankering to rehabilitate racist subcategories that were born centuries ago in every New World slave society except the United States—which made do with a categorical black/white distinction? Or would turn to primitive fascination with blood as a mystical symbol of group membership, and to genealogical investigation reminiscent of the *estatutos de limpieza de sangre* that once identified Jews for persecution in Spain and Spanish America? Yet it is today's news. In early 2009, the Project RACE organization's website editorialized about two pending bills that it supported as components of a single agenda. One, "The California School Racial Equality Designation Act" (AB1281), "outlined a way for *any* educational system to allow biracial and multiracial children the respect and dignity they deserve ... ." The other, "The California Umbilical Cord Collection Program" (AB 52), had general application, but it would "also help save the lives of multiracial children and adults, as a medical program similar to bone marrow donation."[114]

On April 24 of that year, the California Assembly passed AB 52 with wording that, without fully endorsing the bogus medical claims, allowed the activists to declare victory. It passed AB 1281 as well.[115] In advertising the presence of six "multiracial"

---

113   National Marrow Donor Program, "Learning About Bone Marrow or Cord Blood Transplants," http://www.marrow.org.

114   "Legislation Introduced in California!" archived at www.projectrace.com (emphasis in the original). Project RACE: "Leading the movement for a multiracial classification. A brief summary appears at aablooddriveandmarrowregistry4sicklecellawareness.webs,cin/ab52cord bloodbill.htm. Accessed on 22 June 2010.

115   Susan Graham, "Unanimous Passage of California Legislation!," April 28, 2009, archived at www.projectrace.com. The bill can be read at http://info.sen.ca.gov. The governor vetoed AB 52 on October 11, 2009.

employees in his office, the politician who godfathered AB 52 implied that those employees would share in the life-saving medical benefits. The suggestion was nonsense. Like the far more numerous people of mixed descent not classified as multiracial, those employees will be saved from nothing by this pastiche of last-headline science and make-believe genetics. Set aside the medical nonsense, though, and notice the wide-awake shrewdness applied to repackaging the stuff of nightmares. This purposefully encoded, politically deployed racecraft serves as a reminder that what depends on imagination and action is more flexible than nature, and has the power to create a quasi-nature more convincing than nature itself.

How Americans Look

This tour began with aspects of racecraft that depend on what another person looks like, at a glance, to a viewer observing quickly and superficially. Deference rules, variable sumptuary codes, mistaken shootings by police, and border monitoring of segregated spaces all stand in reference to a person as a seen "object." That reference entails, besides, a seeing object and of course a seeing subject. These varied sightlines of racecraft are not separate phenomena. They occur together or in rapid sequence, and in constantly shifting perspective. To conclude, therefore, our tour examines in close-up the intimate yet public practices that organize individual perception of physical appearance, including one's own, as subject. If physical appearance belonged to nature, it would be no more meaningful to a casual viewer than the pattern of stripes on a zebra's back. In fact, Americans observe themselves and each other through their own eyes and those of others, all the while classifying and evaluating. Thus racecraft has an inner horizon that turns out to be densely populated with sometimes peculiarly selected physical traits. A living person, to be met presently, ascribes meaning to the shape of his jawbone. And Jefferson preferred the skin color of white people, with its "fine mixtures of red and white," to that of black people, "that external monotony, that immovable veil of black which covers all the emotions."[116]

That "veil of black" can also unleash emotions, as happened when the portrait of a dark-skinned woman appeared on the cover of a scholarly journal. The artist intended to illustrate an article about the "morally destructive" content of Aunt Jemima as a representation of Afro-American women.[117] As provocative as the essay was in content and form, the image proved to be more so. The artist had painted a young black woman, standing or seated nowhere in particular, with the skin color, nose, lips, and stocky build that many black women have. She had tied her hair with a colorful scarf (as black women, and not only black women, often do, especially on bad-hair days). She wore no lipstick and no smile. And her remarkable eyes looked straight ahead with a neutral expression. What she might be thinking, and what to think about her, the artist left to the viewer's imagination. The viewers did, indeed, imagine. Many who wrote to protest, black and white, saw a reinforcement of the very stereotype that the author had set out to overthrow. The author of the article herself objected to the illustration, writing that "the Aunt Jemima logo in some form" would have been "a more accurate image."[118] In fact, the young woman of the cover is unlike the Aunt Jemima of the pancake box. Aunt Jemima is middle-aged, wears lipstick, smiles, and is understood to be at work in someone's kitchen.

So what sparked the commotion? One correspondent hinted at a truth that the others avoided: that the artist's unsmiling

---

116   Thomas Jefferson, *Notes on the State of Virginia*, in *Writings* (New York: Library of America, 1984 [orig. ed. 1787]), 264–5.

117   Emilie M. Townes, "The Cultural Production of Evil: Some Notes on Aunt Jemima and the Imagination," *Harvard Divinity Bulletin* (Winter 2006), 30–42.

118   Emilie M. Townes, "Cover Questions," *Harvard Divinity Bulletin* (Spring 2006), 9–10, and letters from other individuals and from the Standing Committee on Diversity at Harvard Divinity School.

young woman was too dark-skinned to refute the caricature. To succeed, though, a racist caricature must have the viewer's assent to its point of view. Neither the pancake-box image nor the portrait can make dark skin, in and of itself, hard to look upon. The viewer must bring that reaction to the picture or, for that matter, to a real person. Physical features simply are what they are.[119] But they are also what they can become in a workaday encounter: in a grocery line, taxi, country club pool, and so on; or, indeed, in a police operation like the one that ended in tragedy when a white police academy graduate killed his black classmate, having failed to recognize him.[120] In that dreadful instance, split-second judgment explosively merged a person with a stereotype. That judgment exposed parts of racecraft's inner horizon that inhabit perception itself.

Our tour ends on an Internet site where Americans can be overheard thinking aloud about perception. Does physical appearance register ancestry and, if so, how? An "Undecided Question" appeared at Answers.yahoo.com in April 2008, at the height of that year's presidential primary election: "Why do Caucasian people have ethnic traits sometimes?"[121] We neither analyze nor edit the responses, but simply note that most respondents posed further questions, such as: "Do I look fully caucasian in these pictures?" "I don't have a Hispanic-like jaw I have a caucasian jaw why?" "Why is there full Hmong people with Caucasian features such as blond, reddish hair Colored eyes, etc.?" "Are freckles caucasian traits?" (The "Best Answer" to the last question, decided by vote, was "no its not," for which its contributor, "bAdHaBi," offered proof by signing off as "black n rican with freckles.") "In MIXED RACE

119   Karen E. Fields, "Cover Questions II," *Harvard Divinity Bulletin* (Autumn 2006), 2.

120   Tina Kelley, "Calls for Calm after Shooting of Policeman by Colleagues," *New York Times* (January 30, 2000), Sect. I, 14; Marion Davis, "Did Cornel Young Jr. Die in Vain?," *The Providence Phoenix* (January 23–29, 2004).

121   Googling "Caucasian" and "traits" yielded these results.

people, why are Caucasian traits expressed LESS than the other race's traits? I'd like to understand WHY genes seem to be 'subordinate' or 'submissive' when they mix with another racial group. I've been curious about this for a long time." "Why do Caucasians have a wider range of physical traits, like hair color and texture and eye color, than other races?"

A reply from "Overeducated" redirects the conversation: "Maybe because all these white supremacists (although I'm white) are wrong in thinking the Caucasian race is a single, pure race … maybe the Caucasian race is a little more mixed up than they'd like to admit." Three months later, an answer came from "Richard. yo," who in the meantime had looked up "Caucasian" in a reference book: "Here is the anthropology definition. 'Of or being a major human racial classification traditionally distinguished as very light to brown skin pigmentation and straight to wavy hair, and including peoples indigenous to Europe, northern Africa, western Asia, and India. No longer in scientific use." Therefore, he concludes, "It covers a wide variety of people, it's to be expected that they would have a wider range of physical traits." Alongside this exchange, an unidentified questioner in the sidebar wonders: "Once you are born, can you genetically change your eye color or hair color genes?"

Taking up the subject of variation, "68 charger" suspected that "we are the most mixed race but have no facts to substantiate that claim. Maybe someone more knowledgeable than myself will." "King of Sexytown" rejoined: "Maybe we are all one race and the range of physical traits is just that wide." Here speaks "only humane": "Lets go back to the beginning. Lets take Adam. Adam was created from the earth from the lightest hue to the darkest, the smoothest to the roughest. We are children of Adam and Eve, Eve was also created from Adam (one of his ribs) so knowing that In My Opinion it leads me to believe that we are all related all races, regions and climates can contribute for our more distinctive features but the features of some race groups can come out at any time in any race. I think its Gods way of reminding us who's in control. Just a thought."

In his study of European witchcraft, from the vantage point of nineteenth-century Britain, W. E. H. Lecky sought to identify the moment when "the idea of absurdity" began to travel alongside stories of "old women riding on broomsticks," the moment when the improbability of such stories could be felt, at long last.[122] What seemed obviously true to his long-dead historical subjects seemed as odd to him, in his day, as it does to Americans of the present. Since our task is to look forward from today's America, we try in the coming chapters to put on display the oddness of social beliefs and practices that Americans continue to take for granted, to show where they come from historically, and to share the clues we have about how they work. We conclude that racecraft has nothing to recommend it or to redeem it as truth about the world. Accordingly, we invite our fellow Americans to explore how the falsehoods of racecraft are made in everyday life, in order to work out how to unmake them. Once we Americans learn to see them for what they are, we can make sense of our past and therefore of our present. Then we may at last be ready to write a new chapter.

122   W. E. H. Lecky, *History of the Rise and Influence of the Spirit of Rationalism in Europe*, with an Introduction by C. Wright Mills (New York: George Braziller, 1955 [1982]), 34.

2 Individual Stories and America's Collective Past

To write a new chapter requries awareness of a past that all Americans share, whatever their ancestry. The wizardry of racecraft makes Jim Crow appear to have affected black Americans alone. It also makes slavery appear to have involved the South alone and to have vanished without repercussions when the Civil War blew it away in 1865. In the teaching of American history, perhaps the most difficult lesson to convey is that slavery once held the entire country in its grip. It was not just the business of enslaved black people, slaveholders, or the South. Slavery engaged an immense geography of connected activities that no Americans could escape, whoever they were and wherever they lived. What is more, slavery does not belong only to America's past, but is the heritage of all Americans alive today, including those of recent vintage. Slavery enthroned inequality both among free citizens and between slaves and owners and, in the manner of its ending, left inequality as a permanent bequest to America's future.

The "history writ large" of most schoolbooks is better at linking events in the past than at discerning continuity between past and present. Stories about actual people and their lives in real worlds of the past dramatize that continuity. In our first appearance on a platform together, at the Fourth Southern Conference on Women's History at the College of Charleston in June 1997, we presented the script that follows to other teachers, and publish it here for the first time. The stories it recounts concern Americans, in diverse historical circumstances, who *differ by ancestry, class, economic predicament, and national origin. The earliest story dates from 1862 and the most recent from 1991.*

Introduction (Karen)

Good afternoon. This is going to be fun for us. It is the first time Professor Fields and I have shared the same platform, let alone attempted a duet. Our subject, above and beyond what the title says, is the connection between scholarly research and teaching.

Even though this is the first time we have tried a duet, we have worked together for many years. We work in different disciplines, history and sociology, but we regularly exploit each other's scholarship. I footnote Professor Fields; Professor Fields footnotes me. We assign each other's writings to our classes, and lecture on them. We have long talks over the phone about ideas, and we read work in progress to each other. We also share a fascination with language, and especially with ordinary turns of phrase that derail thought. What is more, we approach our work in similar ways. In particular, we both hold the philosophical view that means and ends should cohere in all human endeavor, a rule that applies to scholarly research in the social sciences (no matter what discipline), and, I daresay, more generally, to research in any field. If the goal of research is to learn about the nature of our world, then research only fulfills itself in close connection with teaching.

That is true even though some of the time, of course, we do research for ourselves and for the sheer solitary joy of it; sometimes, too, we do it with our professional peers in mind; but often, we do it while imagining that very special re-telling we feel privileged to do as teachers of the young. We follow a profession that is not only honorable but critical. Classically and now, teaching has a civilizational mission: It is the main source and resource of human continuity, hence of community. As this gathering consists mainly of people who are, in one way or another, teachers, we thought we would spend the brief time at our disposal discussing with you some stories and documents to which we often recur in our teaching, and that turn on two themes that constantly engage anyone trying to understand the American past. These themes stand out most clearly, perhaps, if expressed in terms of two sets of apparent opposites: individual experience versus collective experience and separate histories versus joint histories. We will illustrate these points with the help of seven stories, to which we have assigned personal names: "John Boston"; "Rebecca Garvin"; "Aubrey Welch"; "Mrs. Samuel Burden"; "Downtown White People"; "William Faulkner"; and "Toni Morrison."

Racial Divide (Karen)

With the contrast "separate versus joint," we indicate a distinction that only sometimes makes sense, between something called "African American history" and something called, simply, "American history." We insist that what we call in our title "America's collective past" cannot be understood or taught without both and, furthermore, that neither can be understood separately from the other. In making those claims, however, we run up against certain common terms, turns of phrase, and metaphors. If teachers could censor terms for their baneful influence on education, we would go after "racial divide." Its nearest semantic parallel is perhaps the "continental divide," which refers to a physical separation that popular imagination used to visualize in terms of Boston "back east" and Dodge City "out west." That metaphor of separation confuses thought and leads it in the wrong direction.

Afro-Americans and Euro-Americans have always lived not separately but in close quarters, as our stories will illustrate. Equally, and for the same reason, we would impose severe zoning restrictions on the range of the term "segregation." For all its dividing black from white by law and custom, Jim Crow was a historically specific set of arrangements for living separate lives together. How that was managed is the American story, not just the Afro-American story, that research should uncover and teaching should pass on. The metaphor of "racial divide" produces illogical formulations that are as hard to uproot as dandelions, even in the face of contrary facts. For example, my students read the great Frederick Douglass's *Narrative*, with its vivid close-up of his owners' religious conversions, style of consumption, speech habits, and general character, but, despite all that, retain the notion that slavery belongs to the past of black Americans alone.

Individual versus Collective (Barbara)

Finding the right balance between the individual and the collective not only helps us to make sense of the past; it helps us to engage our students with that past in a way that will serve them better as citizens who have work to do in fashioning from the past a more civilized and humane present and future. Unfortunately, it is easy to get the balance wrong. Our very language often tempts us to do so. We talk, for example, about "oral history," as though interviews with witnesses and participants (valuable, certainly, as a way to get at individual experience) were a type of history, when they are actually a type of evidence: no different, in principle, from any other type. Evidence, whether interviews, government documents, private papers, or archeological remains, cannot speak for itself and never adds up to history until it is scrutinized, evaluated, and ordered in light of other evidence. Similarly, talk of "recovering voices" from the past or "letting voices speak" is either a self-delusion or a confidence game. Reduced to their shared fallacy, these tricks of speech represent the elevation of individual experience to the point that it overshadows collective experience, which, after all, is the only kind that affords us a handhold on the machinery of our destiny as human beings.

As deceptive as overemphasis on the individual is the elaboration of a collective picture so grand and encompassing that it blots out individual experience. The danger is not just that we may lose touch with individual experience, but that, in the process, we may falsify the big picture itself. My sister likes to recall the essay at the end of a McNeil-Lehrer Report some years ago, in which Roger Rosenblatt referred to Eisenhower as "the sleepy conservative president who launched the Civil Rights Movement." With the turn of a phrase, the essayist performed a disappearing act on the lives of those Afro-American Southerners who risked life and livelihood, and often lost both, so that Eisenhower might be forced to play his bit part, and Lyndon Johnson his supporting role, in the drama of the Civil Rights Movement. It is not just the lives of the true soldiers of the movement that got falsified in the shuffle; it was the history of the nation in that crucial era. President-itis (the disease that leads otherwise sane people to argue that Eisenhower launched the Civil Rights Movement, Lincoln freed the slaves, Roosevelt cured the depression, and Nixon ended the war in Vietnam) is a common example, but not the only one, of a big picture that proves false because its individual components have gotten lost.

John Boston (Barbara)

Set the "racial divide" metaphor alongside the following story about the Civil War, and notice how uncomfortably the two fit together. John Boston is a humble individual who is nevertheless part of that very big story, and I propose to introduce him to you through a letter that he addressed to his wife in 1862. The very provenance of the document tells you how grand is the drama in which his individual life became suddenly engulfed. After all, how many letters from a husband to his wife end up in the National Archives, in the records of the Adjutant General's Office, which is where this one landed? It landed there because John Boston, a slave in Maryland, escaped from his owner and, having found refuge with the soldiers of a Union regiment encamped in neighboring

Virginia, wrote to inform his wife of his successful escape and to
provide her with details of his whereabouts, so that she could write
to him. His wife may never have seen the letter, but Boston's owner
certainly saw it, and so did a member of the Maryland legislature
to whom the owner complained, and so in turn did the governor
of Maryland, to whom the legislator referred the matter, and so
did General George McClellan, to whom the governor addressed
an indignant demand to know just what Union soldiers thought
they were doing, harboring the runaway slaves of loyal citizens
of Maryland. The letter finally reached the Secretary of War,
although I do not know whether he troubled himself to read it,
complaints from Maryland slaveholders about runaway property
having become a dime a dozen in those days.

So the person I am about to introduce to you was certainly
involved in big doings. But what about him as an individual?
Before I introduce him to you in his own words, perhaps I should
let you imagine him as he might have been imagined (let us say)
by the film-makers who gave us the movie *Glory*: as ragged, dirty,
unkempt, illiterate, inarticulate, and naive as the enlisted men of the
54th Massachusetts Volunteer regiment so memorably slandered in
that movie. Ragged, dirty, unkempt Boston may have been. As to
the rest, let us meet him in his own words.

> My Dear Wife it is with grate joy I take this time to let you know
> Whare I am   I am now in Safety in the 14th Regiment of Brooklyn
> this Day i can Adress you thank god as a free man   I had a little
> truble in giting away   But as the lord led the Children of Isrel to
> the land of Canon So he led me to a land Whare fredom Will rain
> in spite Of earth and hell.

Not knowing whether he and his wife would ever see each other
again, Boston tried to offer comfort: "i trust the time Will Come
When We Shal meet again   And if We dont met on earth We Will
Meet in heven Whare Jesas ranes." Finally, he entreated his wife

to write to him at once and told her how to do so: "I Want you to rite To me Soon as you Can Without Delay   Direct your letter to the 14ᵗʰ Reigment New york State malitia Uptons Hill Virginea In Care of Mʳ Cranford Comary."[1]

As you listen to that language, picture the letter itself. It has no punctuation, the capitalization is erratic, and the spelling is phonetic. It is the work, clearly, of a person having little or no formal education. But "uneducated" does not mean "inarticulate." Boston is no tongue-tied naif, as in the movie *Glory*, awaiting the discipline of sympathetic white officers to teach him that he is a man. Nor does he communicate with his wife in black English (a concept, by the way, that fools people who would not for a moment fall for anything called "white English," though people of European descent have their own distinctive ways of speaking English just as do people of African descent). Boston's diction is that of the King James Bible, his eschatology conventionally Christian ("if We dont met on earth We Will Meet in heven Whare Jesas ranes"), his understanding of marriage, family, and romantic love between husband and wife firmly mainstream. "Separate lives lived together" we might indeed call those of John Boston and the white people who owned him, owned his wife, and defined the terrain on which he and his wife could seek to build a marriage and raise a family. And, as if to drive the point home, Boston could not even tell his wife how to write to him without at the same time informing his owner. Indeed, I suspect (though I cannot prove it) that Boston expected his owner to intercept the letter and intended to gloat, to dare his owner to try to get him back, when he gave his wife precise instructions about how to reply: "Direct your letter to the 14ᵗʰ Reigment New york State malitia Uptons Hill Virginea In Care of Mʳ Cranford Comary."

---

1   Ira Berlin, Barbara J. Fields, Steven F. Miller, Joseph P. Reidy, and Leslie S. Rowland, eds., *Free At Last: A Documentary History of Slavery, Freedom, and the Civil War* (New York: New Press, 1991), 29–30.

Rebecca Garvin Set-Up (Barbara)

Someone I never met, though she is closer to me than John Boston,
may help to illustrate our point about the need to understand
together the separate lives of those divided and those joined by
the color line. What follows is a story about Rebecca Garvin, our
great-grandmother, a story told by her daughter, our grandmother.
It happened in Charleston, South Carolina, in an area reserved for
white people. I will let my sister, Grandmother Fields's collabora-
tor, tell you the story, and then I will ask you to notice something
about it:

Rebecca Garvin (Karen)

When my son Rob was small, Mother used to take him out every
day, to Colonial Lake, which was in the middle of downtown
[Charleston]. She carried him in a special carriage I bought for him
from Hartmann's mail-order house. Few in the city had anything
like my carriage. It was ivory-colored wickerwork, and it had a
reversible top—as you walked, you could look at the baby. Mother
got busy and crocheted an ivory blanket, which she laced through
with blue ribbon around the sides and then caught with blue bows.
Then she covered some pants guards (which men used in those
days, when riding their bicycles) to pull the ends of the blanket
through so it would drape nicely. I don't think, by the time she
got through, that anybody in town, black or white, had a fancier
baby carriage. It entertained her to go along President Street and
then up Calhoun to the lake, talking and laughing with Rob. The
only drawback was that if she got tired, she couldn't sit down. The
benches by Colonial Lake were for white only.

But anyway, Mother went almost every day. One day, a big,
burly, Irish policeman came up to her to admire this rich baby
and play with it too. He smiled, but when he looked in and saw it
was a black baby in the carriage, that was the end of the smiling.

"Where did you get that carriage?" "I didn't get it. His mother got it. Ask her." And she stood there, looking him right in the face, just daring him to touch anything, *daring him*, and mad enough to spit. When he found out it was a black baby she had been pushing every day, he tried to forbid her to come down. She just kept looking at him, right in his red face, until he got through talking. Then she carried on walking around Colonial Lake, round and round and *round*, as much as she was able. Mother said the Lord gave her strength that day, to keep on walking around that lake. The police-man couldn't do anything, because many black women walked with white babies down there. It wasn't forbidden for a black woman to take any color baby to Colonial Lake; she just couldn't sit down.[2]

Rebecca Garvin Conclusion (Barbara)

For most of you, that story is the conventional story of white racism, as epitomized in the stereotypical relationship between Negro and Irish immigrant. But what I want you to notice is the figure who dominates its action, without appearing in person at all: the white Charleston aristocrat, the one to whom the Irish policeman was supposed to show deference. That figure's aura of superiority was so great that his (or her) symbolic presence in the form of a hidden baby was enough to suspend the etiquette of the color line, so far as the behavior of the policeman toward a black woman in a semi-forbidden place was concerned. Why did that policeman grin at Rebecca Garvin every day? Not to express his goodwill toward her or his delight to find her out walking on a fine day. He grinned because the fine carriage and fittings led him to assume that she was the servant of his own betters, tending the child of his betters. Correspondingly, his anger when he discovered his mistake grew from the realization that he had mistakenly offered courtesy to a

2   Mamie Garvin Fields with Karen E. Fields, *Lemon Swamp and Other Places: A Carolina Memoir* (New York: Free Press, 1983), 9–10.

black woman, thinking he was offering it to her white employer. In the same way, Jim Crow on the railways offered an exemption for the Afro-American servant attending her mistress or the mistress's child.

It is easy to overlook the fact that the apparatus of Jim Crow, like that of slavery, imposed relations of dominance and subordination among Euro-Americans, not just between Afro-Americans and Euro-Americans. In other words, among the separate lives divided by the color line, lives that we must analyze together if we are to make sense of them, are those of white people whose rank with respect to each other requires examination. One group of white people outranked the other precisely because it was in a position to oppress and exploit black people. A vast reservoir of bitterness and violence might overflow at any moment against the Afro-American whose words or actions, or whose simple being, reminded a white person of his subservience to another white person.

Aubrey Welch Set-Up (Karen)

Although such encounters certainly offered periodic reminders of one white person's subservience to another, it is more accurate to say that segregation promoted intermittent amnesia on the matter. So when history writ large floodlights segregation, it brings out the black/white distinction while leaving white/white class distinctions hidden in shadow. The disappearance effect applies only at a distance, however. In the next story, Grandmother Fields delivers, in a slow-motion close-up, the class resentments of the white poor that might suddenly erupt in violence.

The background to the story is the constant diplomacy by which Grandmother Fields sought to obtain improvements, of one kind and another, for her school on James Island. Her interlocutor is Mr. Welch, a prosperous landowner who served as the superintendent. On this occasion, her agenda is to obtain "certain extra things" for the Rosenwald Day program.[3] Polished recitations and artful props may say a forbidden thing—that black children are the equals of their white age-mates—silently, without a dangerous word. Danger looms, however, the moment Grandmother Fields discloses to Mr. Welch her intention to invite all the white neighbors to Rosenwald Day. Listen to her.

Aubrey Welch (Barbara)

... Aubrey Welch hurried up to tell me *wait a minute, hold on*: I must invite the "white people" and leave the "crackers" alone because, "The cracker don't want you to have even a painted bench!" And if the "cracker" had reason to think that the school was getting too good for the "nigra," why he might burn it down. Now the "white people" thought different and would "he'p ya too." Uh huh. "Well, Mr. Welch, who are the white people I should invite?" As soon as he let me know who and who and who were the "white people," I made it my business to invite them all.

Always fast on her feet, Grandmother Fields managed to seize the unexpected arrow in mid-air and turn it to practical use, getting a globe for the classroom, a bus for a school trip, all sorts of "extra things." "The 'white people' did give help to the school over the years," she recalls, "and no 'crackers' ever did come to burn down what was too grand for the 'nigras.'" But that night, "when I got home with what Mr. Welch said, Bob and I laughed until we cried."[4] Can you imagine what made them giddy with laughter? I howled as she told the story and did not ask myself why until years later. I suspect that they were savoring the ruin of an illusion, a white supremacy under which all white people were created equal. In their generation (as in ours) black children were taught early

---

3   Named for Julius Rosenwald, a Northern philanthropist who had helped to build and staff rural schools for Afro-American children.

4   Fields and Fields, *Lemon Swamp*, 209–10.

on, for safety's sake, that you'd best "watch yourself" around poor white people, frightening because they were "resentful," elongated in Charlestonian speech as "res*ay*antful." Until that day, it had not occurred to Grandmother and Grandfather Fields that higher-class white people saw poor white people in pretty much the same way.

Mrs. Samuel Burden Set-Up (Barbara)

That is why I prefer, in my teaching, to speak of "Jim Crow," rather than "segregation." *Segregation* is too small a concept to encompass the reality lived by those caught up in Jim Crow. With the end of slavery, in which owners exploited laborers by owning their persons, employers commanded labor by controlling access to the means of labor, subsistence, and livelihood. The power of controlling such access takes many forms, and those seeking access understand full well the protean quality of the force that blocks them, as well as the complicated rituals through which they must dramatize their own subjection. Education could be a militant act in and of itself, on the part of both teacher and student. And so it was in the case of Mrs. Samuel Burden, an elderly woman Grandmother Fields encountered while teaching on James Island during the 1920s.

Mrs. Samuel Burden (Karen)

Mrs. Burden was a military widow, collecting a pension, which meant that she had to collect her money from the white powers-that-be in downtown Charleston. So when my grandmother opened special classes for the parents and grandparents of her day pupils, Mrs. Burden made it her business to be there. People asked Mrs. Burden why she bothered and asked Grandmother Fields why she bothered with a pupil so old. Old as she was, she was going to learn to sign her name. So Mrs. Burden kept coming to school, and,

Grandmother Fields said, brought her teacher "more eggs than the law allows."

Let me open a parenthesis. It is often said that, both during slavery and after, Afro-Americans had a faith in education that verged on the religious: "Seek ye first the kingdom of the Book, and all else shall be added unto you." It is less often said that, both during slavery and after, the comparably fervent conviction of some white Americans pushed in the opposite direction. They became as unconvinced of Afro-Americans' intellectual capacity to benefit from schooling as they were already convinced of Afro-Americans' superior aptitude for planting, tending, and harvesting crops. In 1908, the year Grandmother Fields was finishing her training to teach, a South Carolina school official wrote that "education carries a Negro to the penitentiary faster than anything." So, Grandmother Fields was crossing and re-crossing a battlefield, well known to black and white James Islanders, as she walked from farm to farm urging black families to send their children to school, and perhaps even more when she created literacy classes for adults. Let me now close the parenthesis and come back to the scene of Mrs. Burden's enthusiasm over seventy years ago.

Mrs. Burden was determined to be able to walk into that office of downtown white folks one day and sign for her pension properly. She was determined to stop having to put herself down as "X." Grandmother Fields said, "The day Mrs. Burden could go into that office and sign 'Mrs. Samuel Burden,' she almost didn't need her walking stick." In the Jim Crow South, black and white Americans knew that schooling really was about where one stood in the polity. Mrs. Burden knew it; so did the people who saw her coming that fine day. After long preparation, she executed her mission as a private in the long guerrilla war in America that preceded the conventional phase that finally pressed a "sleepy conservative" like Dwight D. Eisenhower to a strange sort of generalship.

"Segregation-integration" does not encompass what Mrs. Burden's struggle, as opposed to Eisenhower's, was about. Who in the world ever sat down in a hot church in the evening, or at a segregated lunch counter at noonday, or faced dogs and water hoses and cattle prods singing, "O integration…" But surely some of you remember the real civil rights song: "O freedom."[5]

Downtown White People Set-up (Barbara)

What is more, "segregation-integration" conjures up a stick-figure diagram of life under Jim Crow, rather than life as people actually lived it. From a distance, it looks like a predictable world organized by general rules, explicit scripts, identifying costumes (that is, physical appearance) and, infrequently, written signs, with local knowledge doing the rest. The view from close up only now and then fit the diagram. For Mrs. Burden's battlefield planning and preparation, "downtown" served as her fixed objective, for that was the symbolic locus of power in Charleston, and it generally looked the part. In reality, and in accord with the nature of power, the battlefield moved to meet people wherever they were, whatever they might be doing. "In the midst of life, we are in death," intones the officiant at funeral ceremonies according to the tradition in which we were reared. While Jim Crow was not death (at least not always), it did loom up suddenly, like death, in the midst of everyday activities, with unexpected features revealing themselves in different guises from moment to moment.

---

5   Barbara borrowed the illustration from a lecture delivered in her class many years ago by Martha Prescod Norman Noonan, a veteran of SNCC's Mississippi Freedom Summer. At the time of the Charleston conference, our audience, and, indeed, most adult Americans, would still have been familiar with the song, whose first lines are: "O freedom, O freedom." The invocation of those lines with "integration" substituted for "freedom" brought instant laughter and comprehension from the audience, and everyone joined in the singing of the legitimate stanza. The same illustration in a classroom today requires that the teacher sing the entire stanza for the class: "O freedom, O freedom, O freedom over me, And before I'd be a slave, I'd be buried in my grave, And go home to my Lord and be free."

Such was the case on a morning during the 1920s. In her bedroom slippers and with a coat thrown hastily over her nightgown, Grandmother Fields had driven Grandfather Fields to work in their recently acquired Model T and was on her way home. "Since not too many Negro women drove cars," she recalled, "you were recognized and you had to stop and greet people." To drive right by when you recognized someone, and the someone recognized you, was not done. That morning, Grandmother Fields saw Mr. Crawford, pushing his vegetable cart.

Downtown White People (Karen)

Anyway, she slowed her progress and, although Mr. Crawford saw her and stopped, a car coming alongside him did not:

So, BAM, a wreck; and out of this wreck comes a white man. Good Lord! Now, out of the other wreck comes a Negro woman in her houseshoes. And I was a sight, trying to hold up my gown with my hands through the coat pockets and standing there in my worn-out slippers. In fact, my car wasn't really a "wreck," I only had a small dent, but the other one looked bad. As my witness, Mr. Crawford sent a boy for a cop and waited with me, all of us more or less "on display" out in the middle of the avenue.

"Miz Fields, now don't you worry," Mr. Crawford said. But to tell you the truth, neither one of us knew what mightn't happen. The only thing I knew about the other driver was that he came from Vermont, which I read off his plates. He didn't talk to me, and I didn't talk to him. When the cop got there, he walked around the two Model Ts, not saying much either—at first. But then, all of a sudden, Praise the Lord, the cop began to shout and carry on, "You damn Yankees so-and-so. You damn Yankees such-and-such." From the time I heard that, I kept on not saying a word, I kept quiet sure enough. I was not the "damn Yankee."

What came next blurred the lines of the segregation-integration diagram:

> Well, sir, the Rebels took the whole thing in charge. Instead of all the white men getting together to say that I was not in the right (which I was), the white Charlestonians took sides with the black Charlestonian, against the "damn Yankee." First we must go to the court. Now just imagine. There I was, going up past the brass-work and the woodwork, marble everywhere, in my houseslippers, a half-dressed colored woman going in the courthouse in a group of white men. I can't imagine what an onlooker mightn't have thought! ... Finally, we must go to a certain lawyer on Broad Street (near the Battery), where the "aristocratic" lawyers stayed. They sure enough fixed the thing. That poor fellow had to pay everybody a hundred dollars.[6]

William Faulkner Set-up (Barbara)

The landscape of Jim Crow can also be envisioned as a minefield: a person may traverse it safely by not stepping on the mines, but can discover where mines are buried only by stepping on one. Like all analogies, this one is imperfect. Its weakness is that the buried hazards of Jim Crow, unlike those in a minefield, are not in set positions, waiting to go off when stepped on. Instead, the actions of those involved in any given encounter determine the placement of the mine, as well as when or whether it goes off. The participants produce the outcome as the encounter unfolds. William Faulkner offered a brilliant example of the pertinent dynamics in the encounter between three auto thieves and a mud farmer in his novel, *The Reivers*. In the process, he illustrated the role of laughter in the complex etiquette of racist subordination.

Ned McCaslin, an Afro-American employee (and wrong-side-

6   Fields and Fields, *Lemon Swamp*, 166–7.

of-the-blanket relation) of the Priest family, has gone on an illicit
excursion to Memphis, in a car borrowed without permission
from Grandfather Priest, in company with Priest's eleven-year-
old grandson and a white employee of the family. En route to
Memphis, the car gets stuck in a mud puddle deliberately cultivated
by a white farmer who makes his living by offering passing motor-
ists the loan of his mules to extract their cars. As the farmer, in the
course of hard bargaining with the white employee over the fee to
be paid for the service, offers to pull the car from a second puddle
free of charge, Ned gets involved in a conversation with him:

> There's another hole just this side of the bridge that I'm throw-
> ing in free ... He said to Ned: "What we call the reserve patch up
> thisaway."
> "You means the Christmas middle," Ned said.
> "Maybe I do," the man said. "What is it?"
> Ned told him. "It's how we done at McCaslin back before the
> Surrender when old L.Q.C. was alive, and how the Edmonds boy
> still does. Every spring a middle is streaked off in the best ground
> on the place, and every stalk of cotton betwixt that middle and the
> edge of the field belongs to the Christmas fund, not for the boss but
> for every McCaslin nigger to have a Christmas share of it. That's
> what a Christmas middle is. Likely you mud-farming folks up here
> never heard of it." The man looked at Ned awhile. After a while
> Ned said, "Hee hee hee."
> "That's better," the man said. "I thought for a minute me and
> you was about to misunderstand one another."[7]

In Faulkner's telling, the incident is humorous; but he does not
miss, or permit his readers to miss, the undercurrent of menace
and violence lurking in the transaction. This incident ends with a
giggle; but it might easily have ended with fire and a rope.

7   William Faulkner, *The Reivers* (New York: Random House, 1962), 89–90.

Toni Morrison (Karen)

Faulkner's incident ended with neither fire nor rope, but with laughter—laughter not as mirth but as means, a social artifact mutually available to Ned and the mud farmer. Another novelist, Toni Morrison, has provided us with an illustration from our own time, of laughter as a means of negotiating separate lives lived together. This time, however, we see the laughter from the perspective of the one who enjoys it, rather than the one who deploys it: the mud farmer, as it were, rather than Ned.

Toni Morrison has drawn attention to the points Senator John Danforth chose to emphasize when he introduced Clarence Thomas as a nominee for the Supreme Court.

> He is his own person. That is my first point ... Second, he laughs ... To some, this may seem a trivial matter. To me, it's important because laughter is an antidote to that dread disease, federalitis. The obvious strategy of interest groups trying to defeat a Supreme Court nominee is to suggest that there is something weird about the individual. I suggest that there is something weird about Clarence Thomas. It's his laugh. It's the loudest laugh I have ever heard. It comes from deep inside, and it shakes his body. And here is something at least as weird in this most up-tight of cities; the object of his laughter is often himself.

"Every black person who heard those words understood," Morrison affirms. (Ned would have agreed with her.) She continues:

> How necessary, how reassuring were both the grin and its being summoned for display. It is the laughter, the chuckle, that invites and precedes any discussion or association with a black person. For whites who require it, it is the gesture of accommodation and obedience needed to open discussion with a black person and certainly to continue it. The ethnic joke is one formulation, the obligatory

recognition of race and possible equanimity in the face of it. But in the more polite halls of the Senate, the laugh will do ... It is difficult to imagine a sponsor introducing Robert Bork or William Gates (or that happy exception, Thurgood Marshall) with a call to this most clearly understood metonym for racial accommodation.[8]

Conclusion (Barbara)

Perhaps the juxtaposition of these two very different novelists, William Faulkner and Toni Morrison, is an appropriate way to close. Both have drawn out the collective meaning of an individual act: laughter; but laughter not as terms of endearment but as rules of engagement. Both unforgettably portray the dimly understood protocols that have served to join separate and unequal, yet joint and simultaneous, existences. Beyond that, there they stand: two people who epitomize separate lives lived together. Two people who, had their paths crossed, probably could not have conversed as peers. And yet, they analyzed their separate yet together worlds in uncannily kindred ways. From their different points of view evolves an honest vision of America's collective past.

It should be our ethical aim as teachers to equip ourselves and our students to gaze upon that past with the breadth and honesty that the task requires.

---

8   Toni Morrison, "Introduction: Friday on the Potomac," in Toni Morrison, ed., *Race-ing Justice, En-gendering Power: Essays on Anita Hill, Clarence Thomas, and the Construction of Reality* (New York: Pantheon, 1992), xii–xiii.

3 Of Rogues and Geldings

"Race" too often recommends itself as a guiltless word, a neutral term for an empirical fact. It is not. Race appears to be a neutral description of reality because of the race-racism evasion, through which immoral acts of discrimination disappear, and then reappear camouflaged as the victim's alleged difference. This chapter documents the career of that evasion and examines its pernicious corollaries. In the symposium in which the article was first published, a distinguished historian set out to interpret America's history as the story of "ethnoracial mixture" among immigrants of varying origins, including European. To read the entire symposium is to be reminded that early twentieth-century racists—and bio-racists—did not spare notionally white people.[1]

David Hollinger has performed a valuable service by insisting on the historical uniqueness of the Afro-American experience, rejecting the false history, spurious logic, and expedient politics that collapse the situations of Afro-Americans, Latino Americans, Asian Americans, and indigenous Americans into a single category. He correctly insists that there is no counterpart for any other descent group to the one-drop or any-known-ancestry rule that, with minor exceptions, has historically identified Afro-Americans. He criticizes the bankrupt politics that has resulted from treating

---

1 Originally published as "Of Rogues and Geldings," in AHR Forum, *American Historical Review* 108 (December 2003), 1397–1495.

a multi-century history of enslavement and racist persecution as a simple variation on the immigrant experience. (He might have added that the immigrants-all version of American history, while labeling as immigrants Africans and Afro-Caribbeans who arrived as slaves, as well as Indians and Mexicans whose country was taken over by outsiders, omits from its central narrative persons of African descent who truly were immigrants.[2]) And when he gets too close to some of the very misconceptions that his own analysis ought to preclude, his good sense draws him back; as when, after speculating that greater recognition of mixed ancestry offspring might result in greater acceptance of unambiguous African ancestry, he quickly acknowledges that greater isolation is just as likely. But the focus on "ethnoracial mixture" with the suggestion that historians should "see the history of the United States as, among other things, a story of amalgamation" is a different matter. It brings to mind an anecdote about an Irishman who, when asked the way to Ballynahinch, responds: "If I were you, I wouldn't start from here at all."[3]

Starting from "ethnoracial mixture" leads to the great evasion of American historical literature, as of American history itself: the substitution of "race" for "racism." That substitution, as I have written elsewhere, "transforms the act of a subject into an attribute of the object."[4] Disguised as race, racism becomes something

---

2   See Winston James, "Explaining Afro-Caribbean Social Mobility in the United States: Beyond the Sowell Thesis," *Comparative Studies in Society and History* 44 (April 2002): 218–62; Roy Bryce-Laporte, "Black Immigrants: The Experience of Invisibility and Inequality," *Journal of Black Studies* 3 (1972), 29–56.

3   Eric Hobsbawm tells a version of this universal joke in "On the Revival of Narrative," in *On History* (London: Weidenfeld and Nicolson, 1997), 191. David A. Hollinger, "Amalgamation and Hypodescent: The Question of Ethnoracial Mixture in the History of the United States," *American Historical Review* 108 (December 2003), 1389, 1386.

4   Barbara J. Fields, "Whiteness, Racism, and Identity," *International Labor and Working-Class History* 60 (Fall 2001), 48.

Afro-Americans are, rather than something racists do. Racists and apologists for racism have long availed themselves of the deception. "Don't blame me because you're colored," a white homeowner in Westchester, New York, told Hugh Mulzac, an Afro-Caribbean, when refusing to sell him a house—as though Mulzac's ancestry, rather than the homeowner's refusal, had aborted the sale. Similarly, a *Washington Post* columnist, during an effort to mitigate the killing of a blameless and unarmed African immigrant by New York City police officers, characterized as "race—but not racism" the commonplace refusal of cab drivers to stop for Afro-American passengers.[5] It is as though real estate transactions, the braking of motor vehicles, and the discharge of firearms were controlled—perhaps through telekinesis or some other paranormal or supernatural process—by the victim's appearance or ancestry, without the aggressor's will or participation.

Thomas Jefferson pioneered the race-instead-of-racism ideological maneuver, and his *Notes on the State of Virginia* is its *locus classicus*.[6] Judging slavery essential to the project of extending the sovereignty of the United States over the American continent, he tried to resolve the contradiction between enslavement and the natural right to freedom by interpreting slavery as a fact of the slaves' inferior nature.[7] To that end, he formulated the notion of race, draping its ideological nakedness in a tissue of purported scientific argument so thin that he would surely have seen through it on any subject less central to his nation-founding project than slavery: the American mammoth, let us say, or the intellectual

5   Martha Biondi, *To Stand and Fight: The Struggle for Civil Rights in Postwar New York City* (Cambridge, MA: Harvard University Press, 2003), 115; Richard Cohen, "Profile of a Killing," *Washington Post*, March 16, 2000, A27.

6   Thomas Jefferson, *Notes on the State of Virginia* (1787; Chapel Hill, NC: University of North Carolina Press, 1982).

7   "Those holding liberty to be inalienable and holding Afro-Americans as slaves were bound to end by holding race to be a self-evident truth." See Chapter 4, p. 121.

potential of the American Indians.[8] Significantly, he addressed both of those subjects in a query about nature, whereas he sketched his argument about the inferiority of the Negroes in a query about civilization.[9] Jefferson's ingenuity could not free him from his bind, however. As surely as he knew that slavery was essential to his project, he also knew that it could wreck his project by lodging a deadly flaw at the heart of American sovereignty and in the government that embodied that sovereignty.

Knowing with equal profoundness two irreconcilable truths— that slavery was vital to the nation and, at the same time, likely to destroy it—Jefferson could not sustain, even to the end of his book, the self-deceiving transformation of racism into race. Into the famous query on "Manners," he dropped as if from nowhere a hyperbolic account of slavery as "a perpetual exercise of the most boisterous passions" (not much time for cultivating tobacco if that were literally true) and, for good measure, referred to the slaves as citizens and implied their moral and intellectual equality with their enslavers.

> With what execration should the statesman be loaded, who permit-
> ting one half the citizens thus to trample on the rights of the other,
> transforms those into despots, and these into enemies, destroys the

---

8   For example, in dismissing the claim of the Indians' inferiority, Jefferson insists on the importance of investigating them in a proper context: "To form a just estimate of their genius and mental powers, more facts are wanting, and great allowance to be made for those circumstances of their situation that call for a display of particular talents only." But, in pronouncing black people devoid of the talent Indians display in handicraft arts and oratory, he sees no comparable need for context, asserting baldly that "it would be unfair to follow them to Africa for this investigation." Jefferson, *Notes*, Query VI, 62, and Query XIV, 139.

9   Jefferson's ruminations about the mammoth and his vindication of the American Indians appear in *Notes*, Query VI, "Productions Mineral, Vegetable and Animal." His speculation about the Negroes' biological inferiority appears in Query XIV, "Laws."

morals of the one part, and the amor patriae of the other. For if a slave can have a country in this world, it must be any other in preference to that in which he is born to live and labor for another: in which he must lock up the faculties of his nature, contribute as far as depends on his individual endeavors to the evanishment of the human race, or entail his own miserable condition on the endless generations proceeding from him.[10]

Abruptly contradicting his own earlier rationale, he revealed race to be racism; and slavery, rather than something slaves were, became something slaveholders did—to the corruption of themselves, the injustice of the slaves, and the probable destruction of the country. Thereafter, Jefferson masked his eyes from the glare of that momentary insight, so confounding that it caused him, for a split second, to abandon rationalism and secularism along with racism, and to ponder supernatural interference in human history.

Indeed I tremble for my country when I reflect that God is just: that his justice cannot sleep for ever: that considering numbers, nature and natural means only, a revolution of the wheel of fortune, an exchange of situation, is among possible events: that it may become probable by supernatural interference![11]

Jefferson's successors (one scholar has called him America's first racial pundit[12]) have proved more adept than he at the race-racism

---

10   Jefferson, *Notes*, Query XVIII, 162–3. See Lewis P. Simpson's remarkable analysis in "Land, Slaves, and Mind: The High Culture of the Jeffersonian South," in *Mind and the American Civil War: A Meditation on Lost Causes* (Baton Rouge, LA: Louisiana State University Press, 1989), esp. 25–8.

11   Jefferson, *Notes*, 163. Simpson argues that Query XVIII marks a crisis in Jefferson's faith in the capacity of reason to solve the problems of human society and human history; see his *Mind and the American Civil War*, 25–8.

12   Michael R. West uses the expression in *The Education of Booker T. Washington: The Negro Problem, Democracy, and the Idea of Race Relations* (New York: Columbia University Press, 2006), 38.

evasion, indulging in it without Jefferson's outburst of compensatory hyperbole. "Race" appears in the titles of an ever-growing number of scholarly books and articles as a euphemism for slavery, disfranchisement, segregation, lynching, mass murder, and related historical atrocities; or as unintentionally belittling shorthand for "persons of African descent and anything pertaining to them."[13] The more dutifully scholars acknowledge that the concept of race belongs in the same category as geocentrism or witchcraft, the more blithely they invoke it as though it were both a coherent analytical category and a valid empirical datum. In place of Jefferson's moment of impassioned truth-telling, his successors fall back on italics or quotation marks, typographical abbreviations for the trite formula, "race is a social construction."[14]

The formula is meant to spare those who invoke race in historical explanation the raised eyebrows that would greet someone who, studying a crop failure, proposed witchcraft as an independent variable. But identifying race as a social construction does nothing to solidify the intellectual ground on which it totters. The London Underground and the United States of America are social constructions; so are the evil eye and the calling of spirits from the vasty deep; and so are murder and genocide. All derive from the thoughts, plans, and actions of human beings living in human societies. Scholars who intone "social construction" as a spell for

---

13 Examples include *The Wages of Whiteness: Race and the Making of the American Working Class*; *Whiteness of a Different Color: European Immigration and the Alchemy of Race*; *Race, Rock, and Elvis*; *Race and Reunion: The Civil War in American Memory*; *Appalachians and Race: The Mountain South from Slavery to Segregation*; *Disowning Slavery: Gradual Emancipation and "Race" in New England, 1789–1860*; *The Death of Reconstruction: Race, Labor, and Politics in the Post–Civil War North, 1865–1901*; *Race, War, and Surveillance: African Americans and the United States Government during World War I*.

14 Scholars often identify the truism that race is "socially constructed" as the argument of "Slavery, Race, and Ideology in the United States of America," (Chapter 4, below). But (minus the tedious language) that is the article's starting point, not its conclusion.

the purification of race do not make clear—perhaps because they
do not themselves realize—that race and racism belong to different families of social construction, and that neither belongs to
the same family as the United States of America or the London
Underground. Race belongs to the same family as the evil eye.
Racism belongs to the same family as murder and genocide. Which
is to say that racism, unlike race, is not a fiction, an illusion, a superstition, or a hoax. It is a crime against humanity.

No operation performed on the fiction can ever make headway
against the crime. But the fiction is easier for well-meaning people
to handle. (*"Race,"* I have written elsewhere, "is a homier and
more tractable notion than *racism*, a rogue elephant gelded and
tamed into a pliant beast of burden."[15]) Confronted with the intellectual arguments against the concept of race, my undergraduates
react by grasping for another word to occupy the same conceptual
space.[16] "I don't feel comfortable saying 'race' after your class. But
I don't know what else to call it," is a characteristic response. At
the suggestion, "Why not 'ancestry,' if that's what you're talking
about?" they retreat into inarticulate dissatisfaction. Instinctively,

15 Fields, "Whiteness, Racism, and Identity," 48.
16 In this, they are not alone. The noted scholar Steven Pinker, determined
to salvage some vestige of biological race from the "popular" view that "races
do not exist but are purely social constructions," commits the common error of
confusing genetic distinctions with racial distinctions. (See his *The Blank Slate:
The Modern Denial of Human Nature* [New York: Viking, 2002], 143–4.) He
thereby twists a scientifically justifiable view of race as a statistical abstraction—
that is, an imaginary entity comparable to the per capita annual income or the
body mass index—to fit the old and discredited view of race as a group of people
defined by particular characteristics. He mentions Tay-Sachs and sickle cell
anemia, often tagged by true believers as racial characteristics. But both are,
in fact, uncharacteristic, afflicting only a minority even within the populations
most affected by them. On Pinker's own showing, statistical generalizations
about "the large inbred families we call races" no more define individuals or
groups than does average height or per capita income in a person's county of
residence. Races "exist," therefore, only in the sense that the equator, the body
mass index, or the per capita annual income "exists."

they understand that, while everyone has ancestry, only African ancestry carries the ultimate stigma. Therefore, what they are unknowingly searching for is a neutral-sounding word with racism hidden inside, which is what "race" is. The apparently blameless word permits students to reabsorb into the decorum of the routine something whose essence is not just indecorum but monstrosity: the attachment to fellow human beings of a stigma akin to leprosy in medieval Europe, only worse, in that it sets beyond the pale of humanity not the leper alone but the leper's progeny ad infinitum.

Domesticating such a monstrosity for presentation in civilized company requires believers in race to attempt cosmetic repairs of its most obnoxious peculiarities. One such peculiarity is the fact that, effectively, there can be only one race, since the one-drop-of-blood or any-known-ancestry rule applies only to African ancestry;[17] indeed, the rule ceases to function at all if applied to more than one type of ancestry. The cosmetic applied to the resulting asymmetry and invidiousness is "whiteness," whose champions purport to discover "racialization"—and therefore races—all over the shop. A further sleight of hand defines race as identity so that "white" also becomes a race.[18] Similar cosmetic embellishments claim "agency" for the victims in creating race or deodorize it by tracing its origin to "culture" rather than racism. But people no more fasten the stigma of race upon themselves than cattle sear the brand into their own flesh. And, no matter how slipshod the definition of culture, no one can seriously assert that one culture unites those whom American usage identifies without hesitation as one race.[19]

---

17   See Chapter 4, 115.

18   Fields, "Whiteness, Racism, and Identity," 48–51. Rogers Brubaker and Frederick Cooper, in "Beyond 'Identity'," *Theory and Society* 29 (2000), 1–47, pours a needed bucket of cold water on the ubiquitous concept of "identity."

19   Raymond Williams, *Keywords* (London: Fontana, 1988), 87–93; and Terry Eagleton, *The Idea of Culture* (Oxford: Blackwell, 2000), explore some of the byways in the history and politics of the word and the many things it has stood for.

Even language can be squeezed into the glass slipper of race by a sufficiently ruthless pruning of the foot. According to believers in something known as "black English," the deep structures of African languages—in other words, the speakers' African-ness—accounts for the speech habits of Afro-Americans. But African linguistic structures cannot explain why, despite the much greater survival of Africanisms in Jamaican creole, the children of Jamaican migrants to Britain do not speak "black English"; instead, they speak English as white Britons of their class and region do. (Nor can such structures explain why there is no such thing as black French, black Portuguese, or black Spanish.) The speech patterns of Afro-Americans testify not to the greater strength of African linguistic survivals among Afro-Americans as compared to Afro-Caribbean migrants in Britain but to the greater prevalence and rigidity of segregated schooling, housing, and sociability, especially among the working class, in the United States, as compared to Britain.[20] Racism, in other words, not race.

Once the race-racism evasion has seated monstrosity in the realm of the normal, corollary evasions follow. Two scholars, one of them a member of the Civil Rights Commission at the time, defended the disfranchisement of law-abiding Afro-Floridians during the presidential election of 2000 against the charge of racism. They did so on the grounds that a higher proportion of Afro-Floridians than Euro-Floridians have felony convictions and are therefore not entitled to vote. No matter that law-abiding Afro-Floridians have exactly the same rate of felony convictions (zero) as law-abiding Euro-Floridians, and that punishing one person for

20   Barbara J. Fields, "Origins of the New South and the Negro Question," *Journal of Southern History* 67 (November 2001), 824–6. See below, Chapter 5, p. 168. See also Mervyn Alleyne, "A Linguistic Perspective on the Caribbean," in Sidney W. Mintz and Sally Price, eds., *Caribbean Contours* (Baltimore, MD: Johns Hopkins University Press, 1985), 155–79. Alleyne notes the presence of creole languages in the Francophone Caribbean, their absence in the Hispanophone Caribbean, and their presence in some parts of the Anglophone Caribbean and absence in others.

another's conduct negates the basic premises of a law-governed democratic society. Under cover of the evasion that attributes race to the disfranchised rather than racism to the disfranchiser, the authors have smuggled in a charter for collective punishment.[21] Presumably, they would not defend stripping citizens of the right to vote because of felony convictions among persons sharing their occupation, hobbies, astrological sign, or shoe size. But, according to these scholars' reasoning, innocent persons may legitimately be punished for the conduct of those who share their ancestry— which is racism by definition.[22]

Another widely read author defends collective punishment even more explicitly while discussing the refusal of cab drivers to stop for black passengers. He calls the refusal "rational discrimination" and concludes that it is based on "group differences, which are real." He concedes that such discrimination, while rational, may not be moral; not, however, because it violates basic rules of justice by punishing one person for the alleged misconduct of another but because it "penalizes minorities for physical characteristics that they cannot change." The issue, in that view, is intolerance rather than injustice.[23]

Tolerance itself, generally surrounded by a beatific glow in American political discussion, is another evasion born of the race-racism switch. Its shallowness as a moral or ethical precept is plain. ("Tolerate thy neighbor as thyself" is not quite what Jesus said,

---

21 Abigail Thernstrom and John R. Lott, Jr., Letters, *New York Times*, June 1, 2002.

22 It is symptomatic of the abrogation of democracy by racism that the United States maintains a penal system in which arrest, charge, conviction, and sentence depend heavily on one's ancestry and that, alone among supposedly advanced democracies, it permanently disfranchises persons who have served out their time in prison.

23 Dinesh D'Souza, *The End of Racism* (New York: Simon & Schuster, 1995), 245–88. Thernstrom, Lott, and D'Souza appear untroubled that their defense of group discrimination contradicts individualism, which otherwise ranks among their highest political values.

Edward Mendelson, a colleague in the Columbia English department, reminds students in his classes.) As a political precept,
tolerance has unimpeachably anti-democratic credentials, dividing society into persons entitled to claim respect as a right and
persons obliged to beg tolerance as a favor. The curricular fad
for "teaching tolerance" underlines the anti-democratic implications. A teacher identifies for the children's benefit characteristics
(ancestry, appearance, sexual orientation, and the like) that count
as disqualifications from full and equal membership in human
society. These, the children learn, they may overlook, in an act
of generous condescension—or refuse to overlook, in an act of
ungenerous condescension. Tolerance thus bases equal rights on
benevolent patronization rather than democratic first principles,
much as a parent's misguided plea that Jason "share" the swing
or seesaw on a public playground teaches Jason that his gracious
consent, rather than another child's equal claim, determines the
other child's access.

Tolerance as an alternative to equality is so firmly rooted in
good intentions that practitioners fail to recognize the evil. Reed
Whittemore probably felt no pang about claiming, in a review of
Ralph Ellison's *Shadow and Act*, that, by writing the book, Ellison
had "decided it was possible to join the human race, and so did so."
Whittemore contrasted Ellison favorably with white artists who
were "trying to secede" from the human race.[24] White persons,
he implied, are human beings until they choose not to be; black
persons are not human beings until they earn the privilege, one
at a time, by performing a meritorious act (such as writing a book
Whittemore approves of).

Hannah Arendt illustrates another corollary of the race-
racism evasion by insisting that the denial of human and citizenship rights is divisible into parts, some worthier of condemnation

---

24   Reed Whittemore, "Beating That Boy Again," *New Republic*, November
14, 1964, 26. Michael R. West kindly drew my attention to this instance of well-
meant racism.

than others, and prohibition of intermarriage the worst of all. But what makes prohibition of marriage across the color line worse than forbidding someone to vote, sit on a jury, move about freely, get an adequate education, express political views without fear, or even enjoy safety of life and limb? Arendt was probably tempted into error by a belief that intermarriage would promote assimilation, which would eliminate the problem by eliminating the problem people. Such a solution appears logical if one attributes the problem to the race of the prey, rather than the racism of the predator.

The historical precedents have long since discredited that solution, in any case. The descendants of Portuguese and Spanish Jews who had converted to Christianity under duress during the fifteenth century were still "New Christians" to their persecutors in the seventeenth and eighteenth centuries. Under the statutes of purity of blood (*estatutos de limpieza de sangre*), candidates for posts in government, the military, cathedrals and chapters, monastic and religious orders, and universities had to be certified as free from Jewish ancestry through elaborate genealogical searches. Persons whose families had been Christian for centuries could find themselves stigmatized by the discovery of a remote Jewish antecedent unknown to them; and the disability extended, with greater or lesser efficiency depending on the time and place, to the American colonies of Spain and Portugal. The Jews' very compliance with their persecutors' demand for conversion kindled greater anger against them, their enemies interpreting centuries of Christian practice as deep cover for a crypto-Jewish menace boring from within.[25]

25   Yosef Hayim Yerushalmi, *Assimilation and Racial Anti-Semitism: The Iberian and the German Models* (New York: Leo Baeck Institute, 1982), 11–14, 22, 44n; C. R. Boxer, *The Portuguese Seaborne Empire, 1415–1825* (London: Hutchinson, 1969), 266–72, 333–4; Stuart B. Schwartz, "Colonial Brazil, c.1580–c.1750: Plantations and Peripheries," in *The Cambridge History of Latin America*, Vol. 2, Leslie Bethell, ed. (Cambridge: Cambridge University Press, 1984), 494–6. *Estatutos de limpieza de sangre* also policed the color line in Latin America. For example, see Jay Kinsbruner, *Not of Pure Blood: The Free People of*

Whether called assimilation or amalgamation, the goal of blending in the discordant element operates on the rationale rather than on the problem. Framing questions in those terms guarantees that the answers will remain entangled in racist ideology. For example, a pair of sociologists investigating the degree of Afro-Caribbean immigrants' assimilation into American society unquestioningly adopt as their measure of assimilation the rate of intermarriage between Afro-Caribbeans and native white Americans, rather than the much higher rate of intermarriage between Afro-Caribbeans and native Afro-Americans.[26] The American ancestry of most native Afro-Americans goes back to the seventeenth or eighteenth century, whereas native white Americans are apt to be only first or second-generation Americans. Racism thus enters unannounced and unnoticed, to define eleventh or twelfth-generation black natives as less American than the children and grandchildren of white immigrants.

The race evasion compounded by the equation of race with identity explains why the siren song of multiracialism attracts so many people. The point is best approached by way of a question: What is wrong with racism? One answer, whose historical pedigree includes such antecedents as David Walker, Frederick Douglass, Wendell Phillips, W. E. B. Du Bois, A. Phillip Randolph, and Martin Luther King, Jr., holds that racism is wrong because it violates the basic rights of human being and citizen. Most decent people would assent to that view, if it were put to them in so many words. But the ever-widening campaign for recognition of a "multiracial" category of Americans suggests a different answer. What is wrong with racism, in that view, is that it subjects persons of provably mixed ancestry to the same stigma and penalties as persons of unambiguously

Color and Racial Prejudice in Nineteenth Century Puerto Rico (Durham, NC: Duke University Press, 1996), 36–7, 120, 128.

26   Suzanne Model and Gene Fisher, "Unions Between Blacks and Whites: England and the US Compared," *Ethnic and Racial Studies* 25 (September 2002), 728–54.

African ancestry. The anguish of the Jean Toomer or the Anatole Broyard rests, ultimately, on a thwarted hope to be excused, on grounds of mixed ancestry, from a fate deemed entirely appropriate for persons of unambiguous African ancestry.[27]

Such a view, for all the aura of progressivism and righteousness that currently surrounds multiracialism, is not a cure for racism but a particularly ugly manifestation of it. For Jean Toomer and Anatole Broyard, as for today's apostles of multiracialism, it is mixed ancestry, rather than human status, that makes racism wrong in their case. If there is pathos in their predicament (bathos seems closer to the mark), it arises from that fact that American racism, while making no room for fractional pariahs, vaguely supposes that, logically, it ought to. White Americans have conceded little space for those claiming immunity by reason of mixed ancestry, generally regarding passing as a particularly insidious form of deceit. The Anatole Broyard who passes without detection is like a leper who neglects to strike his clapper dish and shout "Unclean!" before approaching an inhabited area. Still, a latent strain of sentimentality has sympathized with the predicament of the person of mixed African and European ancestry: the tragic mulatto of racist literature and pop culture. Consistency seems to require that injustice be visited on the pariahs according to their quantum of pariah blood. But the imitation-of-life, tragic-mulatto plot-line works and appears tragic only if the audience simultaneously accepts two conflicting views, both racist: on the one hand, that the penalty for

---

27 Jean Toomer, described by one scholar as "a signal light for the writers of the Harlem Renaissance," seethed at publishers' expectation that he should go on producing what they and their readers would recognize as "Negro" literature. Eventually, he denied outright any trace of African ancestry. See Darwin Turner, "Introduction," *The Wayward and the Seeking: A Collection of Writings by Jean Toomer* (Washington, DC: Howard University Press, 1982), 11–12; and his introduction to Toomer, *Cane* (New York: Norton, 1988), 136. Henry Louis Gates, Jr., discusses Broyard's explicitly racist contempt for black people in *Thirteen Ways of Looking at a Black Man* (New York: Random House, 1997), 201–2.

African taint should be proportioned to its extent; on the other, that there can be no such thing as a fractional pariah: one either is or is not.

Persons of mixed background like Jean Toomer, Anatole Broyard, and Tiger Woods, along with their well-meaning but misguided champions, have reached the understanding that the categories imposed by racism are too restrictive to fit persons of ambiguous ancestry. They have not reached the deeper understanding that these categories are too restrictive to fit anyone. They were too tight for Amadou Diallo, the African immigrant mistakenly killed by New York City police officers, and he died of the constriction. Diallo probably defined himself as a member of his nation or tribe or lineage, rather than as "black." But, under the American system, it was the officers' definition of him, not his definition of himself, that held the balance between life and death.

Racism is a qualitative, not a quantitative, evil. Its harm does not depend on how many people fall under its ban but on the fact that any at all do. And the first principle of racism is belief in race, even if the believer does not deduce from that belief that the member of a race should be enslaved or disfranchised or shot on sight by trigger-happy police officers or asked for identification when crossing the campus of the university where he teaches, just as believing that the sun travels around the earth is geocentrism, whether or not one deduces from the belief that persons affirming the contrary should be hauled before an inquisition and forced to recant. Once everyone understands that African descent is not race and that African ancestry differs from others only in the racism with which Euro-America has stigmatized it, the problem changes: what is needed is not a more varied set of words and categories to represent racism but a politics to uproot it.

4 Slavery, Race, and Ideology in the United States of America

Our analysis of racecraft lays out various mechanisms by which an ideology takes on the appearance of uncontroversial everyday reality—universally understood rituals regarding deference and consumption, self-confirming enactment in practical activities of all kinds, and continuously renewed barriers against the everyday flow of refuting evidence. The roots of witchcraft ideology are ancient, but America's racecraft ideology is comparatively recent. This chapter establishes how and when it arose. Against the promptings of that ideology, still to be reckoned with inside and outside classrooms, the chapter argues that the assignment of black Americans to slavery did not follow automatically from their color or ancestry. Rather, it occurred as part of a historical process in which the enslavement of Africans made possible the freedom of Europeans, and then cast a long shadow over subsequent history. Out of that process emerged an elaborate public language of "race" and "race relations" that disguised class inequality and, by the same stroke, impoverished Americans' public language for addressing inequality.[1]

1   Originally published as "Slavery, Race, and Ideology in the United States of America," *New Left Review* 181 (May–June 1990), 95–118. The author wishes to acknowledge the helpful comments of David Brion Davis on an earlier version of this essay. She has benefited from discussions with Karen E. Fields, Leslie S. Rowland, Julie Saville, and Michael R. West, and from the spirited reaction of audiences who heard the paper in Brazil at the Universidade Federal de Ouro

In 1988, a sports announcer in the United States lost his job because he enlarged indiscreetly—that is, before a television audience—upon his views about "racial" differences. Asked why there are so few black coaches in basketball, Jimmy "the Greek" Snyder remarked that black athletes already hold an advantage as basketball players because they have longer thighs than white athletes, their ancestors having been deliberately bred that way during slavery. "This goes all the way to the Civil War," Jimmy the Greek explained, "when during the slave trading ... the owner, the slave owner would breed his big black to his big woman so he could have a big black kid, you see." Astonishing though it may seem, Snyder intended his remark as a compliment to black athletes. If black men became coaches, he said, there would be nothing left for white men to do in basketball at all. Embarrassed by such a rank and open expression of racism in the most ignorant form, the network fired Jimmy the Greek from his job. Any fool, the network must have decided, should know that such things may be spoken in the privacy of the locker-room in an all-white club, but not into a microphone and before a camera. Of course, Jimmy the Greek laid no claim to being educated or well informed. Before he was hired to keep audiences entertained during the slack moments of televised sports events, he was famous as a bookie. He claimed expert knowledge about odds and point spreads, not about history, biology or human genetics. But those claiming to be educated—and employed on that basis—have proved to be just as superstitious as Jimmy the Greek. Belief in the biological reality of race outranks even astrology, the superstition closest to it in the competition for dupes among the ostensibly educated. Richard Cohen, the house liberal of the *Washington Post*, wrote a column defending the

Preto in Mariana, the Universidade Federal de São Paulo, and the Universidade Federal Fluminense in Niterói; and in the United States at the University of California, San Diego; the University of North Carolina at Chapel Hill; the University of Mississippi in Oxford; and Columbia University in New York City.

underlying assumption of Jimmy the Greek's remark, if not its specific content. According to Cohen, Jimmy the Greek was wrong for overestimating what can be accomplished by the deliberate breeding of human beings, not for believing in physical race. "Back in my college days," Cohen began, "I dabbled in anthropology. In physical anthropology we had to do something called 'racing and sexing' of skulls. That entailed looking at a skull and determining whether it was once a man or a woman—and which race." The circular logic of first defining certain characteristics as "racial," then offering differences in those same characteristics as proof that the "races" differ, did not trouble him, even in retrospect. In matters of virtually religious faith, logic carries no weight. Cohen capped that shameful display with a tag that ought to have warned him of the intellectual quagmire into which he had strayed: "Yes, Virginia, the races are physically different."[2]

Most Americans, though perhaps few others, will recognize the allusion. Many years ago, a newspaper editor answered a query from a troubled child named Virginia, who was experiencing her first painful doubts that Santa Claus was a real person and who had written to the newspaper to get an authoritative answer. The answer came in a famous editorial entitled "Yes, Virginia, There Is a Santa Claus." Cohen spoke more truth than he realized in thus equating his own—and, presumably, his readers'—need to believe in race with a child's need to believe in Santa Claus. Anyone who continues to believe in race as a physical attribute of individuals, despite the now commonplace disclaimers of biologists and geneticists,[3] might as well also believe that Santa Claus, the Easter Bunny and the tooth fairy are real, and that the earth stands still while the sun moves.

---

2   Richard Cohen, "The Greek's Offense," *Washington Post National Weekly Edition*, January 25–31, 1988.

3   For example, see Stephen Jay Gould, *The Mismeasure of Man* (New York: Norton, 1981); Richard Lewontin, Steven Rose, and Leon Kamin, *Not in Our Genes* (New York: Pantheon, 1984).

Newspaper and television journalists are entitled to be as silly and irresponsible as they wish, and it usually does no harm, since nobody in his right mind pays attention to them. (Richard Cohen underlined his scientific illiteracy by speaking of "white genes"— entities known to no geneticist that I am aware of.)[4] But in May of 1987, the Supreme Court of the United States provided a much more serious example—more serious precisely because it *was* the Supreme Court and not a half-baked journalist. The Court had to decide whether Jewish and Arab Americans could seek relief under civil rights law for acts of discrimination against them. Instead of taking its stand on the principle that discrimination against anybody is intolerable in a democracy, the Court chose to ask whether Jews and Arabs are racially distinct from "Caucasians." If so, then civil rights laws forbidding "racial" discrimination might be applied to them. The Court decided that, because Jews, Arabs, and a variety of other nationalities were regarded as racial groups in the late

4 Cohen is by no means alone. An NBC network broadcast during the spring of 1989, anchored by the gullible Tom Brokaw and vigorously defended by one of its producers in the columns of the *New York Times*, similarly affirmed the essence of Jimmy the Greek's instinctive prejudice. The broadcast featured an Israeli doctor who, by measuring muscular movements of world-class athletes, claimed to identify typical "racial" characteristics. No one asked whether ordinary people use their muscles the same way world-class athletes do; that is, whether his experiment proved something about typical racial characteristics or something about exceptional athletes. Nor did anyone ask whether athletes classed as black are more likely than those classed as white to have learned their moves from coaches and fellow athletes also classed as black; that is, whether the experiment dealt with race or training. Needless to add, no one ventured to ask the most embarrassing question of all, the one that stumped the scientific racists of the late nineteenth and early twentieth centuries: how to assign the subjects of the experiments to one "race" or the other without assuming the very racial distinction the experiment is supposed to prove? Try as they would, the scientific racists of the past failed to discover any objective criterion upon which to classify people; to their chagrin, every criterion they tried varied more within so-called races than between them. It is likely that Brokaw's neo-racist would find the same true of muscular movements had he the honesty and intelligence to pose the question.

nineteenth century, they may therefore be so considered today.[5] In other words, the Court knew no better way to rectify injustice at the end of the twentieth century than to re-enthrone the superstitious racial dogma of the nineteenth century. In fact, the Supreme Court had little choice, bound as it is by American precedent and history—bound, that is to say, by its participation in those rituals that daily create and re-create race in its characteristic American form. The Supreme Court acts, no less than Jimmy the Greek, within the assumptions, however absurd, that constitute racial ideology in the United States. Unfortunately, so do historians and other academic specialists, who vitally need to take a distance from these assumptions in order to do their job.

The Single "Race"

One of the most important of the absurd assumptions, accepted implicitly by most Americans, is that there is really only one race, the Negro race. That is why the Court had to perform intellectual contortions to prove that non-Negroes might be construed as members of races in order to receive protection under laws forbidding racial discrimination. Americans regard people of known African descent or visible African appearance as a race, but not people of known European descent or visible European appearance. That is why, in the United States, there are scholars and *black* scholars, women and *black* women. Saul Bellow and John Updike are writers; Ralph Ellison and Toni Morrison are *black* writers. George Bush and Michael Dukakis were candidates for president; Jesse Jackson was a *black* candidate for president.

Moreover, people in the United States do not classify as races peoples of non-European but also non-African appearance or descent, except for purposes of direct or indirect contrast with people of African descent; and even then, the terms used are likely

---

5 St. Francis College, et al. v. Majid Ghaidan Al-Khazraji, and Shaare Tefila Congregation v. John William Cobb et al., May 18, 1987.

to represent geography or language rather than biology: *Asian* or *Hispanic*.[6] Even when terms of geography designate people of African descent, they mean something different from what they mean when applied to others. My students find it odd when I refer to the colonizers of North America as *Euro-Americans*, but they feel more at ease with *Afro-Americans*, a term which, for the period of colonization and the slave trade, has no more to recommend it. Students readily understand that no one was really a European, since Europeans belonged to different nationalities; but it comes as a surprise to them that no one was an African either, since Africans likewise belonged to different nationalities.

A second absurd assumption inseparable from race in its characteristic American form takes for granted that virtually everything people of African descent do, think, or say is racial in nature. Thus, anyone who followed the news commentaries on the presidential election primaries of 1988 learned that, almost by definition, Afro-Americans voted for Jesse Jackson because of racial identification—despite polls showing that Jackson's supporters were far more likely than supporters of any other candidate to identify him with specific positions that they agreed with on issues that mattered to them. Supporters of the others regarded their men as interchangeable, and were likely to

---

6   That is not, of course, to deny the well-justified annoyance of Japanese-, Chinese-, Korean-, Vietnamese- and Indian-Americans at being classed together as *Asian-Americans* or, still more inaccurately, as simply *Asians*. Nor is it to overlook the nonsense that flourishes luxuriantly around the attempt to set terms of language and geography alongside the term that supposedly represents biological race. Survey researchers for the United States government often ask "Hispanics" whether they wish to be considered "white" or "black." The resulting classifications can divide members of a single family. As often as not, the report of the results proceeds to distinguish *Hispanics* from *blacks* and *whites*. Moreover, the government regards Portuguese-speaking Brazilians as "Hispanic" and requires that they so identify themselves when applying for a social security number, as the Brazilian novelist Jorge Amado discovered during a recent visit.

switch again and again, in response to slick advertising spots or disparaging rumors.[7]

Perhaps most intellectually debilitating of all is a third assumption: namely, that any situation involving people of European descent and people of African descent automatically falls under the heading "race relations." Argument by definition and tautology thereby replaces argument by analysis in anything to do with people of African descent. Probably a majority of American historians think of slavery in the United States as primarily a system of race relations—as though the chief business of slavery were the production of white supremacy rather than the production of cotton, sugar, rice, and tobacco. One historian has gone so far as to call slavery "the ultimate segregator."[8] He does not ask why Europeans seeking the "ultimate" method of segregating Africans would go to the trouble and expense of transporting them across the ocean for that purpose, when they could have achieved the same end so much more simply by leaving the Africans in Africa. No one dreams of analyzing the struggle of the English against the Irish as a problem in race relations, even though the rationale that the English developed for suppressing the "barbarous" Irish later served nearly word for word as a rationale for suppressing Africans and indigenous American Indians.[9] Nor does anyone dream of analyzing serfdom in Russia as primarily a problem of race relations, even though the Russian nobility invented fictions of their innate, natural superiority over the serfs as preposterous as any devised by American racists.[10]

---

7   *New York Times*, March 10, 1988, A26.

8   John Anthony Scott, "Segregation: A Fundamental Aspect of Southern Race Relations, 1800–1860," *Journal of the Early Republic* 4 (Winter 1984), 425. Scott did not originate this preposterous assertion. Nevertheless, he endorses it enthusiastically.

9   Edmund S. Morgan, *American Slavery, American Freedom: The Ordeal of Colonial Virginia* (New York: Norton, 1975), Chapter I; Leonard P. Liggio, "English Origins of Early American Racism," *Radical History Review* 3, 1976.

10   See Peter Kolchin, *Unfree Labor: American Slavery and Russian Serfdom*

Loose thinking on these matters leads to careless language, which in turn promotes misinformation. A widely used textbook of American history, written by very distinguished historians, summarizes the three-fifths clause of the United States Constitution (Article I, Section 2) thus: "For both direct taxes and representation, five blacks were to be counted as equivalent to three whites."[11] The three-fifths clause does not distinguish between *blacks* and *whites*—even, using more polite terms, between black and white *people*. (Indeed, the terms *black* and *white*—or for that matter, *Negro* and *Caucasian*—do not appear anywhere in the Constitution, as is not surprising in a legal document in which slang of that kind would be hopelessly imprecise.) The three-fifths clause distinguishes between *free Persons*—who might be of European or African descent—and *other Persons*, a euphemism for *slaves*. The issue at stake was whether slaveowning citizens would hold an advantage over non-slaveowning citizens; more precisely, whether slaves would be counted in total population for the purpose of apportioning representation in Congress—an advantage for slaveholders in states with large numbers of slaves—and of assessing responsibility for direct taxes—a disadvantage. The Constitution answered by saying yes, but at a ratio of three-fifths, rather than the five-fifths that slaveholders would have preferred for representation or the zero-fifths they would have preferred for taxation. When well-meaning people affirm, for rhetorical effect, that the Constitution declared Afro-Americans to be only three-fifths human, they commit an error for which American historians themselves must accept the blame.

When virtually the whole of a society, including supposedly thoughtful, educated, intelligent persons, commits itself to belief in propositions that collapse into absurdity upon the slightest examination, the reason is not hallucination or delusion or even simple

(Cambridge, MA: Harvard University Press, 1987), 170–91.

11   Winthrop D. Jordan, Leon F. Litwack et al., *The United States*, combined edition, 5th edition (Englewood Cliffs, NJ: Prentice Hall, 1982), 144.

hypocrisy; rather, it is ideology. And ideology is impossible for anyone to analyze rationally who remains trapped on its terrain.[12] That is why race still proves so hard for historians to deal with historically, rather than in terms of metaphysics, religion, or socio-(that is, pseudo-) biology.

Nothing so well illustrates that impossibility as the conviction among otherwise sensible scholars that race "explains" historical phenomena; specifically, that it explains why people of African descent have been set apart for treatment different from that accorded to others.[13] But *race* is just the name assigned to the

12   A well-known historian once illustrated this fact for me in the very act of denying it. Challenging me for having made a statement to the same effect in an earlier essay (Barbara J. Fields, "Ideology and Race in American History," in J. Morgan Kousser and James M. McPherson, eds., *Region, Race, and Reconstruction: Essays in Honor of C. Vann Woodward* [New York: Oxford University Press, 1982]), he declared: "Someone could accept the evidence that there is a racial disparity in IQ and still believe in integration." Well-intentioned, but trapped in racial ideology, he cannot bring himself to question the scientific status of race itself, let alone IQ. Nor, although an accomplished user of statistical methods, can he perceive the fallacy of statistical studies claiming to have eliminated the social determinants of intelligence and isolated the genetic ones, while perforce using social criteria—there are no others—to assign subjects to their proper "race" in the first place.

13   Inseparable from this conviction is the reification of race that impels many scholars to adopt and impose on others, as a pious duty, the meaningless task of deciding whether race is more or less "basic" to historical explanation than other—and similarly reified—categories; a waste of time to which I drew attention in "Ideology and Race in American History," p. 158. Someone might as well undertake to decide in the abstract whether the numerator or the denominator is more important to understanding a fraction, instead of settling down to the more sensible task of trying to define and specify each one, recognizing their difference as well as their relationship and their joint indispensability to the result. An example is David Roediger, "'Labor in White Skin': Race and Working-Class History," in Mike Davis and Michael Sprinker, eds., *Reshaping the US Left: Popular Struggles in the 1980s* (London: Verso, 1988), 287–308. Roediger apparently believes that distinguishing analytically between *race* and *class* necessarily implies "privileging" one over the other (to use his slang). And, in defending the identification of racism as a "tragic flaw"

phenomenon, which it no more explains than *judicial review* "explains" why the United States Supreme Court can declare acts of Congress unconstitutional, or than *Civil War* "explains" why Americans fought each other between 1861 and 1865.[14]

Only if *race* is defined as innate and natural prejudice of color does its invocation as a historical explanation do more than repeat the question by way of answer. And there an insurmountable problem arises: since race is not genetically programmed, racial prejudice cannot be genetically programmed either but, like race itself, must arise historically. The most sophisticated of those who invoke race as a historical explanation—for example, George Fredrickson and Winthrop Jordan—recognize the difficulty. The preferred solution is to suppose that, having arisen historically, race then ceases to be a historical phenomenon and becomes instead an external motor of history; according to the fatuous but widely repeated formula, it "takes on a life of its own."[15] In other words, once historically acquired, race becomes hereditary.

that helps to explain American history, rather than as part of the history that needs explaining, he confuses a rhetorical device with a historical explanation.

14   Alden T. Vaughan's "The Origins Debate: Slavery and Racism in Seventeenth-Century Virginia," *Virginia Magazine of History and Biography* 97 (July 1989), is a good example of the use as explanation of the very facts needing to be explained. The argument ends in explicit tautology: "It may be more useful to see Anglo-American racism as a necessary precondition for a system of slavery based on ancestry and pigmentation." That is, Anglo-American racism is a necessary precondition for Anglo-American racism. The argument ends as well in unseemly agnosticism about the possibility of rational explanation: "Racism was one cause of a particular type of slavery, though it may be better to avoid the term *cause*, for causation is itself a shaky concept in complex situations." The quoted sentences appear on page 353.

15   George Fredrickson has attempted to retread the old tire once again in "Race, Class and Consciousness," the introduction to his collection *The Arrogance of Race: Historical Perspectives on Slavery, Racism, and Social Inequality* (Middletown, CT: Wesleyan University Press, 1988). See also Winthrop D. Jordan, *White Over Black: American Attitudes Toward the Negro, 1550–1812* (Chapel Hill, NC: University of North Carolina Press, 1968).

The shopworn metaphor thus offers camouflage for a latter-day version of Lamarckism.

The History of an Ideology

Race is not an element of human biology (like breathing oxygen or reproducing sexually); nor is it even an idea (like the speed of light or the value of π) that can be plausibly imagined to live an eternal life of its own. Race is not an idea but an ideology. It came into existence at a discernible historical moment for rationally understandable historical reasons and is subject to change for similar reasons. The revolutionary bicentennials that Americans have celebrated with such unction—of independence in 1976 and of the Constitution in 1989—can as well serve as the bicentennial of racial ideology, since the birthdays are not far apart. During the revolutionary era, people who favored slavery and people who opposed it collaborated in identifying the racial incapacity of Afro-Americans as the explanation for enslavement. American racial ideology is as original an invention of the Founders as is the United States itself. Those holding liberty to be inalienable, and holding Afro-Americans as slaves, were bound to end by holding race to be a self-evident truth. Thus we ought to begin by restoring to race—that is, the American version of race—its proper history.

As convenient a place as any to begin a brief summary of that history, along with that of plantation society in British North America, is in seventeenth-century Virginia. Virginia foundered during its early years and survived only through the good will and, when the colonists had exhausted that, the extorted tribute of the indigenous Indians. But during the second decade of the seventeenth century, Virginia discovered its vocation: the growing of tobacco. The first boom in what would eventually become the United States took place during the 1620s, and it rested primarily on the backs of English indentured servants, not African slaves. Not until late in the century, after the boom had passed, did landowners begin buying slaves in large numbers, first from the West Indies and then, after 1680, from Africa itself.[16] During the high years of the boom it was the "free-born" Englishman who became, as one historian put it, "a machine to make tobacco for somebody else."[17] Indentured servants served longer terms in Virginia than their English counterparts and enjoyed less dignity and less protection in law and custom. They could be bought and sold like livestock, kidnapped, stolen, put up as stakes in card games, and awarded— even before their arrival in America—to the victors in lawsuits. Greedy magnates (if the term is not redundant) stinted the servants' food and cheated them out of their freedom dues, and often out of their freedom itself, when they had served their time. Servants were beaten, maimed, and even killed with impunity. For expressing opinions unfavorable to the governor and the governing council, one man had both his arms broken and his tongue bored through with an awl, while another lost his ear and had to submit to a second seven-year term of servitude to a member of the council that had judged his case.[18]

Whatever truths may have appeared self-evident in those days, neither an inalienable right to life and liberty nor the founding of government on the consent of the governed was among them. Virginia was a profit-seeking venture, and no one stood to make a profit growing tobacco by democratic methods. Only those who could force large numbers of people to work tobacco for them stood to get rich during the tobacco boom. Neither white skin nor English nationality protected servants from the grossest forms of brutality and exploitation. The only degradation they were spared was perpetual enslavement along with their issue in perpetuity, the fate that eventually befell the descendants of Africans.

---

16   Edmund S. Morgan estimates that Virginia's black population numbered fewer than 500 in 1645 and fewer than 2,000 in 1660. See Morgan, *American Slavery, American Freedom*, 298.

17   Ibid., 129.

18   Ibid., 14–30.

Scholars occasionally maintain that English indentured servants escaped that fate while Africans fell victim to it because Europeans would go only so far and no farther in oppressing people of their own color. But they really only believe such folklore when they are floating in the twilight world of racial ideology, a world in which even the Supreme Court of the United States finds itself mentally disarmed. Once restored to honest daylight, they know better. They know that the Greeks and Romans enslaved people of their own color. They know that Europeans held other Europeans in both slavery and serfdom, and that the law in Tudor England provided for the enslavement of vagabonds. They know that the English considered no brutality too extreme in bringing to heel the supposedly savage and undoubtedly fair-skinned Irish. Oliver Cromwell sold survivors of the Drogheda massacre as slaves in Barbados, and his agents systematically auctioned Irish children off to planters in the West Indies. Nazi concentration camps swallowed up not only Jews and Gypsies but also partisans, resistance fighters, and Communists, whom even the United States Supreme Court would be hard-pressed to define as racial groups. From Peterloo to Santiago, Chile, to Kwangju, South Korea, to Tiananmen Square and the *barrios* of San Salvador, humanity has learned again and again that shared color and nationality set no automatic limit to oppression. Ultimately, the only check upon oppression is the strength and effectiveness of resistance to it.

Resistance does not refer only to the fight that individuals, or collections of them, put up at any given time against those trying to impose on them. It refers also to the historical outcome of the struggle that has gone before, perhaps long enough before to have been hallowed by custom or formalized in law—as "the rights of an Englishman," for example. The freedoms of lower-class Englishmen, and the somewhat lesser freedoms of lower-class Englishwomen, were not gifts of the English nobility, tendered out of solicitude for people of their own color or nationality. Rather, they emerged from centuries of day-to-day contest, overt and covert, armed and unarmed, peaceable and forcible, over where the limits lay. Moral scruples about what could and what could not be done to the lower classes were nothing but the *shoulds* and *should nots* distilled from this collective historical experience, ritualized as rules of behavior or systematized as common law—but always liable to be put once again on the table for negotiation or into the ring for combat.[19] Each new increment of freedom that the lower classes regarded as their due represented the provisional outcome of the last round in a continuing boxing-match and established the fighting weights of the contenders in the next round.

Custom and Law

In the round that took place in early colonial Virginia, servants lost many of the concessions to their dignity, well-being, and comfort that their counterparts had won in England. But not all. To have degraded the servants into slaves *en masse* would have driven the continuing struggle up several notches, a dangerous undertaking considering that servants were well armed, that they outnumbered their masters, and that the Indians could easily take advantage of the inevitably resulting warfare among the enemy. Moreover, the enslavement of already arrived immigrants, once news of it reached England, would have threatened the sources of future immigration. Even the greediest and most shortsighted profiteer could foresee disaster in any such policy. Given how fast people died in Virginia, the lifetime's labor of most slaves would probably have amounted to less than a seven-year term of servitude (fifteen thousand immigrants between 1625 and 1640 only increased the population from

19 For illustration, see Rodney Hilton, *Bond Men Made Free: Medieval Peasant Movements and the English Rising of 1381* (London: Methuen & Co., Ltd., 1977); Thomas A. Green, *Verdict According to Conscience: Perspectives on the English Criminal Trial Jury, 1200–1800* (Chicago: University of Chicago Press, 1985); and C. S. L. Davies, "Slavery and Protector Somerset: The Vagrancy Act of 1547," *Economic History Review*, 2nd ser., December 19, 1966.

some thirteen hundred to seven or eight thousand).[20] And the prospect of gaining enslaveable children in the future—an uncertain prospect, considering how few women arrived during the boom years[21]—could not compensate for the certain loss of adult immigrants in the present.

Some of these same considerations argued against employing African-descended slaves for life on a large scale; others did not. Needless to say, adverse publicity did not threaten the sources of forced migration as it did those of voluntary migration. Much more important: Africans and Afro-West Indians had not taken part in the long history of negotiation and contest in which the English lower classes had worked out the relationship between themselves and their superiors. Therefore, the custom and law that embodied that history did not apply to them. To put it another way: when English servants entered the ring in Virginia, they did not enter alone. Instead, they entered in company with the generations who had preceded them in the struggle; and the outcome of those earlier struggles established the terms and conditions of the latest one. But Africans and Afro-West Indians did enter the ring alone. Their forebears had struggled in a different arena, which had no bearing on this one. Whatever concessions they might obtain had to be won from scratch, in unequal combat, an ocean away from the people they might have called on for reinforcements.

Africans and Afro-West Indians were thus available for perpetual slavery in a way that English servants were not. Indeed, Virginians could purchase them ready-enslaved and pre-seasoned; and so they did in the earliest years of the traffic. Only much later did this become a matter of what we now call race. It took time, indeed, to become systematized as slavery. Although African or African-descended slaves dribbled in from 1619 on, the law did not formally recognize the condition of perpetual slavery or systematically mark out servants of African descent for special treatment

---

20 Morgan, *American Slavery, American Freedom*, 159.
21 Men outnumbered women more than five to one in 1624. Ibid., 111.

until 1661. Indeed, African slaves during the years between 1619 and 1661 enjoyed rights that, in the nineteenth century, not even free black people could claim.[22] Simple practicality decided the matter. Until slavery became systematic, there was no need for a systematic slave code. And slavery could not become systematic so long as an African slave for life cost twice as much as an English servant for a five-year term, and stood a better-than-even chance of dying before five years could elapse.[23]

Not until the 1660s did that morbid arithmetic change, and by then other things had changed as well. The price of tobacco had fallen, and so had the numbers of English servants emigrating to America. Afro-Americans began living long enough to be worth enslaving for life, and Euro-Americans began living long enough to claim both the freedom and the freedom dues—including land—to which they were entitled at the end of their terms of servitude. This last provoked countermeasures by those whose fortunes depended on the labor of servants. One such countermeasure was to concoct excuses for extending servants' terms, and that the Virginia Assembly set about with a vengeance during the 1650s, '60s, and '70s. Another was to engross all the available land in the tidewater, forcing freed servants either to rent from the landowners (and thus continue working for the landowners' enrichment) or to settle in frontier regions, remote from water transportation and exposed to reprisals by Indians, who understandably resented this new encroachment by the aliens who had already driven them from the tidewater. By the 1670s, the rulers of Virginia faced a potentially serious problem: a large class of young (white) freedmen, landless, single, discontented—and well-armed.[24]

---

22   Willie Lee Rose, ed., *A Documentary History of Slavery in North America* (New York: Oxford University Press, 1976).

23   Morgan, *American Slavery, American Freedom*, 197–8.

24   Ibid., 297, 215–49, 404; Allan Kulikoff, *Tobacco and Slaves: The Development of Southern Cultures in the Chesapeake, 1680-1800* (Chapel Hill, NC: University of North Carolina Press, 1986), Chapter 1.

Sure enough, trouble arrived on cue. In 1676, a group of just such young freedmen, joined by servants and slaves as well, launched the largest popular rebellion of colonial America, plundering the property of the well-to-do, burning the capital, and sending the royal governor and his cronies temporarily into hiding on Virginia's Eastern Shore. The rebellion ended abruptly, without accomplishing—or for that matter attempting or proposing—changes in the prevailing system of power and authority. What it did succeed in doing was planting suspicion and fear of the growing white lower class in the minds of the rich and powerful.[25]

It was a fortunate circumstance—fortunate for some, anyway —that made Africans and Afro-West Indians available for plantation labor at the historical moment when it became practical to buy slaves for life, and at the same time difficult and dangerous to continue using Europeans as the main source of plantation labor. The importation of African slaves in larger and larger numbers made it possible to maintain a sufficient corps of plantation laborers without building up an explosive charge of armed Englishmen resentful at being denied the rights of Englishmen and disposing of the material and political resources to make their resentment felt.[26]

Eventually, European settlement pushed into the interior, and freedmen—declining in numbers anyway as the immigration of servants slowed down—found it possible to take up land of their own. As the labor of slaves for life replaced that of servants for a term, the problem of providing for freedmen receded into the past. (So far into the past, indeed, that when providing for freedmen appeared once again on the nation's agenda, during the Civil

25 Morgan, *American Slavery, American Freedom*, 250–70.
26 Slaves imported into Virginia came first from the West Indies and then, beginning in the 1680s, increasingly from Africa. By the first decade of the eighteenth century, three-quarters of black people in Virginia were of African origin. Ira Berlin, "Time, Space, and the Evolution of Afro-American Society on British Mainland North America," *American Historical Review* 8 (February 1980), 71.

War era, the ancient precedent of freedom dues had been all but forgotten. When Abraham Lincoln and his contemporaries spoke of compensated emancipation, they did not feel a need to specify compensation for whom. No one talked of freedom dues, only of the folly of offering Negroes an unearned "gift.")

From Oppression to Inferiority

Race as a coherent ideology did not spring into being simultaneously with slavery, but took even more time than slavery did to become systematic. A commonplace that few stop to examine holds that people are more readily oppressed when they are already perceived as inferior by nature. The reverse is more to the point. People are more readily perceived as inferior by nature when they are already seen as oppressed. Africans and their descendants might be, to the eye of the English, heathen in religion, outlandish in nationality, and weird in appearance. But that did not add up to an ideology of racial inferiority until a further historical ingredient got stirred into the mixture: the incorporation of Africans and their descendants into a polity and society in which they lacked rights that others not only took for granted, but claimed as a matter of self-evident natural law.[27]

All human societies, whether tacitly or overtly, assume that nature has ordained their social arrangements. Or, to put it another way, part of what human beings understand by the word "nature" is the sense of inevitability that gradually becomes attached to a predictable, repetitive social routine: "custom, so immemorial that it looks like nature," as Nathaniel Hawthorne wrote. The feudal nobility of the early Middle Ages consisted of people more powerful than their fellows through possession of arms or property or both. No one at that time, not even they themselves, considered them superior by blood or birth; indeed, that would have been heresy. But the nobleman's habit of commanding others, ingrained

27   See Fields, "Ideology and Race in American History," 143–77.

in day-to-day routine and thus bequeathed to heirs and descendants, eventually bred a conviction that the nobility was superior
by nature, and ruled by right over innately inferior beings. By the
end of the fifteenth century, what would have been heresy to an
earlier age had become practically an article of faith.[28] The peasants did not fall under the dominion of the nobility by virtue of
being perceived as innately inferior. On the contrary, they came to
be perceived as innately inferior by virtue of having fallen under
the nobility's dominion.

Facts of nature spawned by the needs of ideology sometimes
acquire greater power over people's minds than facts of nature
spawned by nature itself. Some noblemen in tsarist Russia sin-
cerely believed that, while their bones were white, the serfs' bones
were black;[29] and, given the violence that prevailed in those times,
I must presume that noblemen had ample occasion to observe the
serfs' bones at first hand. Such is the weight of things that must
be true ideologically that no amount of experimental observation
can disprove them. But because tsarist Russia had no conception of
absolute equality resting on natural law, it did not need as consistent or radical a version of absolute inequality resting on natural law
as developed in the United States in the wake of the Revolution.[30]
When self-evident laws of nature guarantee freedom, only equally

28   Jerome Blum, *Our Forgotten Past: Seven Centuries of Life on the Land*
(London: Thames and Hudson, 1982), 34–6.

29   Kolchin, *Unfree Labor*, 170.

30   In explaining why slaveholders in the American South developed a more
thorough and elaborate pro-slavery ideology than Russian lords of serfs, Kolchin
comes to the brink of this conclusion, only to back away from it into tautology.
He argues that the presence of a "racial" distinction between owner and slave
that did not exist between lord and serf "partly" accounts for the difference. But,
as he quickly concedes, owners of African-descended slaves elsewhere in the
Americas did not develop a thorough or consistent pro-slavery argument either.
The racial distinction did not "exist" in either the American South or Russia,
but was invented in one and not the other. The "racial" distinction between
Southern owners and their slaves does not explain anything, but is itself part of
what needs to be explained.

self-evident laws of equally self-evident nature can account for its denial.

Historians can actually observe colonial Americans in the act of preparing the ground for race without foreknowledge of what would later rise on the foundation they were laying. A law enacted in the colony of Maryland in 1664 established the legal status of slave for life and experimented with assigning slave condition after the condition of the father. That experiment was soon dropped. Paternity is always ambiguous, whereas maternity is not. Slaveholders eventually recognized the advantage of a different and unambiguous rule of descent, one that would guarantee to owners all offspring of slave women, however fathered, at the slight disadvantage of losing to them such offspring as might have been fathered on free women by slave men. Nevertheless, the purpose of the Maryland experiment is clear: to prevent the erosion of slaveowners' property rights that would result if the offspring of free white women impregnated by slave men were entitled to freedom. The language of the preamble to the law makes clear that the point was not yet race: "And forasmuch as divers freeborne English women forgettfull of their free Condicon and to the disgrace of our Nation doe intermarry with Negro slaues by which alsoe diuers suites may arise touching the Issue of such woemen and a great damage doth befall the Masters of such Negroes...."[31]

"Freeborne English women"—not white women—were forgetting their free condition and disgracing their nation—not yet forgetting their color and disgracing their race. And from their forgetting and disgracing arose "diuers suites" and "a great damage" to the slaveowners. *Race* does not explain that law. Rather, the law shows society in the act of inventing race.[32] Practical needs—the

---

31   "An Act Concerning Negroes & other Slaues," in Rose, ed., *A Documentary History of Slavery in North America*, 24.

32   A law enacted in colonial Virginia illustrates the pitfall of anachronism awaiting historians who handle such material ahistorically. An entry under "Negroes" in the index to a compilation of Virginia's laws refers readers to a

need to clarify the property rights of slaveholders and the need to discourage free people from fraternizing with slaves—called forth the law. And once practical needs of this sort are ritualized often enough either as conforming behavior or as punishment for non-conforming behavior, they acquire an ideological rationale that explains to those who take part in the ritual why it is both automatic and natural to do so.

During the heyday of the cotton empire in the nineteenth century, slavery continued to perform the service it had pioneered in colonial times: that of limiting the need for free citizens (which is to say white people) to exploit each other directly and thereby identifying class exploitation with racial exploitation. But it also did much more than that. The domination of plantation slavery over Southern society preserved the social space within which the white yeomanry—that is, the small farmers and artisans who accounted for about three-fourths of the white families in the slave South just before the Civil War—could enjoy economic independence and a large measure of local self-determination, insulated from the realm of capitalist market society. By doing so, slavery permitted and required the white majority to develop its own characteristic form of racial ideology.

The White Yeomanry

Two-thirds of the people of the Old South were free and white. Of these, most owned no slaves and the few who did used them mainly for hunting, fishing, general farming, and household chores, not

provision against Negroes "Lifting hand against a white man," and that is how Ira Berlin characterizes the law (*Slaves Without Masters: The Free Negro in the Antebellum South* [New York: Pantheon, 1974], 8). But the index was prepared for a compilation published in 1823. The law itself, enacted in 1680, provides a penalty for "any negroe or other slave [who] shall presume to lift up his hand in opposition against any christian." William Waller Hening, *The Statutes at Large; Being a Collection of all the Laws of Virginia, From the First Session in the Legislature, in the Year 1619*, vol. 2 (New York, 1823), 481, 602.

for growing cash crops like cotton and tobacco. They tended to live in the backcountry, in areas too hilly, rocky, sandy, infertile, chilly, or far from navigable water to be of interest to planters. In fact, many had seen their parents or grandparents driven from better land as the slave plantations expanded to the west.[33] For reasons of their own self-interest, slaveholding planters did not wish either to antagonize non-slaveholders in their backcountry sanctuaries (since the yeomen outnumbered and thus potentially outvoted them) or to interfere in their local communities. Schools, roads, railroads, and other improvements in the backcountry would require the planters to tax themselves—something they did as little as possible. For their part, the yeomen were jealous of their local independence and self-determination. They did not want the state telling them to send their children to school, and many mistrusted railroads, with their land speculators and pirates and their locomotives that might set fields ablaze or run over children and livestock.[34]

33 Ulrich B. Phillips, "The Origin and Growth of the Southern Black Belts," in *The Slave Economy of the Old South: Selected Essays in Economic and Social History*, ed. Eugene D. Genovese (Baton Rouge, LA: Louisiana State University Press, 1968).

34 My discussion of the white non-slaveholders rests largely on the important work of Steven Hahn, including *The Roots of Southern Populism: Yeoman Farmers and the Transformation of the Georgia Upcountry, 1850–1890* (New York: Oxford University Press, 1983), esp. part I; "Common Right and Commonwealth: The Stock Law Struggle and the Roots of Southern Populism," in J. Morgan Kousser and James M. McPherson, eds., *Region, Race, and Reconstruction: Essays in Honor of C. Vann Woodward* (New York: Oxford University Press, 1982); and "Hunting, Fishing, and Foraging: Common Rights and Class Relations in the Postbellum South," *Radical History Review* 26 (1982). Also see Orville Vernon Burton and Robert C. McMath, eds., *Class, Conflict, and Consensus: Antebellum Southern Community Studies* (Westport, CT: Greenwood, 1981), and Michael P. Johnson, *Toward a Patriarchal Republic: The Secession of Georgia* (Baton Rouge, LA: Louisiana State University Press, 1977). J. Mills Thornton III, *Politics and Power in a Slave Society; Alabama, 1800–1860* (Baton Rouge, LA: Louisiana State University Press, 1978), and Lacy K. Ford, Jr., *Origins of Southern Radicalism: The South Carolina Upcountry, 1800–1860* (New York: Oxford University Press, 1988), offer interpretations of the white

Within their local communities, the white non-slaveholders developed a way of life as different from that of the slaveowning planters as from that of farmers in those Northern states where capitalist agriculture already prevailed. They grew only enough cash crops (that is, cotton or tobacco, because rice and sugar were chiefly plantation crops) for home use or to pay for those few purchases that required cash. For the rest, they concentrated on food crops—grain, potatoes, vegetables—and livestock. A custom long defunct in the Northern states permitted anyone to graze livestock or to hunt and fish on any land, public or private, that was not fenced. Thus, even people who owned little or no land could still keep livestock. The non-slaveholders traded in local markets, not national and international ones, and usually on the basis of barter or "swap-work." ("Swap-work" meant that someone might, for example, repair the roof of his neighbor's barn in exchange for the neighbor's putting a new wheel on his wagon or making him a pair of boots.) Local stores sold mainly commodities that the community could not produce—for example, firearms and ammunition, molasses, and nails—since the community was largely self-sufficient in food, furniture, shoes and clothing. Nearly every household owned a spinning wheel, with which homegrown cotton could be turned into yarn for making the family's clothes. A network of indebtedness held the community together, at the same time that it started arguments and lawsuits: everybody owed something to somebody else. The local store did not even charge interest until a debt was over a year old. The law itself recognized the rules of basic justice that prevailed within the non-slaveholders' communities. Most states of the lower South had a law known as the "homestead exemption." Even if the head of a household went bankrupt, his creditors could not strip him of his house and its furnishings and land—enough to permit him to retain his social and economic independence.

---

yeomanry differing from Hahn's, but much of their evidence tends rather to sustain it.

Strong belief in the value of social independence led the non-slaveholders to share with planters a contempt for both the hireling laborers of the North and the chattel slaves of the South; it also bred in them an egalitarian instinct that never gracefully accepted any white man's aristocratic right to rule other white men—a right the planters never doubted with regard to the lower classes of whatever color. The racial ideology of the yeomanry therefore could not possibly replicate that of the planters. Instead, it emerged as a byproduct of the practical, day-to-day business of the yeomen's lives. This is perhaps a good moment to say a few words about what ideology is and what it is not, because without an understanding of what ideology is and does, how it arises and how it is sustained, there can be no genuinely historical understanding of race. Ideology is best understood as the descriptive vocabulary of day-to-day existence through which people make rough sense of the social reality that they live and create from day to day. It is the language of consciousness that suits the particular way in which people deal with their fellows. It is the interpretation in thought of the social relations through which they constantly create and re-create their collective being, in all the varied forms their collective being may assume: family, clan, tribe, nation, class, party, business enterprise, church, army, club, and so on. As such, ideologies are not delusions but real, as real as the social relations for which they stand.

Ideologies are real, but it does not follow that they are scientifically accurate, or that they provide an analysis of social relations that would make sense to anyone who does not take ritual part in those social relations. Some societies (including colonial New England) have explained troublesome relations between people as witchcraft and possession by the devil. The explanation makes sense to those whose daily lives produce and reproduce witchcraft, nor can any amount of rational "evidence" disprove it. Witchcraft in such a society is as self-evident a natural fact as race is to Richard Cohen of the *Washington Post*. To someone looking in from outside, however, explaining a miscarriage, a crop failure, a sudden illness, or a death by invoking witchcraft would seem absurd, just as explaining slavery by invoking race must seem absurd to anyone who does not ritually produce race day in and day out as Americans do. Ideologies do not need to be plausible, let alone persuasive, to outsiders. They do their job when they help insiders make sense of the things they do and see—ritually, repetitively—on a daily basis.

So much ideology is. Here is what it is not. It is not a material entity, a thing of any sort, that you can hand down like an old garment, pass on like a germ, spread like a rumor, or impose like a code of dress or etiquette. Nor is it a collection of disassociated beliefs—"attitudes" is the favored jargon among American social scientists and the historians they have mesmerized—that you can extract from their context and measure by current or retrospective survey research. (Someday the reification of conduct and demeanor in "attitudes" will seem as quaint and archaic as their reification in bodily "humors"—phlegmatic, choleric, melancholic, sanguine—does now.) Nor is it a Frankenstein's monster that takes on a life of its own.

Ideology is not the same as *propaganda*. Someone who said, "Anti-slavery *ideology* infiltrated the slave quarters through illicit abolitionist newspapers," would be talking rather about propaganda than about ideology. The slaves' anti-slavery ideology could not be smuggled to them in alien newsprint. People deduce and verify their ideology in daily life. The slaves' anti-slavery ideology had to arise from their lives in slavery and from their daily relations with slaveholders and other members of slave society.[35]

---

35 The slaves' religion arose in the same way. In an astute and eloquent passage, Donald G. Mathews diagnoses the error of supposing that the slaves should or could have had a "correct" version of Christianity transmitted to them by an outside agency. To argue that way, Mathews correctly insists, presupposes that the slave could "slough off his enslavement, ancestry, traditional ways of viewing the world, and sense of selfhood in order to think the oppressor's thoughts after him ... The description of action in which the slave is expected to remain passive while receiving a discrete body of ideas and attitudes which exist

Frederick Douglass was not propounding a paradox but speaking the simple truth when he said that the first anti-slavery lecture he ever heard was delivered by his master in the course of explaining to his mistress why slaves must not be taught to read. By the same token, slaves who decided at the first shot of the Civil War—or even earlier, with Lincoln's election—that emancipation was finally on the nation's agenda were not responding to prevailing Northern propaganda (which, indeed, promised nothing of the kind at that time). It was their experience with slaveowners, not least the slaveowners' hysterical equation of the Republican Party with abolition, that made slaves see Lincoln as the emancipator before he saw himself that way. And, I might add, it was the slaves' acting on that foreknowledge that forced Lincoln to become the emancipator.

Ideology, Propaganda, and Dogma

To insist that ideology and propaganda are not the same is not to suppose that they are unrelated. The most successful propagandist is one who thoroughly understands the ideology of those to be propagandized. When propagandists for secession before the American Civil War emphasized the danger that the Northerners might encroach upon Southerners' right of self-determination, they emphasized a theme that resonated as well with the world of non-slaveholders as with that of planters, even though the two worlds differed as night from day. "We will never be slaves" was good secessionist propaganda. "We must never let them take our slaves" would have been poor propaganda and the secessionists knew it; just as today "Strategic Defense Initiative" makes a good advertisement for a weapons program, whereas "Strategic Offensive Initiative" or "First-Strike Initiative" would not.

apart from social and cultural conditions reveals one of the most mischievous and flawed assumptions which scholars make." Donald G. Mathews, *Religion in the Old South* (Chicago: University of Chicago Press, 1967), 187.

Neither is ideology the same as *doctrine* or *dogma*. Pro-slavery *doctrine* might well hold, for example, that any white person's word must take precedence over any black person's. But the push-and-shove reality of any planter's business would tell him or her that some situations call for accepting a slave's word over an overseer's.[36] After all, overseers came and went, but slaves remained; and the object was to produce cotton or sugar or rice or tobacco, not to produce white supremacy. The perfect subordination of the slaves to the overseer, if coupled with poor production, would spell disaster for a planter. Thus, the ideology of a planter—that is, the vocabulary of day-to-day action and experience—must make room for contest and struggle (perhaps couched in paternalistic or racist language), even if doctrine specified an eternal hierarchy. Doctrine or dogma may be imposed, and they often are: dissenters can be excommunicated from a church or expelled from a party. But ideology is a distillate of experience. Where the experience is lacking, so is the ideology that only the missing experience could call into being. Planters in the Old South could have imposed their understanding of the world upon the non-slaveholders or the slaves only if they could have transformed the lives of the non-slaveholders and slaves into a replica of their own.

An ideology must be constantly created and verified in social life; if it is not, it dies, even though it may seem to be safely embodied in a form that can be handed down.[37] Many Christians still think of kneeling with folded hands as the appropriate posture for prayer, but few now know why; and the few who do know cannot, even if they choose, mean the same thing by it as was meant by those to whom the posture was part of an ideology still real in everyday social life. The social relations that once gave explicit meaning to

---

36   Eugene D. Genovese, *Roll, Jordan, Roll: The World the Slaves Made* (New York: Pantheon, 1974), 16.

37   Some people imagine that ideology can indeed be handed down in the form of law. If that were so, then the law could do without courts, lawyers, judges, and juries.

that ritual gesture of the vassal's subordination to his lord are now as dead as a mackerel, and so, therefore, is the ideological vocabulary —including the posture of prayer—in which those social relations once lived.

The foregoing line of argument raises the question of how one group's understanding of reality, its ideology, appears to prevail over others when it comes to real and effective political power. Depending on who poses the question, it is the problem of social order, of converting power into authority, or of political hegemony. The most obvious answer—force—is not an answer. There is never ultimately enough force to go around, particularly since submission is hardly ever an end in itself. If the slaveholders had produced white supremacy without producing cotton, their class would have perished in short order. A colonial ruler does not just want the natives to bow down and render obeisance to their new sovereign. The natives must also grow food, pay taxes, go to work in mines and on estates, provide conscripts for the army, and help to hold the line against rival powers. For these activities to proceed, the natives must not just submit, they must cooperate. Even in those few cases in which submission *is* an end in itself, force is never enough in itself. Slaveholders, colonial rulers, prison guards, and the Shah's police have all had occasion to discover that when nothing remains except force, nothing remains—period. The rule of any group, the power of any state, rests on force in the final analysis. Anyone who gives the least thought to the matter reaches that conclusion, and thinkers as different in other respects as Weber, Marx, Machiavelli, and Madison would have no trouble agreeing on that. Rule always rests on force in the last analysis. But a ruling group or a state that must rely on force in the first analysis as well is one living in a state of siege, rebellion, war or revolution.

It will not do to suppose that a powerful group captures the hearts and minds of the less powerful, inducing them to "internalize" the ruling ideology (to borrow the spurious adjective-verb in which this artless evasion has so often been couched). To suppose that is to imagine ideology handed down like an old garment, passed on like a germ, spread like a rumor, or imposed like a dress code. Any of these would presuppose that an experience of social relations can be transmitted by the same means, which is impossible.

And yet, power does somehow become authority. A red light, or the upraised palm of a traffic policeman, brings people to a stop (at least in places where people tend to obey them) not by the exercise of power—neither a light nor a hand can stop a moving automobile—but by the exercise of authority. Why? Not, surely, because everyone shares a belief, an "attitude," about the sanctity of the law, or holds the same conception of a citizen's duty. Many citizens who would unhesitatingly stop for a red light, even at a deserted intersection at 2:00 a.m., would painstakingly calculate the relative cost and benefit of breaking laws against environmental pollution, insider-trading in securities, or failing to report income to the Internal Revenue Service, and then obey or violate the law according to how the calculation worked out.

It is not an abstract belief or attitude that brings people to stop at a red light. Rather, people discover the advantage of being able to take for granted what everyone else will do at a busy intersection. Or, to be more exact, they have grown up in a society that constantly ritualizes that discovery—by making people stop again and again for red lights—without each person having to make the discovery anew by ad hoc calculation at every intersection. Both parts are necessary: the demonstrable advantage of stopping and the constant re-enactment of the appropriate conduct, a re-enactment that removes the matter from the realm of calculation to that of routine. The ritual repetition of the appropriate social behavior makes for the continuity of ideology, not the "handing down" of the appropriate "attitudes." There, too, lies the key to why people may suddenly appear to slough off an ideology to which they had appeared subservient. Ideology is not a set of attitudes that people can "have," as they have a cold, and throw off the same way. Human beings live in human societies by negotiating a certain

social terrain, whose map they keep alive in their minds by the collective, ritual repetition of the activities they must carry out in
order to negotiate the terrain. If the terrain changes, so must their
activities, and therefore so must the map.

Shaping the Terrain

Let me pursue a bit further this analogy of terrain. But imagine
a physical landscape: trees here, a river there, mountains, valleys,
quicksand, desert, and so on. And imagine an observer at the alti-
tude of an earth satellite, who for some reason can follow the paths
of people over the terrain, but cannot see the details of the landscape. The observer sees people tunneling under, climbing over,
jogging to left or right, moving with odd swimming motions,
even disappearing unceremoniously into the quicksand. Given
a modicum of training in the orthodox tradition of American
history, he might conclude that people in this part of the landscape
have "attitudes" calling for one kind of movement, while people
in that part have "attitudes" calling for another kind—all of these
"attitudes" possessing a "life of their own." Given a modicum
of wisdom, he would realize that the key to understanding some
people's movements is to analyze the terrain.

Therein, also, lies the key to understanding how one group
acquires authority, imposes order, or achieves hegemony.
Exercising rule means being able to shape the terrain. Suppose that
the ruling group wants everyone in our landscape to move east,
and therefore starts fires in the forests to the west. Mission accomplished: everybody moves east. Because they all share a conviction,
an "attitude," glorifying the virtues of easterly movement? Not
necessarily. All that order, authority, or hegemony requires is that
the interest of the mass in not getting burned alive should intersect
the interest of the rulers in moving everyone to the east. If easterly
movement subsequently becomes part of the routine by which the
masses organize their lives independently of the rulers, so that such

movement becomes part of a constantly repeated social routine, a vocabulary will soon enough explain to the masses—not analytically, but descriptively—what easterly movement means. And that vocabulary need not and cannot be a duplicate of the one spoken by the rulers.

Racial ideology supplied the means of explaining slavery to people whose terrain was a republic founded on radical doctrines of liberty and natural rights, and, more important, a republic in which those doctrines seemed to represent accurately the world in which all but a minority lived. Only when the denial of liberty became an anomaly apparent even to the least observant and reflective members of Euro-American society did ideology systematically explain the anomaly. But slavery got along for a hundred years after its establishment without race as its ideological rationale. The reason is simple. Race explained why some people could rightly be denied what others took for granted: namely, liberty, supposedly a self-evident gift of nature's God. But there was nothing to explain until most people could, in fact, take liberty for granted— as the indentured servants and disfranchised freedmen of colonial America could not. Nor was there anything calling for a radical explanation where everyone in society stood in a relation of inherited subordination to someone else: servant to master, serf to nobleman, vassal to overlord, overlord to king, king to the King of Kings and Lord of Lords.

It was not Afro-Americans, furthermore, who needed a racial explanation; it was not they who invented themselves as a race. Euro-Americans resolved the contradiction between slavery and liberty by defining Afro-Americans as a race; Afro-Americans resolved the contradiction more straightforwardly by calling for the abolition of slavery. From the era of the American, French, and Haitian revolutions on, they claimed liberty as theirs by natural right.[38] They did not originate the large nineteenth-century

38 Eugene D. Genovese, *From Rebellion to Revolution: Afro-American Slave Revolts in the Making of the Modern World* (Baton Rouge, LA: Louisiana

literature purporting to prove their biological inferiority, nor, by
and large, did they accept it. Vocabulary can be deceptive. Both
Afro- and Euro-Americans used the words that today denote race,
but they did not understand those words the same way. Afro-
Americans understood the reason for their enslavement to be, as
Frederick Douglass put it, "not *color*, but crime."[39] Afro-Americans
invented themselves, not as a race, but as a nation. They were not
troubled, as modern scholars often are, by the use of racial vocabulary to express their sense of nationality. Afro-American soldiers
who petitioned on behalf of "These poor nation of color" and "we
Poore Nation of a Colored rast [race]" saw nothing incongruous
about the language.[40]

Racial ideology in its radical American form is the ideology to
be expected in a society in which enslavement stands as an exception to a radically defined liberty so commonplace that no great
effort of imagination is required to take it for granted. It is the ideology proper to a "free" society in which the enslaved descendants
of Africans are an anomalous exception. There is no paradox; it
makes good common sense. Indeed, I dare go further. In the wake
of the American Revolution, racial ideology assumed its greatest
importance in the free, bourgeois society of the Northern states,
where both slavery and the presence of Afro-Americans became
increasingly minor exceptions.[41] The paroxysm of racist violence

State University Press, 1979); C. L. R. James, *The Black Jacobins*, 2nd ed., rev.
(New York: Vintage, 1963); Willie Lee Rose, "The Impact of the American
Revolution on the Black Population," in Rose, *Slavery and Freedom*, ed. William
W. Freehling (New York: Oxford University Press, 1982).

39   Frederick Douglass, *My Bondage and My Freedom* (New York: Dover
Publications, Inc., 1969 [1855]), 90.

40   Sargint Wm. White et al. to Dear President, July 3, 1866, document 333,
and Capt. G. E. Stanford et al. to Mr. President and the Cemetery of War, May
30, 1866, document 341, in Ira Berlin, Joseph P. Reidy, and Leslie S. Rowland,
eds., *A Documentary History of Emancipation, 1861–1867*, series 2, *The Black
Military Experience* (Cambridge: Cambridge University Press, 1982), 764, 780.

41   Ralph Waldo Emerson is an excellent illustration of how such racial

that convulsed the South during the years after emancipation, and the ever more detailed legal codification of racist proscription, represent the nationalization of race, an ideology that described the bourgeois North much better than it did the slave South.

For those living within the maturing slave society of the South, racial ideology in its radical American form could not fully account for the social landscape. There, slavery was not a minor exception but the central organizing principle of society, allocating social space not just to slaveholders and slaves but to the free black population[42] and the non-slaveholding white majority as well. Inequality was not a necessary evil to be tolerated only in the instance of uncivilized Negroes, nor was its necessity commonly

---

ideology could become chillingly systematic and loathsome racial *doctrine* in the hands of a first-rate Northern intellectual. Lewis P. Simpson perceptively and relentlessly probes Emerson's bigoted views about Afro-Americans (and, for that matter, his bigoted views about white Southerners) in *Mind and the American Civil War: A Meditation on Lost Causes* (Baton Rouge, LA: Louisiana State University Press, 1989), esp. 52–7, 65–9, 72–3.

42 During the 1850s, the state of Georgia levied a property tax of $0.39 on each slave but a poll tax of $5.00 on each free black person. (For white people, the poll tax was $0.25 and applied to men only.) Annual road duty was required of slave men and white men aged sixteen to forty-five, but of free black men *and* women aged fifteen to sixty. See Peter Wallenstein, *From Slave South to New South: Public Policy in Nineteenth-century Georgia* (Chapel Hill, NC: University of North Carolina Press, 1987), 41, 93. In July 1981, a white citizen of Lynchburg, Virginia, complained to Jefferson Davis, the President of the Confederacy, about the "large number of Free Negroes in this City," branding them at once a "degraded and worse than useless race" and a "class who ... is more than useless," John Lenaham to Hon. Jeff. Davis, 15 July 1861, document 299, in Ira Berlin, Barbara J. Fields, Thavolia Glymph, Joseph P. Reidy, and Leslie S. Rowland, *Freedom: A Documentary History of Emancipation, 1861–1867*, series I, volume I, *The Destruction of Slavery* (Cambridge: Cambridge University Press, 1985), 760. In the eyes of that Virginian and of state and county law in Georgia, slaves and free people of African descent were not the same "race" and neither biology nor ancestry nor prejudice of color had anything to do with it. By word and deed, white citizens in slave society proved that they, unlike many scholars, were not fooled by the language of race into mistaking its substance.

derived from biological science. (In the South, the heyday of scientific racism—as of scientific sexism—came after, not during, slavery.)[43] Inequality was ordained by God, not by science, and was applicable not only to relations between slaveholders and slaves, but also to relations between men and women and between the planter elite and the non-slaveholding majority. Democracy and majority rule did not rank high in the aspirations of the planter class.[44] In fact, the organic intellectuals of the planter class (who rivaled Engels in well-aimed propaganda denouncing the suffering of workers under industrial capitalism) regretted that the white

43 Josiah C. Nott provoked a hostile reaction from other pro-slavery Southerners when he expounded a scientific theory of racism that seemed to contradict scripture. See Drew Gilpin Faust, *The Ideology of Slavery: Proslavery Thought in the Antebellum South, 1830–1860* (Baton Rouge, LA: Louisiana State University Press, 1991), 206–38; Gould, *The Mismeasure of Man*, 69–72. On the nature of white Southerners' arguments for women's subordination during and after slavery, see Elizabeth Fox-Genovese, "The Conservatism of Slaveholding Women: A Comparative Perspective," Porter L. Fortune Chancellor's Symposium on Southern History, University of Mississippi, October 11–13, 1989.

44 For example, John C. Calhoun's doctrine of the "concurrent majority" was explicitly designed to frustrate the will of an anti-slavery majority, should one ever gain control of the United States government, by guaranteeing the slaveholding minority a veto no matter how large the numerical majority arrayed against it. See Calhoun's "A Disquisition on Government," ed. Richard K. Crallé, in *The Works of John C. Calhoun*, vol. 1 (New York: Appleton, 1968). Many historians, following the lead of George Fredrickson, characterize the slave South as a "herrenvolk democracy." It is a specious concept that fails to take account of the ways in which slavery curtailed the political rights of the non-slaveholding white majority, the supposed herrenvolk. An obvious example is the over-representation of slaveholders secured by the three-fifths provision of the United States Constitution (replicated in the constitution of the Confederacy). Another example is the requirement for the posting of bond—ranging from $1,000 to $500,000—that replaced property qualifications for county officers in the plantation districts, ensuring that humble citizens could hold office only under the patronage of their betters. See Steven Hahn, "Capitalists All!," review of James Oakes, *The Ruling Race: A History of American Slaveholders*, in *Reviews in American History* II (June 1983).

laboring poor of their own society could not be brought under the benevolent regime of slavery—called by tactful euphemisms like "warranteeism without the ethnical qualification" and "slavery in the abstract." It would not do, after all, to tell an armed and enfranchised white majority that they, too, would be better off as slaves.[45]

Race Today

The pro-slavery intellectuals' reticence in stating that conclusion publicly and forthrightly goes far to explain why the United States to this day has failed to develop a thorough, consistent, and honest political conservatism. The only historical ground that might have nourished such a tradition—namely, the slave society of the South—was contaminated by the need to humor the democratic aspirations of a propertied, enfranchised, and armed white majority. Few self-styled conservative politicians in the United States today dare argue on principle (at least in public) that hereditary inequality and subordination should be the lot of the majority. Instead, those prepared to defend inequality do so on the basis of a bastard free-market liberalism, with

---

45 Eugene D. Genovese developed this argument long ago in his essay about George Fitzhugh, "The Logical Outcome of the Slaveholders' Philosophy," in *The World the Slaveholders Made: Two Essays in Interpretation* (New York: Pantheon, 1969). A number of historians at first dismissed the argument on the grounds that Fitzhugh was a one-of-a-kind aberration—a charge occasionally repeated even today; for example, George C. Rable, *Civil Wars: Women and the Crisis of Southern Nationalism* (Urbana, IL: University of Illinois Press, 1989), 291. Subsequent work has demonstrated that, although Fitzhugh was indeed one of a kind in some respects, he was no aberration in considering slave society morally superior to capitalist society ("free trade" in his terminology) regardless of the slaves' nationality or descent. See Drew Gilpin Faust, "The Peculiar South Revisited: White Society, Culture, and Politics in the Antebellum Period, 1800–1860," in John B. Boles and Evelyn Thomas Nolen, eds., *Interpreting Southern History: Historiographical Essays in Honor of Sanford W. Higginbotham* (Baton Rouge, LA: Louisiana State University Press, 1987), esp. 102–5; Simpson, *Mind and the American Civil War*, 30–2.

racial, ethnic, or sexual determinism tacked on as an inconsistent afterthought.

Meanwhile, many well-intentioned believers in truth and justice succumb to biological determinism, the armor of the enemy, when they see around them the ugly signs that racism continues to thrive in our world. Weary of the struggle, they throw up their hands and declare that racism, if not genetically programmed, is nonetheless an idea so old and entrenched that it has "taken on a life of its own." They thereby come much closer than they realize to the views of those they ostensibly oppose. Although it is now frowned upon to attribute biological disability to those designated to be a race, it is eminently fashionable to attribute biological disability—or its functional equivalent—to those demonstrated to be racists. Either way, Africans and their descendants become a special category set apart by biology: in the one instance their own, in the other that of their persecutors.

But race is neither biology nor an idea absorbed into biology by Lamarckian inheritance. It is ideology, and ideologies do not have lives of their own. Nor can they be handed down or inherited: a doctrine can be, or a name, or a piece of property, but not an ideology. If race lives on today, it does not live on because we have inherited it from our forebears of the seventeenth century or the eighteenth or nineteenth, but because we continue to create it today. David Brion Davis had the courage and honesty to argue the disturbing thesis that, during the era of the American Revolution, those who opposed slavery were complicit with those who favored it in settling on race as its explanation. We must be courageous and honest enough to admit something similar about our own time and our own actions.

Those who create and re-create race today are not just the mob that killed a young Afro-American man on a street in Brooklyn or the people who join the Klan and the White Order. They are also those academic writers whose invocation of self-propelling "attitudes" and tragic flaws assigns Africans and their descendants to a special category, placing them in a world exclusively theirs and outside history—a form of intellectual apartheid no less ugly or oppressive, despite its righteous (not to say self-righteous) trappings, than that practiced by the bio- and theo-racists; and for which the victims, like slaves of old, are expected to be grateful. They are the academic "liberals" and "progressives" in whose version of race the neutral shibboleths *difference* and *diversity* replace words like *slavery*, *injustice*, *oppression*, and *exploitation*, diverting attention from the anything-but-neutral history these words denote. They are also the Supreme Court and spokesmen for affirmative action, unable to promote or even define justice except by enhancing the authority and prestige of race; which they will continue to do forever so long as the most radical goal of the political opposition remains the reallocation of unemployment, poverty, and injustice rather than their abolition.

The creators and re-creators of race include as well a young woman who chuckled appreciatively when her four-year-old boy, upon being asked whether a young friend whose exploit he was recounting was black, answered: "No, he's brown." The young woman's benevolent laughter was for the innocence of youth, too soon corrupted. But for all its benevolence, her laughter hastened the corruption whose inevitability she laments, for it taught the little boy that his empirical description was cute but inappropriate. It enacted for him, in a way that hand-me-down stereotypes never could, the truth that physical description follows race, not the other way around. Of just such small, innocuous, and constantly repeated rituals, often undertaken with the best of motives, is race reborn every day. Evil may result as well from good as from ill intentions. That is the fallibility and tragedy of human history— or, to use a different vocabulary, its dialectic.

Nothing handed down from the past could keep race alive if we did not constantly reinvent and re-ritualize it to fit our own terrain. If race lives on today, it can do so only because we continue to create and re-create it in our social life, continue to verify it, and thus continue to need a social vocabulary that will allow us to make sense, not of what our ancestors did then, but of what we ourselves choose to do now.

5 Origins of the New South
and the Negro Question

"Race relations," a political formula devised at the end of the nineteenth century, is close kin to the race-racism maneuver: both divert the mind's eye from the shell that hides the pea. The race-racism maneuver transforms racist action (invidious treatment) into race (inborn difference). In a cognate maneuver, the formula "race relations" drew a sentimental curtain of Old South symbols across the New South's class relations and politics. While the curtain concealed the South's cheap labor, black and white, it also muffled the noise of anti-democratic struggles to build white supremacy. To understand that double mission of white supremacy—to hold down black people and white people alike—there exists no better source than Origins of the New South, *by the great American historian C. Vann Woodward.*[1]

Not the least remarkable fact about C. Vann Woodward's *Origins of the New South* is that, fifty years ago, Woodward knew better than to attempt what I have been asked to do: to discuss Afro-Americans as a subject apart from the subjects of land, agriculture, and rural unrest; industrial development and political economy; class warfare, class alliances, and politics; and literature, the

1   Originally published as "*Origins of the New South* and the Negro Question," *Journal of Southern History* 57 (November 2001), 811–26. I would like to thank Michael R. West and Lauren F. Winner for comments on the manuscript.

sciences, and the arts. Then (as now), the more usual procedure
was to relegate Afro-Americans to a space of their own, defined as
"race relations" and set apart from the study of history properly
so called. Woodward never fell into that trap. He understood that
the importance of Jim Crow as a subject in no way established its
validity as a method.

Never at any point in *Origins* is Woodward unaware of Afro-
Americans' entire implication within the vital questions of the
New South. Meaningless definitions of their predicament that may
pass muster today, such as *marginalization* and *exclusion*, did not
fool him for a minute. (Marginalized? Excluded? When the planters wanted nothing better than for them to stay conspicuously in
their place, working as before?) The opening sentence of Chapter
1 sets the tone at once (and with as fine an example as I know of
Woodward's flair for mischief). Right there, where no one can
miss it, he writes, "Any honest genealogy of the ruling family of
Southern Democrats would reveal a strain of mixed blood."[2]
The mixture in question was of Whig and Democrat, rather
than of black and white. But, beyond doubt, the metaphor was calculated. Trifling with the hallowed conventions of racism by thus
juxtaposing the sacred and the profane—ruling-class genealogy
and mixed blood—Woodward serves early notice that, in method
as in content, *Origins of the New South* will neither fear nor respect
the color line. Though he may flirt occasionally with the language
of race relations, he only rarely makes concessions to its conceptual apparatus.[3]

2   C. Vann Woodward, *Origins of the New South, 1877–1913* (Baton Rouge,
LA: Louisiana State University Press, 1957), 1. Page numbers for subsequent
references to *Origins* in this essay are inserted parenthetically in the text. The
first edition's pagination is retained in later reprint editions.

3   One of the rare exceptions appears in the chapter on the Atlanta
Compromise (Chap. 13), where Woodward credits Booker T. Washington with
having "framed the *modus vivendi* of race relations in the New South" (356). The
framing as race relations was Washington's work, but Woodward's argument
in the preceding chapters makes clear that the *modus vivendi* itself had been

Race relations as an analysis of society takes for granted that *race* is a valid empirical datum and thereby shifts attention from the actions that constitute racism—enslavement, disfranchisement, segregation, lynching, massacres, and pogroms—to the traits that constitute race. For racists in the New South, those traits might have included the Negroes' ignorance, laziness, brutality, criminality, subjection to uncontrolled passions, or incapacity for the moral and intellectual duties of civilization. For scholars in our own time who accept race, once ritually purified by the incantation *socially constructed*, as a valid category of analysis, the relevant traits are more likely to be "difference," "Other-ness," "culture," or "identity." Either way, however, objective acts, the real substance of racism, take second place to subjective traits, the fictive substance of race; traits that would be irrelevant to explaining racist acts even if their empirical validity could be established.

Quincy Ewing, a white Southerner writing in the *Atlantic Monthly* while Woodward was an infant, refuted on empirical grounds the various racial explanations of the problem: the Negroes' purported ignorance, laziness, criminality, and the like. But such rationales, he maintained, were beside the point in any case. The problem would persist even were there "no shadow of excuse for the conviction that the Negro is more lazy, or more ignorant, or more criminal, or more brutal, or more anything else he ought not to be, or less anything else he ought to be, than other men." Nor, according to

---

determined, as it would continue to be, by means of crop lien and sharecropping, law and constitution, rope and faggot. See Michael R. West, *The Education of Booker T. Washington: American Democracy and the Idea of Race Relations* (New York: Columbia University Press, 2006), 55. Even in *The Strange Career of Jim Crow*, which is much more race-relations-oriented than *Origins*, Woodward betrays his dissatisfaction with the language of race relations: "The peculiarity most often used to distinguish one order from another, however, has been the relation between races, or more particularly the status of the Negro." C. Vann Woodward, *The Strange Career of Jim Crow* (3d rev. ed.; New York: Oxford University Press, 1974), 5. Note the shift from "relation between races" to "the status of the Negro."

Ewing, could the problem be laid to "difference" (an old favorite
that has returned to favor, often graced with a capital *D*): "There is
nothing in the unlikeness of the unlike that is necessarily problematical," he pointed out; "it may be simply accepted and dealt with
as a fact, like any other fact."[4] Like or unlike, Ewing declared, no
race problem arises unless "the people of one race are minded to
adopt and act upon some policy more or less oppressive or repres-
sive in dealing with the people of another race." He concluded:

> The problem, How to maintain the institution of chattel slavery,
> ceased to be at Appomattox; the problem, How to maintain the
> social, industrial, and civic inferiority of the descendants of chattel
> slaves, succeeded it, and is the race problem of the South at the
> present time. There is no other.[5]

Woodward is more attentive than Ewing to how white people
differed among themselves in social and economic standing, objectives and aspirations, and ability to mobilize political power. But,
like Ewing, he recognizes that the essence of the situation was
power and the contest over it: not just the contest (grotesquely
unequal as it was) between white and Afro-American people but
also that among white people themselves. If allowed the rights of
citizenship, Afro-Americans potentially held in their own hands
the balance of power between contending groups of white people.
If stripped of the rights of citizenship, they still potentially held the
balance of power, only not in their own hands. Settling the future

4   Quincy Ewing, "The Heart of the Race Problem," *Atlantic Monthly* 102
(March 1909), 389–97 (first quotation on 390, second on 396). An example of
the current vogue for "difference" as a category of analysis is Patrick Wolfe,
"Land, Labor, and Difference: Elementary Structures of Race," *American
Historical Review* 106 (June 2001), 866–905. Wolfe regards race as "one among
various regimes of difference." After asserting that land and labor are the
key to understanding colonial regimes, he chooses to concentrate instead on
"discourses of miscegenation" (867).
5   Ewing, "The Heart of the Race Problem," 396.

of Afro-Americans in the New South inevitably also meant settling the future of white people there, for better or worse (that is, better for some white people and worse for others).

That is why my title refers to the "Negro Question," rather than to any of the common variations on the theme of race or race relations. *Negro Question* (or *Negro Problem*) has the virtue, as Michael R. West has argued, of setting the predicament of Afro-Americans firmly within, rather than at a tangent from, the major questions of political, economic, and social power that were up for settlement in the New South. It also reveals without euphemism the illegitimacy of the problem in the context of a democratic polity. Proposing to decide the fate of people occupying the nominal status of citizens otherwise than with their participation and assent is a profoundly undemocratic, indeed anti-democratic, undertaking. West argues that *race relations* as an ideological formation of the problem, popularized with genius by Booker T. Washington, arose precisely as a way to disguise the anti-democratic essence of the problem by providing for it both a definition and a solution apparently capable of bypassing the issue of naked power that lay at its core.[6]

From the moment Woodward introduces the Redeemers, discusses their social provenance, and characterizes their political program, he makes clear that the central issue for their regimes was how to forestall democracy. The "most common characteristic" of Redeemer state constitutions, he asserts, was "an overweening distrust of legislatures" (65). Quincy Ewing leaps from chattel slavery before Appomattox to social, industrial, and civic inferiority after. Woodward, however, does not forget that Reconstruction fell between, although he neither exaggerates its extent nor takes at face value the Redeemers' charges against their predecessors. ("The Radical regime in the average state ... lasted less than three and a half years. The amount of good or evil the Radicals could accomplish was limited by this fact if by no other"

---

6   West, *The Education of Booker T. Washington*, 12-19, 55–7. West uses the more brutally honest formulation, "Negro Problem."

[22].) Woodward attributes the intensity of the reaction against democracy to the radicalism of its brief tenure, observing that the investment of freed slaves with citizenship and the franchise was unprecedented (53).[7] He weighs the varied significance that the legacy of Reconstruction held for different groups of white people, as well as for Afro-Americans. White planters of the Black Belt, for example, gained a greater measure of control over white people in the uplands than they had enjoyed under slavery, when their prerogative of casting ballots on behalf of voteless Afro-Americans was three-fifths, instead of five-fifths (79). For Afro-Americans, Reconstruction kindled a hope whose loss Woodward evokes movingly, if briefly, by drawing attention to the somber coincidence that took Frederick Douglass off the stage in the same year that Booker T. Washington emerged onto it (356–7).

The intricacies of fusion, that odd policy of forming tactical political unions with the lesser enemy against the greater, are a sufficient reminder that nothing to do with politics among white Southerners was separate from Afro-Southerners and vice versa. That is especially true of disfranchisement, which, as Woodward makes clear, rested on an old struggle between predominantly white counties and predominantly black counties. The Reconstruction constitutions, sponsored by Republican regimes confident about controlling the votes of the newly enfranchised former slaves,

---

7   Considering the volume of private property expropriated without compensation, the investment of former slaves with citizenship, the franchise, and the right to hold governmental office, and the former slaveholders' loss— albeit temporary—of power within the national state, emancipation in the United States was radical compared to the emancipation of serfs in Europe and slaves elsewhere in the Americas during the nineteenth century. See Barbara Jeanne Fields, "The Advent of Capitalist Agriculture: The New South in a Bourgeois World," in Thavolia Glymph and John J. Kushma, eds., *Essays on the Post-bellum Southern Economy* (College Station, TX: Texas A&M Press, 1985), 73–94; and Steven Hahn, "Class and State in Postemancipation Societies: Southern Planters in Comparative Perspective," *American Historical Review* 95 (February 1990), 75–98.

heightened the struggle by upsetting antebellum arrangements that had limited the power of planters in the Black Belt over the white-majority counties. Some scholars may be tempted to attribute all the fuss and feathers to the working out of something they call "white racial identities." But white residents in white-majority counties were not naive enough to make the same mistake. A Populist newspaper in Louisiana roundly charged the Democrats with "'maintaining white supremacy (?) with the Negro votes'" (276).[8] A white-county delegate at Virginia's disfranchising convention scornfully rejected complaints by Black Belt delegates of Negro domination in their home counties—and not from solicitude for the rights of Afro-American voters: "'I ask you gentlemen of the black belt, ... How do you happen to be here if the Negroes control down there?'" (328). As Woodward makes clear, the question was not white supremacy but *"which whites* should be supreme" (328, Woodward's italics).

White residents in the white-majority counties of Mississippi sought disfranchisement in 1890, according to Woodward, to overthrow their domination by white people in the black counties (329).[9] In the end, they suffered the same fate as the Afro-Americans at whose disfranchisement they had connived. The Mississippi Plan stripped the franchise from the Afro-American majority and lodged with a minority of white people control over the rest. In the face of the resulting hostility, the convention decided against submitting the new state constitution for ratification by the electorate (340–1). Disfranchisement not only directly robbed Afro-American as well as white voters of the franchise, but, according to Woodward, it

8   The question mark appears in Woodward's source.
9   Citing the work of his student J. Morgan Kousser, Woodward later conceded that he had overstated the initial enthusiasm for disfranchisement among white residents of white counties. See C. Vann Woodward, *Thinking Back: The Perils of Writing History* (Baton Rouge, LA: Louisiana State University Press, 1986), 69, 97; and J. Morgan Kousser, *The Shaping of Southern Politics: Suffrage Restriction and the Establishment of the One-Party South, 1880–1910* (New Haven, CT: Yale University Press, 1974).

also prepared the way for the apathy that steadily reduced electoral participation, a trend that has continued up to the present (343–6).

It is not done, however, to interpret these matters as issues of democracy and its abrogation, particularly not where Afro-Americans are concerned. The rubric of the hour is race. Though discredited by reputable biologists and geneticists, race has enjoyed a renaissance among historians, sociologists, and literary scholars. They find the concept attractive, or in any case hard to dispense with, and have therefore striven mightily, though in vain, to find a basis for it in something other than racism. The most recent pedigree papers trace it to culture or identity, at the same time implicating its victims as agents of its imposition. "'Race,' as an embodied category of difference and a constructed aspect of identity, is not imposed by one group upon another," the author of a recent book insists. "It is a product of an ongoing dialogue…"[10]

The effort to redefine race as culture or identity is bound to come a cropper just as did the effort to define race as biology. Indeed, it already has come a cropper, though the fashionable preference for "complicating" analysis may conceal from the unwary the difference between complexity and muddle. Race as culture is only biological race in polite language: No one can seriously postulate cultural homogeneity among those whose racial homogeneity scholars nonetheless take for granted. The only veil hiding the conjuror's apparatus from full view of the spectators is the quicksilver propensity of *culture* to change meaning from one clause to the next—now denoting something essential, now something acquired; now something bounded, now something without boundaries; now something experienced, now something ascribed.[11]

---

10 Joanne Pope Melish, *Disowning Slavery: Gradual Emancipation and "Race" in New England, 1789–1860* (Ithaca, NY: Cornell University Press, 1998), 3–4.

11 A rich discussion of the history of *culture* as a concept, and of the changing

Scholars are quick to assimilate the commonplace that race is "socially constructed"—which a German shepherd dog or even an intelligent golden retriever knows without instruction—to the popular but mistaken view that race is equivalent to identity.[12] For example, Jane Dailey offers as proof "that racial identity in Virginia was neither static nor superficial" a Virginian ex-Readjuster's demand to know "'how many white men in Lynchburg will go back on their race and make negroes of themselves'" by voting for the Mahoneite Readjusters.[13] But of course the remark proves nothing about "racial identity," not even that there is such a thing. No white politician could have suggested, even metaphorically, that Negroes who allied with the opposing faction or, for that matter, who allied with his own faction, thereby turned themselves into white men. Whereas white men might "make negroes of themselves" by improper or undignified conduct, a black man could make a white man of himself only by an act of misrepresentation or concealment that, if discovered, could under the right circumstances land him in jail or at the end of a rope dangling over a bonfire.

Race as identity breaks down on the irreducible fact that any sense of self intrinsic to persons of African descent is subject to peremptory nullification by forcible extrinsic identification. Such

---

relationships among its varied meanings, may be found in Terry Eagleton, *The Idea of Culture* (Oxford: Blackwell, 2000).

12   My own attempt to account historically for the emergence of racial ideology in the United States, attributing it to the juxtaposition of slavery and freedom during the Revolutionary era, is regularly cited as an argument for the "social construction" of race—which is its starting point, not its conclusion. See Barbara Jeanne Fields, "Slavery, Race and Ideology in the United States of America," *New Left Review* 181 (May–June 1990), 95–118. Melish cites this article and sketches a similar historical argument but neglects to attribute the argument to the article. Melish, *Disowning Slavery*, 5.

13   Jane Dailey, *Before Jim Crow: The Politics of Race in Postemancipation Virginia* (Chapel Hill, NC: University of North Carolina Press, 2000), 149 (first quotation), 148 (second quotation).

nullification occurs when police officers shoot an unarmed black civilian or, even more flagrantly, when they shoot a black fellow officer, their identification of him as a black man—and, ipso facto, a candidate for summary execution—lethally overriding his self-definition as a policeman. Whatever Afro-American people's identity may be (and a well-argued recent article proposes doing away with the concept altogether[14]), it cannot be equated with their race. After years of probing them for something of value or use, W. E. B. Du Bois repudiated all efforts to define race as a characteristic or attribute of its victims, whether the definition hinged on biology, culture, or identity (supposing "identity" to mean an individual's or a group's sense of self). The black man is not someone of a specified ancestry or culture, he decided, and certainly not someone who so identifies himself. A black man "is a person who must ride 'Jim Crow' in Georgia."[15]

Forced to ride Jim Crow is the key. Not identity as sense of self, but identification by others, peremptory and binding, figuring even in well-meant efforts to undo the crimes of racism. The victim's intangible race, rather than the perpetrator's tangible racism, becomes the center of attention. Thus, racist profiling goes by the misnomer "racial profiling," and the usual remedy proposed for it is to collect information about—what else?—the victims' "race."[16]

14   Rogers Brubaker and Frederick Cooper, "Beyond 'Identity,'" *Theory and Society* XXIX (February 2000), 1–47.

15   W. E. B. Du Bois, *Dusk of Dawn: An Essay Toward An Autobiography of a Race Concept* (New York, 1940; reprint, New Brunswick, NJ: Transaction Books, 1992), 153. Jane Dailey mistakes Du Bois' blunt definition of race as something imposed by political power for a statement about the "linkages between social interactions and the construction of individual identity." Dailey, *Before Jim Crow*, 133.

16   The columnist Richard Cohen insists that white police officers' automatic identification of a black man as a criminal stems from "race—but not racism," thus implying that mistaken identity is an inborn trait of the mistaken, rather than an act committed by the mistaker. Richard Cohen, "Profile of A Killing," *Washington Post*, March 16, 2000, A27. No doubt Cohen would spot the fallacy at once if police randomly harassed and frisked middle-class white adolescent

Like a criminal suspect required to confess guilt before receiving probation, or a drunk required to intone "I am an alcoholic" as a prerequisite to obtaining help, persons of African descent must accept race, the badge that racism assigns them, to earn remission of the attendant penalties. Not justice or equality but *racial* justice or *racial* equality must be their portion. "In [Ben] Tillman's world," writes Stephen Kantrowitz, "'racial equality' was an oxymoron."[17] In mine, too, I must confess, except that I would replace *oxymoron* with *contradiction in terms*. An oxymoron is a figure of speech. *Racial equality* and *racial justice* are not figures of speech; they are public frauds, political acts with political consequences. Just as a half-truth is not a type of truth but a type of lie, so *equality* and *justice*, once modified by *racial*, become euphemisms for their opposites.

Du Bois' thumbnail summary—forced to ride Jim Crow—represents the end of the odyssey that Woodward chronicles in *Origins*. Woodward offers an equally laconic summary of the beginning of that odyssey:

> Much discussion about the Negro's civil rights, his political significance, his social status, and his aspirations can be shortened and simplified by a clear understanding of the economic status assigned him in the New Order ... The lives of the overwhelming majority of Negroes were still circumscribed by the farm and plantation. The same was true of the white people, but the Negroes, with few exceptions, were farmers without land. (205)

"Farmers without land" makes as good a summary of the starting point of Afro-Americans in the New South as "forced to ride Jim Crow" does of their destination. The same passage reminds us

---

boys on grounds of their color, arguing (correctly) that school mass murderers tend to be white.

17 Stephen Kantrowitz, *Ben Tillman and the Reconstruction of White Supremacy* (Chapel Hill, NC: University of North Carolina Press, 2000), 2.

why Jim Crow will not do as a method of analysis: "It remained
for the New South to find ... a definition of free labor, both black
and white; for the white worker's place in the New Order would be
vitally conditioned by the place assigned to the free black worker"
(205). (Note Woodward's use of "assigned," emphasizing that an
undemocratic settlement where Afro-Americans were concerned
necessarily meant undemocratic limits on white people.)

It is perhaps in order, at this point, to say a few words about
Woodward's observation that "it took a lot of ritual and Jim
Crow to bolster the creed of white supremacy in the bosom of a
white man working for a black man's wages" (211). The phrase
may seem to echo W. E. B. Du Bois' "psychological wage" (the
beloved pet of so-called whiteness studies) and tempt someone to
connect Woodward's argument to arguments about white identity.
In fact, however, Woodward's remark differs from Du Bois' both
in substance and in register. While Du Bois' remark is declara-
tory, Woodward's is sardonic. "It must be remembered," Du Bois
explains, "that the white group of laborers, while they received a
low wage, were compensated in part by a sort of public and psychological wage."[18] To Woodward, "ritual and Jim Crow" is
more a symptom of white people's exploitation than a remedy or
compensation for it. His point is not that Jim Crow compensated
white people for exploitation but, rather, that white people suffered
plenty of exploitation that needed compensating for. A few pages
on in the same chapter, Woodward makes the point explicit:

> The rituals and laws that exempted the white worker from the
> penalties of caste did not exempt him from competition with black
> labor, nor did they carry assurance that the penalties of black labor
> might not be extended to white. The propagandists of the New-
> South order, in advertising the famed cheap labor of their region,

18   W. E. B. Du Bois, *Black Reconstruction in America: An Essay Toward
a History of the Part Which Black Folk Played in the Attempt to Reconstruct
Democracy in America, 1860–1880* (New York: Harcourt Brace, 1935), 700.

were not meticulous in distinguishing between the color of their wares. (221)

Like everything race relations touches, segregation is liable to suffer trivialization on contact, typically in the form of the equation of segregation with separation. That equation is what possessed Joel Williamson to refer to the "peculiar kind of racial integration that slavery required" and John Anthony Scott, in a mirror-image fallacy, to consider slavery "the ultimate segregator."[19] Both are wrong, and for the same reason: Slavery was a system for the extortion of labor, not for the management of "race relations," whether by segregation or by integration. Woodward usually resists the confusion. (Not always: It was in the successive revisions of *Strange Career*, under the influence of various sociological nostrums, that he was most liable to the error.[20])

---

19 Joel Williamson. "Wounds Not Scars: Lynching, the National Conscience, and the American Historian," *Journal of American History* LXXXIII (March 1997), 1233 (first quotation); John Anthony Scott, "Segregation: A Fundamental Aspect of Southern Race Relations, 1800–1860," *Journal of the Early Republic* IV (Winter 1984), 425 (second quotation). The same impulse leads Scott to classify the withdrawal of monastics from the secular world as another, albeit voluntary, manifestation of the same generic phenomenon of isolation. Ibid., 427.

20 In the preface to the third revised edition, Woodward refers to the "strange career of segregation," rather than of Jim Crow—a much narrower concept; and he speculates about Afro-Americans' "ambivalence" toward integration and "yearning for separate racial identity." In "The Career Becomes Stranger," the concluding chapter that he wrote for the third edition, he does not pursue his own insight that the Civil Rights Movement completed a nineteenth-century agenda, rather than tackling a twentieth-century one. He therefore ends on a note of false paradox, emphasizing Afro-Americans' simultaneous demands for integration and separation but losing sight of the social predicament to which both were irrelevant. Woodward, *Strange Career of Jim Crow*, v, vi, vii, 193. See also Howard N. Rabinowitz, "More Than the Woodward Thesis: Assessing *The Strange Career of Jim Crow*," *Journal of American History* LXXV (December 1988), 842–56; and Woodward's response to his critics, "*Strange Career* Critics: Long May They Persevere," ibid., 857–68.

In *Origins*, at least, Woodward understands segregation to be an act of political power, as well as a constitutional and moral wrong—an act of power that, whatever the popular sentiment behind it, gained its force from the authority of the state. Neglecting the act-of-power aspect accounts for scholars' treating the establishment of independent Afro-American churches and the passage of Jim Crow laws as the same phenomenon or as related or similar phenomena. The near-totemic significance often attached to the notion of powerless people's *agency* can lead to the conclusion that initiative in forming independent churches proves agency in bringing about segregation as a legal and political fact. It may also lead to a facile dismissal of segregation laws and the timing of their passage as matters of no importance in themselves, a view from which Afro-Americans who actually lived through the era when segregation laws took effect have dissented.[21] To equate segregation with separation, however (and why ever) accomplished, is to vacate questions of power and citizenship, making a mystery of the New South and, equally, of the Civil Rights Movement. "Freedom now!" was a slogan to inspire the sacrifice of livelihood and even of life. "Integration now!" could scarcely inspire the expenditure of the breath required to shout it.

Woodward presents in *Origins* a relentlessly social-structural argument. He devotes much of his attention to getting a line on the social provenance, political connections, and economic projects and intentions of the ruling class. Letting hitherto unheard "voices" from the past speak, not in order to pose or answer questions deemed to be of moment, but for the pure antiquarian hell of it, is a doubtful enterprise. It did not interest Woodward and, I must say on my own account, is strictly an acquired taste. In our own time, when the overwhelming power of capitalist markets and their protagonists over nation-states and their hapless citizens passes virtually without comment or criticism, Woodward's insistence

---

21   For example, see Mamie Garvin Fields with Karen Fields, *Lemon Swamp and Other Places: A Carolina Memoir* (New York: Free Press, 1983), 45–6.

on getting to grips with capitalism may strike a quaint and rather archaic note. In discussing the proselytizing zeal of the industrialist Daniel Augustus Tompkins, Woodward is at some pains to make clear that it is not just industrialism for which Tompkins and his fellows sounded the trumpets, but "laissez-faire capitalism, freed of all traditional restraints, together with a new philosophy and way of life and a new scale of values" (148).

The moonlight-and-magnolias nostalgia for slavery and the Old South, along with the cult of the Lost Cause, was part of the new order, according to Woodward, not an echo of the old. The "'bonny blue flag,'" symbol of the Confederacy long before Lee's battle flag usurped that role, "'is the symbol of nothing to the present generation of Southern men,'" Henry Watterson said in 1880 (155). (He meant "white Southern men"; that was before otherwise sane people began to believe the legend of a black Confederate phalanx.) Only in the 1890s did the Confederacy become an emotional symbol.[22] Woodward associates the "cult of racism" with that of archaism, all part of a new order seeking to burnish its claim to antiquity (154–7, quotation on 249).

Lynching and racist violence in many forms turn out to be one of the novel elements of the New South. That Woodward's discussion of lynching is brief is now a commonplace observation. Even in its brevity, it is valuable for its insistence that an overall tendency toward violence in the South provides the essential terms of reference for analyzing lynching and pogroms; and for its recognition that racist violence occurred in the context of the political settlement for which Booker T. Washington's Atlanta Exposition address provided the public ratification (350–4). Appropriately, much has been written about lynching since *Origins*. Some of this literature has been worthwhile, answering the questions why, where, who,

---

22 During the civil rights era the battle flag became a symbol of segregationists. Only later did it become a symbol of "white heritage"— whatever that is.

when, under what circumstances, with whose permission, facilitation, or connivance, and with what result.[23] Some of it has added little beyond moral posturing.[24] Some of it has positively darkened counsel. For example, the authors of one study about lynching bend a perceptive observation by John Dollard—"Every Negro in the South knows that he is under a kind of sentence of death; he does not know when his turn will come, it may never come, but it may also be at any time"—into a statement about contingency and agency, rather than a statement about living in fear for one's life. "The kind of contingency Dollard identified was tightly circumscribed, to be sure; it was without doubt criminal and terrible in its living and for a time nurturing of white supremacy," they argue. "But, still, it represented an indeterminateness predicated on and fostering agency."[25]

At every stage of a lynching-in-the-making, the authors inform us, something could happen to make events unfold differently. Their concluding non sequitur is that we had much better attend to the steps along the way rather than the finished process or (still less) the collective and aggregate phenomenon of lynching.[26] The essence of Damocles' predicament, it seems, is the tensile strength of the hair from which the sword hangs, rather than the circumstance that a sword is hanging over him by a hair in the first place.

---

23 See, for example, Jacquelyn Dowd Hall, *Revolt Against Chivalry: Jessie Daniel Ames and the Women's Campaign Against Lynching* (New York: Columbia University Press, 1979); and W. Fitzhugh Brundage, *Lynching in the New South: Georgia and Virginia, 1880–1930* (Urbana, IL: University of Illinois Press, 1993).

24 Williamson, "Wounds Not Scars," 1221–53, is a particularly egregious example.

25 John Dollard, *Caste and Class in a Southern Town* (New Haven, CT: Yale University Press, 1937), 359 (first quotation); Larry J. Griffin, Paula Clark, and Joanne C. Sandberg, "Narrative and Event: Lynching and Historical Sociology," in W. Fitzhugh Brundage, ed., *Under Sentence of Death: Lynching in the South* (Chapel Hill, NC: University of North Carolina Press, 1997), 40–1 (second quotation on 41).

26 Griffin, Clark, and Sandberg, "Narrative and Event," 41–2.

For all his brevity in dealing with lynching, Woodward never forgets the sword or how it came to be hanging by a hair over a man's head. *Origins* is steeped in the South, full of its flavors and textures. Woodward remains alert, nonetheless, to the international context. More important than the direct international comparisons he occasionally makes (for example, in analyzing the credit system [180–1], homicide rates [159], and regional disparities in wealth [111]) is his exploration of foreign investment in the South, during a period when the bourgeoisie of England were scouring the earth for places to invest their surplus capital (118–20). In one of his wonderfully dry, satirical passages, he compares the New South "natives" with those of the European imperialist powers:

> Such wretchedness [as that of white migrants to Arkansas and Texas] belonged to those "backward peoples" whom the leading imperial powers of Western Europe were in those days seeking to "develop," and to whom was applied by common international usage the curious term "natives." The teeming millions of ker-chiefed Negroes in the Black Belt, with their "happy-go-lucky disposition," and the quaint "highlanders" of the mountains, with their "Elizabethan flavor" (invariably noted), fitted conveni-ently into the imperialistic pattern of "backward natives." But the observant traveler from the Northeast found some difficulty in accounting for other millions of Southerners of approximately the same economic status who were not black, who bore English, Scotch, and Irish names, and about whom there was no appreciable Elizabethan flavor. (109)

Despite Woodward's deliberate concentration on power and those who wielded it, he does not treat Afro-Americans as passive objects rather than active subjects of history. His comments about Afro-American Protestant denominations (453), about the Colored Farmers' Alliance (192, 220–1, 255–6), and about Afro-Americans' distaste for fusion in 1894 (277) refute any such accusation. And even the most zealous apostles of "agency" would have to concede that Woodward credits Booker T. Washington with an ample share (356–7). But *Origins* does not, where Afro-Americans or anyone else are concerned, emphasize the inwardness of people's lives for its own sake. Woodward is much less interested in how Afro-Southerners (or, for that matter, Euro-Southerners) made lives for themselves within the cramped space available to them than in how and by whom that space was delimited and what rules governed life within it. Even his treatment of literature, the arts, and the sciences is not a rumination on these matters in, of, or for themselves, but on their relationship to the novel set of social relationships that constituted the New South.

The valid observation that much less secondary literature concerning Afro-Americans was available at the time Woodward wrote *Origins* (and that the book stimulated much of the literature since produced) is not, therefore, an adequate explanation of why *Origins* focuses on some questions to the exclusion of others. Even if the large body of scholarship about Afro-Americans in the South that now exists had been available in 1951, *Origins* would still have emerged as a book about power and its ramifications rather than a book about the self-activity of the powerless. After all, Woodward made broader use than most of his contemporaries of the secondary literature about Afro-Americans, including much that others avoided because it fell on the wrong side of the color line or the line of political acceptability (or both, as in the case of Du Bois). Furthermore, Woodward has attributed great importance to his acquaintance with J. Saunders Redding during his stint at Georgia Tech and with Langston Hughes and other figures of the Harlem Renaissance during study at Columbia University in 1931–2, as well as to his later close intellectual relationship with John Hope Franklin.[27] His footnotes illustrate the debt he owed to such associations. No doubt, had it been available to him, he

27 Woodward, *Thinking Back*, 85–6, 89.

would have drawn upon literature such as Peter J. Rachleff's study of Afro-American working-class political activism in Richmond, Eric Arnesen's study of Afro-American dockworkers in New Orleans, and James D. Anderson's study about educational philanthropy and Tuskegee.[28] Literature of that kind is more relevant to Woodward's questions than the kind in which the self-activity of the exploited and downtrodden is important just because it is self-activity, regardless of its efficacy.

Woodward was capable, of course, as are we all, of errors of judgment and fact. I have never been convinced, for example, by his analysis of class structure among Afro-Americans. "Soon after the war," he writes, "Negroes began to break up into differentiated social and economic classes that eventually reproduced on a rough scale the stratified white society" (218). And later: "One of the most important developments in Negro history ... was the rise of a whole separate system of society and economy on the other side of the color line ... Beginning as a largely undifferentiated class of former slaves, the race was soon sorted out into all the social and economic classes of the white capitalistic society upon which it was modeled" (365–6). Lacking a bourgeoisie, Afro-American society was, at best, a truncated facsimile of the white class structure. It cannot have been a true replica given that those at the bottom of Afro-American society did not answer to those at the top, while those at the top answered to white superiors.

I cannot resist closing with a reflection on an issue—language— that I wish Woodward had dealt with: not because it necessarily belongs in *Origins*, but because he could have dealt with it as no one else will ever do. Woodward did not write about language in *Origins*, though his quotations offer a rich sampling of the varied

---

28   Peter J. Rachleff, *Black Labor in the South: Richmond, Virginia, 1865–1890* (Philadelphia, PA: Temple University Press, 1984); Eric Arnesen, *Waterfront Workers of New Orleans: Race, Class, and Politics, 1863–1923* (New York: Oxford University Press, 1991); James D. Anderson, *The Education of Blacks in the South, 1860–1935* (Chapel Hill, NC: University of North Carolina Press, 1988).

flavors of Southern speech. I wish he had, because his comparativ-
ist instinct and his brisk way with foolishness would have made
short work of the reified entity known to true believers as black
English and attributed by them to the powerful surviving influence of an African meta-language. (I say "African meta-language"
because even the true believers concede that Africans enslaved in
North America spoke many different languages.) Ever the compar-
ativist, Woodward would have wondered why there is no parallel
concept of black Spanish, black Portuguese, or black French, even
though classical Yoruba (not just bits and pieces of grammar and
vocabulary) survived in religious rituals in Cuba and Brazil well
into the twentieth century, while Haiti and the Franco-Caribbean
developed African-descended creole languages that are still spoken
today. He would have noted the entire absence of a creole language
in the Hispanic Caribbean and its presence in some and absence in
other parts of the Anglo-Caribbean.[29]

It would not have taken Woodward long to notice that, despite
a large influx of migrants whose mother tongue is some form of
Jamaican Creole, there is no "black English" in Britain. Though
typically bilingual in English and Creole, second-generation
Caribbean Britons speak English in the accent of their class and
region, just as white Britons do. For the most part, their children
are not even bilingual. They may understand Creole if spoken
slowly and may even be able to say a few heavily accented words
in it, but most are monoglot speakers of a language indistinguishable from that of comparable white Britons. Having reached that
point, Woodward would have found himself on familiar ground:
the history of segregation in America. The speech patterns of
Afro-Americans do not reflect a stronger survival of African

---

29 For a valuable discussion of the origin and current (as of 1985) status
of creole languages in the Caribbean, see Mervyn C. Alleyne, "A Linguistic
Perspective on the Caribbean," in Sidney W. Mintz and Sally Price, eds.,
Caribbean Contours (Baltimore, MD: Johns Hopkins University Press, 1985),
55–79.

linguistic patterns among Afro-Americans, as compared to Anglo-Caribbeans. Instead, they testify to the greater prevalence, strength, and rigidity in the United States, as compared to the United Kingdom, of segregated schooling, residence, and sociability, especially among the working class.

That, of course, is where Woodward came in. All the elaborations and internal linguistic analysis that makes so-called black English seem a product of itself or a reflection of its speakers' identities or a fruitful arena for the exploration of subaltern cultural expression and creativity are secondary, at best, to the central point that it is one of the many outcomes of segregation. Which is to say that it is a result of the power of some people over others; an illustration, not of race (let alone racial identity) but of racism. It is black only in the sense that sharecropping or lynching is black. Precisely because it is an outcome of Jim Crow, a Jim Crow approach cannot account for it.

Woodward's refusal to jim-crow Jim Crow is the great gift that *Origins* has bestowed on the study of Afro-Southerners. Recognizing the centrality of the Negro Question, not just for the aspirations of Afro-Southerners but for those of all Southerners, Woodward placed the issue in the same zone where the big questions were to be engaged. But time does not invariably bring wisdom, and momentum is not necessarily progress. Whether we will put Woodward's gift to appropriate use and build on it—in our politics, our scholarship, our morals, our manners—remains to be seen.

6 *What One Cannot Remember Mistakenly*

Personal Genetic Histories deploy scientific techniques that purport to enable clients to "recover" lost aspects of their individual "history." Quite different techniques deploy the actual memory of individuals to reconstruct a collective history. This chapter shows what careful study can retrieve—albeit with inescapable gaps and ambiguities—*about those Southern places where black and white people lived in close quarters, observed strict rules of engagement, and beheld one another through complex mutual imagining. It follows various byways—a strangely tall public monument, a front-porch encounter between a working-class white man and a black woman schoolteacher, and a teenager's confiscated youth. It draws on stories told by the authors' grandmother, Mrs. Mamie Garvin Fields, who, as a child, witnessed the coming of Jim Crow.*[1]

I chose this title deliberately to provoke. Nothing is more fully agreed than the certainty that memory fails. Memory fails, leaving blanks, and memory collaborates with forces separate from actual past events, forces such as an individual's wishes, a group's suggestions, a moment's connotations, an environment's clues, an

1 Originally presented February 25, 1988 at the Conference on Memory and History, Institute for Oral History, Baylor University, Waco, Texas, and first published in *Oral History, The Journal of the Oral History Society* 17:1 (Spring 1989).

emotion's demands, a self's evolution, a mind's manufacture of order, and yes, even a researcher's objectives. In these collaborations, and in others I have not thought of, memory acquires well-noted imperfections. We seek to understand these imperfections systematically if we are scholars of memory, in itself, and we seek to correct for them if we are scholars who use memory as a source. As researchers, we bind ourselves to skepticism about memory and to a definite methodological mistrust of those rememberers who are our informants. We are fully attentive to the fact that memory fails.

But memory also succeeds. It succeeds enormously and profoundly, for it is fundamental to human life, not to say synonymous with it. A large capacity for memory is an integral component of the complex brain that sets homo sapiens apart. And, without it, the social life that is characteristic of our species would be inconceivable. Thus Nietzsche spoke of memory in terms of our human ability to make, deliver, and collect upon enduring agreements, an ability from which much if not all else is constructed.[2] So although nothing is more certain than that memory fails, equally, nothing is more certain than that memory succeeds. Systematic thought about how it succeeds, and at what, is thus as much in order as the reverse. Otherwise, we who turn to it as a resource fall into paradox.

My work with my grandmother, Mamie Garvin Fields, in her memoir *Lemon Swamp and Other Places*, offers me a starting point for reflection about what memory succeeds in doing and about the ways in which it does its work, for it is important to refine continually our methods of observing and thinking about memory as a matter of scholarly or scientific enterprise. I will also reflect a bit upon this sort of enterprise itself, however, for it is equally

---

2 Friedrich Nietzsche, "Second Essay. 'Guilt,' 'Bad Conscience,' and the Like," in *The Genealogy of Morals: A Polemic*, trans. Horace B. Samuel, ed. Oscar Levy, *The Complete Works of Friedrich Nietzsche*, vol. 13 (New York: Russell & Russell, 1964), 59ff.

important to refine continually our awareness of certain oddities and particularities that shape this enterprise and that therefore shape our inner attitude as we go about our work. As researchers we systematically doubt what we systematically count upon as ordinary human beings in the routine of daily life.

One of the particularities of the enterprise is the paradox we flirt with when we turn, with methodological mistrust, to memory as a source. This danger was present from the beginning of my work on *Lemon Swamp*. I turned to my grandmother as a source about the past, aspects of which I had few or no other ways of knowing. The book deals with public and private events (from submarine infiltration during World War II to her marriage just before World War I), attributes and assumptions current in her milieu (from race consciousness to notions of proper dress), aspirations (from racial "uplift" to middle-class consumption), judgments both collective and personal (Who is an Uncle Tom? To whom is a moral person accountable?), habits about the body (from details of housekeeping to color consciousness), natural and man-made objects in Charleston and elsewhere (from Calhoun's statue on the Citadel green to Lemon Swamp itself), and much more.

At the time of working on this rich material, I liberated myself from the constraints of scholarship or science by refusing to call it sociology, history, or even *oral* history. (The constraints tightened no less if I added to "history" the modifier "oral.") Grandmother's term for what we were about was "stories" (and I will say something about stories later on); in the end, we settled for the term *memoir*—*Lemon Swamp and Other Places: A Carolina Memoir*. I made this liberation clear in the introduction to the book by saying, "It is a subjective, personal account of life and work in South Carolina from 1888 to now."[3] Nonetheless, the two of us then, no less than the reading audience we imagined, thought of it as a source about the past. And since I was trained as a sociologist and

---

3   Mamie Garvin Fields and Karen Fields, *Lemon Swamp and Other Places: A Carolina Memoir* (New York: Free Press, 1982), xiii.

had done historical research, this liberation remained incomplete. It was not possible for me to run methodological red lights unself-consciously—although I most certainly ran them. The running of them occasioned reflection about what some of the green lights permit.

Consider, for example, the predicament that arises when we treat informants with the methodological mistrust that is required. A special existential condition arises between two human beings communicating face to face. Contrary to the "face value" approach of everyday human encounters, ours requires skepticism, suspicion, a certain condescension, and above all a constantly open second channel in which to place those bits of testimony that are destined to float out of the interaction, back toward some source of corroboration. This is alien to normal human communication. (The closest everyday-life kin to it involves police and special agents.) Equally alien to everyday life is the patronizing of an interlocutor with silent knowingness when other information establishes that he or she is wrong or even lying. Suppressing the social common-places regarding contradiction, correction, or dismissal belongs to that special existential condition I am talking about, the one our methodological green lights permit. Now, if the condition of gaining knowledge is first to create a surrogate of human interaction, thereafter deliberately to diminish it, this proceeding demands its own scrutiny—quite apart from the scrutiny the testimony itself gets. This scrutiny amounts to examining our tools in order to see clearly what they are accomplishing above and beyond our intended purpose. When a surgeon sterilizes the knife with which he cuts through flesh in order to repair the heart, he nevertheless still has to attend to the knife's secondary achievements.

I ran the red light that blocks arguing with an informant. Liberated from the constraints of scholarship, I said to Gram one day that I intended to corroborate her testimony about the high regard certain white folks downtown had had over many years for the residents of her street, Short Court. I made my announcement after the departure of an elderly employee of the gas company. (Gram had commented that he must have been coming to her home for sixty-some-odd years.) Gram was outraged: one, that I would consider going around behind her to check on stories; two, that I even had the idea of talking about her to somebody who operates gas meters. She was furious at this multilayered violation of our confidence in one another. At one level, I think she thought I thought she would lie. I argued back that scholarly historical work had to go by crosschecking of this kind. She didn't care about history, then. We fought that afternoon over what would and would not be part of my method. In more usual circumstances of doing research, penetration to this level of what is latent in the routine of interviewing most likely would not have come up.

In the end, I could not establish as "fact" that white folks downtown considered Short Court residents to be "aristocratic," in Gram's terms, although I certainly know from other contexts that white Charleston, for some intents and purposes, distinguished "respectable" black people from others. What our argument did establish is that Gram believed in, and perhaps was invested in, the special distinction, to white eyes, of the stratum to which she belonged. Was Gram remembering an aspiration or a fact? Later on that afternoon, her longtime friend Mrs. DaCosta dropped by to sit a spell on the porch, and Gram by skillful direction obtained corroboration from this dignified lady. (Not only that, we got quite a lot about the special distinction of her own family. I should come over one day and learn more.)

Fighting with my informant was a red light I ran on many afternoons. One of those fights was about what is or is not a relevant set of facts in an account of a public event—in Charleston—for presentation to a public much larger than Charleston's, namely, the future readers of *Lemon Swamp and Other Places*. In this case, Gram did the crosschecking of memory, and it was I who rejected the process. The issue was what can be called the "wedding list" or the "church program" sort of memory. This sort of memory has quite particular features: the utter necessity of getting it right; the methodological assumption of ordinary folks that any mistake is meaningful; a corresponding anxiety about forgetting on the part of the rememberer; the consequential nature of the result; and, last but not least, a god-awful exhaustiveness that can overwhelm all it touches. Everyone knows the gnawing fear that accompanies this kind of remembering. And I daresay as well, no one has not at one time or another upheld it—by drawing conclusions about omissions deemed incapable of being inadvertent, or, from the other side, by clenching jaws and making omissions with cold-blooded intent. The enforcement of flawless memory of this kind is in the nature of many kinds of sociability. It embodies what not only cannot, but must not be remembered mistakenly.

But when we shift to our historical mode in regard to memory, even memory aimed at answering historical questions that are clearly embedded in sociability, the wedding list/church program sort of memory is out of place, an encumbrance, and trivial. Such was the scene for a particularly passionate argument with Gram. Standards imposed by sociability battled with others. Decisions about the inclusion or exclusion of details were subject to different rules for the two of us. Gram was a leader in establishing integrated public day care in Charleston. I put the story in the book's epilogue. The typescript I gave to Gram said that Charlestonians got together to care for the children of working mothers.

> Grandmother Fields will tell you, reeling off the names of Charlestonian places from which people came to help—"Holy Communion Episcopal, Zion Olivet Presbyterian, Plymouth Congregational, to name those in the neighborhood, then St. Phillip's and St. Michael's, which are South of Broad, over toward the Battery, and, of course, Centenary, Old Bethel, and Wesley Methodist." Her list goes on. And you know what? She will go on, reeling off the name of pastors who came forward.[4]

---

4   Ibid., 243.

When Gram saw this, she got down to historical business. She checked with others in a position to know and added, added, added. My epilogue absolutely would not do. It needed to mention Mrs. So-and-So, of Such-and-Such Streets. It could not possibly be published without remembering Pastor This-and-That. Why, these are the people I have worked with for decades. They deserve the credit. These are the people who have been waiting to see my book, who put their names down to buy the first copies off the press. My rejoinder, that no one outside Charleston would care, did not count: the important audience was in Charleston. If the details got tedious to outsiders, well, we couldn't help that. Gram's purpose assigned those details to what cannot, nay, must not be remembered mistakenly. My purpose consigned them to just as obligatory forgetting.[5]

These details are of a category familiar to scholars who try to reconstruct Africa's history using oral tradition. Gram's church-program memory (or anyone's) is an instance of ideologically tainted memory summoned in view of present political purposes. Like that observed among African groups, it has the function of legitimizing and stabilizing a claim to some distinction. And part of its purpose is to perpetuate, by rendering it creditable to those concerned, a respectable consciousness of we-feeling. In that case memory "tainted" by interest is a dead-serious party to the creation of something true. The "mistakes" it may embody represent an imperfection only in light of the particular purposes scholarship has. Our scholarly effort to get the "real" past, not the true past required by a particular present, does not authorize us to disdain as simply mistaken this enormously consequential, creative, and everywhere visible operation of memory. It may be the case that human memory has it as a large-sized portion of its nature to be, in the psychologist Craig Barclay's splendid phrase, "true but not

---

5   I note in this connection that it is very good form in church-program memory to thank people for effort they have not (yet) expended.

veridical."[6] Considerations of this sort carry us back to Nietzsche's identifying memory as a building block of sociability.

Returning again to our own opinions, however, we can take such considerations as a way of reminding ourselves of the biases scholarship requires us to adopt in our vocation to correct for bias in our data and to select what is "significant" in terms of a given research program. In our dealings with informants, we constantly look beyond the encounter toward a scientific horizon where what matters is literal facticity, veracity, representativeness, general applicability, relationship to a set of questions generated by theory, and above all, relevance in terms of a scheme that designates what we need—and what we do not need—to know, what needs to be remembered and what is legitimately forgotten.

Although I did try to compromise, I did not make all my grandmother's amendments, which she crammed into the margins and which still spilled over onto extra pages—publishable remembering required their deliberate forgetting. On the other hand, I have kept them for our archive, well imagining some future historiographic predicament from which these names and places may provide a scholarly exit. Nonetheless, this action did not provide Gram an exit from her social predicament. It has troubled me ever since to reflect that preparing *Lemon Swamp* for publication required of me a certain condescension toward Gram and her compatriots.

This certain condescension was essentially no different from the systematic condescension toward the not-great with which we routinely tax documentary sources. I ask myself, now, how the church list episode with Gram was different from what happened to my grandmother's Great-Great Uncle Thomas, who she said accompanied his owner's sons as their valet when they were sent to Oxford to have the rough edges knocked off their "aristocratic" South Carolina slaveholders' upbringing. Having been taught by

6   Craig Barclay, "Truth and Accuracy in Memory," in M. M. Gruneberg, P. E. Morris, and R. N. Sykes, eds., *Practical Aspects of Memory: Current Research and Issues, Vol I. Memory in Everyday Life* (New York: Academic Press, 1978).

those boys during slavery, Thomas educated his own and others'
children, in a clandestine school—English, Latin, Greek, and
Hebrew, according to Gram. In consequence, Thomas's children
were among those well-educated freedmen whom the missionary
churches recruited to be leaders. Face-to-face with a remarkable
set of facts, and trained to mistrust such claims, I deputized a
friend, off to Oxford for studies, to find out what he could about
slaves resident in the colleges in the 1830s or thereabouts. The
answer: records of who lived there 150 years ago were scarce, and
names of servants resident with them were nonexistent—because
irrelevant. What would have been the conceivable purpose of
remembering one "Thomas" (now known to have been "James"[7]),
who laundered the shirts of Masters So-and-So and Such-and-Such
Middleton? Those details held no more interest then than somebody else's church program list does for us now—or that Gram's
list of Charleston luminaries in the day-care movement has. Only a
then unimaginable future historiography could make the names of
slave servants resident at Oxford worth remembering. So while the
contents of my grandmother's communication about her Great-
Great Uncle Thomas are rich and suggestive about a number
of issues, Gram's communication could not be transformed into
information.

I did, however, take one more stab at transforming Gram's story
about Thomas Middleton into information about Charleston's
past. The source for most of the stories about dead Middleton kin
had been Anna Eliza Izzard, whom everyone called Cousin Lala.
Lala had graduated from Avery Institute, a private high school for
freedmen established by the America Missionary Association, and
then from Claflin University, established by the Methodist Church.
(One of Thomas's sons, J. B. Middleton, was among those recruited
to Claflin's first board of trustees.) After earning her B.A., Lala

---

7   Research conducted twenty years since the publication of *Lemon Swamp*
has revealed that "Tom" actually was "James Middleton," who died in 1889 just
short of his hundredth birthday.

established a private school at her parents' home in Short Court. There she taught "black history," part of which was family history, including the saga of Thomas. Now, sometime in the 1920s a black doctoral student named T. Horace Fitchett had come to Charleston to collect oral testimony from local black people. Gram told me he collected a great deal from Lala. Thereafter he had taught for many years at Howard University. Reasoning that his notes and papers might yield corroboration, I contacted Howard's Moorland Collection, and through it, his widow. Mrs. Fitchett told me his papers would eventually be turned over but that tragic circumstances at present made my consulting them impossible. Thus ended for purposes of the book my attempt either to make of Gram's story a bit of information or to discredit it as that. The historical fact that neither could be done appears in the text as the naming of Gram's sources, mainly Lala and a less distinct figure called "Aunt Jane." Therewith I abandoned a would-be "fact" on the less respectable territory, so far as scholarship is concerned, of mere communication.

But then, not long ago, I happened to read an essay that made me think further about this respectable territory of verifiable fact: "The Storyteller," by Walter Benjamin.[8] In it he observes that the main form communication takes in the modern world is that of information, a form which, in his words, "lays claim to prompt verifiability." He goes on to characterize this development not as an advance but as an impoverishment. Storytelling dies, he says, as this new form of communication arises. Storytelling's successor, information, represents an impoverishment because, and to the degree that, the producer of information accomplishes precisely what we scholars strive to do: namely, to induce some body of material to deliver up explanation of its own accord, without our adding anything to it. "But the finest stories," according to Benjamin, "are characterized by the lack of explanation." Because the hearer or

---

8   Walter Benjamin, *Illuminations*, trans. Harry Zohn, ed. Hannah Arendt (New York: Harcourt, Brace & World, 1968), 83–109.

reader is left to interpret according to his own understanding, "the narrative achieves an amplitude that information lacks." If it involves our own participation, achieving this "amplitude that information lacks" is precisely what we as researchers strive not to do. Therefore while we seek narrative from our informants, we are specifically precluded from handling it in such a way that it remains what it was at birth.

According to Benjamin, it is the nature of every real story to contain "openly or covertly, something useful." And the utilities of stories include "counsel." "Counsel," he goes on, "is less an answer to a question, than a proposal concerning the continuation of a story that is just unfolding. To seek this counsel one would first have to be able to tell the story ... Counsel woven into the fabric of real life is wisdom. The art of storytelling is reaching its end because the epic side of truth, wisdom, is dying out." Anyone who said in a conference on oral historical method that the researcher sought "wisdom" or "counsel" from his informants would, I believe, be met with stunned silence. We are usually free not to attend to these possible features of what we hear. But when we exercise this freedom to disregard an inborn feature of what we encounter, what does this do to memory contained in it? What have we done, and what have we foregone, by carrying out surgery so as to put "fact" in a specimen bottle while throwing the unexamined rest of the body into the disposal unit?

My own freedom from the constraints of scholarship went along with unfreedom in this regard. Since the project of doing *Lemon Swamp* did not change the relationship of grandmother and granddaughter, the elements of "wisdom" and "counsel" were not ignorable and hidden but explicit and obligatory. She was, after all, addressing the child of her child. Gram was didactic. My attempt to transform another of her communications into information, into something that laid claim to prompt verifiability, engendered another fight. In this case, the offending deed was to take a photograph of the Calhoun statue for inclusion in the book, offering readers thereby a kind of "proof" for an observation of Gram's, thus replicating the trip I made to see the object she referred to. Key points of the story were not verifiable, as I will now show. Let me start by quoting her on the subject of the statue of Senator John C. Calhoun, the indefatigable defender of slavery and states' rights:

> We all hated all that Calhoun stood for. Our white city fathers wanted to keep what he stood for alive. So they named after him a street parallel to Broad—which, however, everybody kept on calling Boundary Street for a long time. And when I was a girl, they went further: they put up a life-size figure of John C. Calhoun preaching and stood it up on the Citadel Green, where it looked at you like another person in the park. Blacks took that statue personally. As you passed by, here was Calhoun looking you in the face and telling you, "Nigger, you may not be a slave, but I am back to see you stay in your place." The "niggers" didn't like it. Even the "nigger" children didn't like it. We used to carry something with us, if we knew we would be passing that way, in order to deface that statue—scratch up the coat, break the watch chain, try to knock off the nose—because he looked like he was telling you there was a place for "niggers" and "niggers" must stay there. Children and adults beat up John C. Calhoun so badly that the whites had to come back and put him up high, so we couldn't get to him. That's where he stands today, on a tall pedestal. He is so far away now until you can hardly tell what he looks like.[9]

The point of that story, made repeatedly in many different ways, was that even during the ascendency of Jim Crow, even when it appeared from the outside that black people had capitulated to their defeat, they resisted; even the children resisted. The counsel was, you resist, too. Be a worthy descendent of Thomas and J. B. and Lala and the others. You do it, too. "You do it, too" is not

9   Fields and Fields, *Lemon Swamp*, 57.

something we researchers are prepared to take seriously from informants. Indeed, this aspect of the narratives we hear for our scholarly purpose raises a danger flag, marking bias, ideological special pleading, and the like. The flag marks a familiar site of mis-remembering, where the "should-have-been" displaces the "was," where wishes fill the blanks where facts are to be placed by dint of our own industry.

I proceeded with industry. I made myself conspicuous in the reading room of the Charleston Historical Society, depository of many documents pertaining to the past of a very historically conscious city. Conspicuous: because I, like other black people of Southern heritage, still do not enter such formerly segregated places unselfconsciously or unnoticed. I spent two days search-ing for "information": I expected or hoped to learn that "rowdy" members of the "colored race" had vandalized this public work of art. Instead I learned something that prevented the facts from speaking for themselves, which pushed to a dead end my search for mere information. What I discovered was much more interesting. It opened out instead of pinning down Gram's story.

It turns out that in 1854, the year Calhoun died, the Ladies' Calhoun Memorial Association began planning the memorial. In 1879, they were finally able to commission A. E. Harnisch of Philadelphia to execute a bronze statue of Calhoun on a Carolina granite pedestal, surrounded by allegorical figures—Truth, Justice, the Constitution, and History—at a cost of forty thousand dollars. But Harnisch in the end built the memorial with only one of the female figures—and she in such a state of disrobement that some of the ladies are said to have fainted at the unveiling. When the white folks recovered themselves sufficiently for straight thinking, they found historical fault with the clothing besides the aesthetic fault with the nakedness: Harnisch had put Calhoun into a Prince Albert coat, an anachronism. Black Charlestonians figured in the citywide uproar in a curious way. The public work of art began to be called, in Gullah syntax, "Calhoun and he wife." A newspaper article says, "Because of the female figure's state of disattire, the nickname greatly distressed the ladies of Charleston and Mrs. Calhoun who was still alive."

Besides, the statue's construction was poor, the pose bad, and "his right index finger pointed in a different direction from the others, a habit peculiar to him in speeches, but in this instance exaggerated to the point of deformity." The various discomfitures continued until 1895, when the *Charleston Post* was able to report that, "the old statue which has so long been a thorn in the flesh of the ladies of the Calhoun Monument Association … to say nothing of the general public, will be taken down and consigned to oblivion." Massey Rhind of New York won the commission to execute Mr. Calhoun No. 2, erected in June 1896. No. 1 found his resting place in the Confederate Home Yard. A finger (it is not said which) was placed in the Charleston Museum. There ends the story obtainable at the Charleston Historical Society.

There is no mention of the oddly tall pillar that stands on top of the grand, wide conventional pedestal with its luxuriating scrolls at the corners and its dignified plaques of speeches on each side. No explanation is offered for the remarkable disproportion of line that the pillar creates nor for the fact that if you want to study Calhoun's features with your eye, or with that of a camera, you are interfered with by the sun and sky. Nothing I could find notices certain Charlestonians' notice of the statue beyond the raucous Negro laughter implied by the nickname "Calhoun and he wife."

Gram and I fought about the picture I took of the statue. Innocently, I had intended it to illustrate her story. Gram said she would never have a picture of *that man* in her book. She was still passionate about a personage dead by then for nearly a century and a half. She intended, with malice aforethought, to exclude him from the list of guests—just as surely as the ladies' society intended to include him on their own.

I have already devoted more time to topics regarding the color line than my grandmother would have approved of. I need to pause to say something about this fact. Gram would be the first to say that *Lemon Swamp* is about her own life, not about the racist system that partly enclosed it. Matters of race and color are a permanent presence without being her principal subject. They are constituent to life, but they do not define life. So, for example, Gram fondly remembers the details of her very fancy wedding—a black affair, from beginning to end—but yet notices that curious white people from the neighborhood slipped into Wesley Church's gallery, silently, to behold the occasion's splendor. On the other hand, when she decided to go to Boston to get her trousseau and took the Clyde Line Ship, she did not at first remember whether it was segregated. The point was the adventure. She did not pay attention to where white people were on the ship. And in her story of the time she collided with a car driven by a white man, the initial subject had been proper dress, the motto mothers and aunts of all colors tell their nieces and daughters, "Dress, you never know." It turned out that she had thrown a coat atop her nightgown on the day of that accident. Her Aunt Harriet, severe exponent of "Dress, you never know," was proved right (such women usually are!) as Grandmother made her way through downtown offices after the accident. But the fact that all the officials were white and all the aftermath unfolded downtown, among "downtown white folks," colors for her in a distinctive way a comeuppance anyone could have had. I would call these features "involuntary memory," if the term had not already been filched from Proust and assigned a technical meaning. I use the term "unintended memory" instead, and I sometimes think it is also unintendable.

Even so, such features are often not the main subject of the story, from Gram's point of view. This fact needs emphasis because, as I continue exploring matters of race and color here, I acknowledge that these did not command Gram's front-burner attention as they do mine. For her, they are there in the way Mount Kilimanjaro is there in Africa. For many intents and purposes, it is *merely* there, rising to its snow-capped peaks over the luxuriant tropicality of the town of Moshi. The mountain is hardly to be missed, yet hardly to be noticed, at once native and alien to the life around it. Tourists are the ones who preoccupy themselves with looking at it. I am saying this to give warning that, as Gram's interlocutor, I was a tourist to her life with a tourist's habit of gawking. Gram criticized me more than once for my preoccupation. She called me "angry." Once she even called me "ugly" on the subject and asked, "What must those people be doing to you up there?" ("Up there" was Massachusetts at the time.) So I invite you to exercise methodological mistrust in my case, to be suspicious of the selections I have made in my own exercise of remembering. It is a fact that I cannot help gazing at Kilimanjaro.

The Kilimanjaro I gaze at, when uncovered by clouds and mist, often comes into view in the form of unintended memory. That inner horizon of the South's racial order is not the aspect we generally tend to think of first. It is easier to think of the South's Jim Crow regime in its outward and visible signs—its laws, its segregated spaces, its economic arrangements, its intermittent physical atrocities, and its civic iconography, items such as Calhoun's statue. But one learns through the testimony of inhabitants that it can at the same time be mapped out as an inward and invisible topography. It has objects analogous to mountains, rivers, and the like, which must be climbed, crossed, circumambulated, avoided, or otherwise taken into account. At the same time that these are not visible to the naked eye, and not immediately obvious to aliens on the scene, they are to insiders, much of the time, not specifically noteworthy. They remain, in the phrase of Harold Garfinkel, "seen but unnoticed" features of social life.[10] As such, they enter memory. They often emerge in oral testimony as unintended memory. In actual life they are manifest, above all, as social order.

Whenever we start from a remove in time or space, these topographical features begin to seem less substantial than they are. We

---

10   Harold Garfinkel, *Studies in Ethnomethodology* (Englewood Cliffs, NJ: Prentice Hall, 1967).

tend to think of them as movable by a mere movement of thought. Consider, for example, the seventeenth-century English revolutionaries whom Christopher Hill describes in *The World Turned Upside Down*. These people embark on militant political projects by shaking and quaking, talking in tongues, and listening to the voice of prophecy. To us, they seem to be making a bizarre detour around a God present on the ground of ordinary experience that we nevertheless cannot see. To us, it seems there are more practical, straight-ahead routes. It is as though we watch from above as human beings walk, as we might walk, across a flat heath. But, unlike us, they then turn to walk around what seems to us a nonexistent obstacle. Of course the obstacle is really there, unavoidably and materially there; but the knowledge of what it is, where it is, and *that* it is, they carry in memory.

The memory I am talking about is not the individual's own. It is instead the fruit of collaboration among the inhabitants of a common social locale. Having said this much, I think I can avoid the troubling yet expressive term "collective memory,"[11] although I mean something like it. Or, rather, I mean to say that fundamental features of human memory are not grasped at the level of the isolated individual. Upbringing—or, to use my discipline's term, socialization—provides the context in which the human brain's, and mind's, imperfect capacity for memory develops. It is also a process by which human beings acquire things that cannot be remembered mistakenly. I want to present one example of this process that emerged as unintended memory.

Last spring while I visited my grandmother, a middle-aged woman dropped by. This woman and her brother had been Gram's pupils on James Island. They started to reminisce about those school days over forty years ago. After a time, Gram spoke about

---

11 This notion is explored in a fascinating way, with all its riches and some of its vexations, in Bogumil Jewsiewicki, "Collective Memory and the Stakes of Power: Reading Popular Zairian Discourses," *History in Africa* 13 (1986), 195–223.

the brother. What a fine, bright pupil he had been over the years. And very cute as a little fellow—his mother had liked to dress him in outfits with Peter Pan collars. And, oh, he was smart; he had a grand future because of his mind. The conversation seemed to be humming along in trivial sociability (generous recollections about someone's family being very good form), but then I heard my grandmother saying, "What they did to him was such a tragedy. How they could take that fine young man and put him in jail for all those years! How it broke the mother down!" They both shook their heads in commiseration. My antennae went up. When I finally got my question in between the headshaking, the sister turned to me. Well, he didn't do it. The other boy did it, but he never would admit, *never would admit*, so all those years my brother was in jail for what he did. He walked all around among us big as day, year in, year out, may he rot … and so forth in that vein, the anger at the other boy coming alive again, boiling, and engulfing the English syntax. Well, what happened? What happened: He never did ask for no drink of water, they said he sassed that white girl, talking about how he want some water, my brother ain't do that, know better than that. Ain't stop to ask that girl nothin'. That other boy did, and *my* brother went to jail, never would own up that *he* ask for that drink of water. My brother went to jail in place of him. In a rush of renewed emotion, the woman had arrived at an invisible mountain and begun to walk around it.

I piped up that neither one of them should have gone to jail for twenty years over asking for a drink of water, not your brother and not the other boy either. If I hadn't seen the mountain yet, the awful way she looked up at me, and then ignored me, let me see it. I let further comment die in my mouth. I then saw what she saw, a black teenager who allowed his friend to be convicted in his place. She did not see what I suddenly saw, a Southern tableau: the impressionable white girl and her oppressive male kin (or perhaps the oppressive girl and her impressionable kin) enforcing an unjust etiquette of domination. A black young man did not ask a white young woman to address any sort of personal or bodily need. Her outrage at the one injustice but not the other revealed the Jim Crow order with an immediacy that intentional testimony never could. For this kind of unintended memory, I submit that crosschecking is redundant.

For those of us who try to glean from personal testimony the movement of history, as well as history's congealment in an order, what is interesting in the end is the ferment. We want to glean from people's recollection what territory remained unsubdued, perhaps unsubduable, by the Jim Crow regime's obligatory remembering. We want to find out when and how they came to note, and wonder at, the positively audacious presence of Kilimanjaro. Not accidentally, it is in the domain of education that we find continuous evidence of such ferment and continuous guerrilla war, for education is about what we agree that the young should carry in their minds: what schoolbook lessons and what non-schoolbook lessons they should receive, about where they stand in the world and what that world is made of. In the 1950s, when the issue was desegregation, the guerrilla battles to fill the mind differently made the transition to conventional warfare.

But in the 1920s and 1930s, Gram's heyday, this fight proceeded in the South on a personal or local scale, underground, and hit and run. But I would maintain that the larger fight that later entered national awareness is inconceivable without it. One recent Tuesday night, PBS's "MacNeil-Lehrer Newshour" ended with one of its learned essays about national life. Roger Rosenblatt invited us to contemplate how Dwight D. Eisenhower, the "sleepy conservative" president, surprised those who had elected him, by "launching the civil rights era." His memory could not have been more mistaken. The launching was done by the people whose business it was.

This launching was done not only by those who put their hand on the plow, and their eyes on the prize, in the 1940s and 1950s, but also by others who began long before that. Gram loved to tell the story of old Mrs. Burden, who lived on the same James Island where black people in a thousand ways were inculcated with the unjust etiquette I described. No doubt in many of those ways Mrs. Burden was inculcated, too. But as a military widow, she was collecting a pension, which meant that she had to collect her check from the downtown white powers-that-be. When Gram began to teach her pupils' parents and grandparents, Mrs. Burden made it her business, old as she was, to learn to sign her name. People asked her why she bothered and asked Gram why she bothered with a pupil so old. But Mrs. Burden kept on coming and brought the teacher, Gram said, "more eggs than the law allows." She was determined to be able to walk into that office of downtown white folks one day and sign for her pension properly. Mrs. Burden was after a schoolbook lesson; and she was after a non-schoolbook lesson. She was determined to stop having to put herself down as "X." Gram said, "The day Mrs. Burden could go into that office and write 'Mrs. Samuel Burden,' she almost didn't need her walking stick." In fights as small-scale and personal as this one—the fight to be known by one's own name—the guerrilla war went on in the worst of times, blasting away bit by bit the invisible mountains of the Jim Crow South.

Let me close by saying that, during my time of liberation from scholarly constraint, Gram assigned me a part in a continuing guerrilla war in which memory is not only a source of information about the past but also a force in creating the future. But, in a development that gave me many hours of methodological bad conscience, coming to grasp history in this immediately human sense involved departing from rules that define its incomparably paler counterpart, a mode of scientifically disciplined study. In the process, I had to think again about what this scientific discipline is for, what a present-day scholar's pursuit of knowledge is and is not, and after thinking again, to see how called-for modesty is about what it can add to civilization. What does inquiry disciplined by the ideals of science accomplish—if it is neither here nor there in terms of the growth of the individual, if it must by its nature remain silent, as my mentor Max Weber says, on the question What shall we do, and how shall we live?, if it paradoxically says that one way we shall live, as researchers, is according to an ethics of research that pertains to research and naught else, if it cuts through the flesh of human communication to expose for viewing an internal organ but marvels not at the act of surgery, if it is passionately committed to a search for truth that is not, cannot, and must not be a quest for wisdom?

None of this is meant to disparage the scientific model of knowledge; but it is meant to take note of the possibility that the very prestige of this model in an Age of Information may obscure what is particular and odd about it and thus obscure what vital tasks this mode of pursuing knowledge leaves undone, unconceived, perhaps even unconceivable. With this conundrum about method, I leave off speaking for myself, and let the Polish poet Czeslaw Milosz say what I think I have come to understand.

"To see" means not only to have before one's eyes. It may mean to preserve in memory. "To see and to describe" may also mean to reconstruct in imagination. A distance achieved thanks to the mystery of time must not change events, landscapes, human figures into a tangle of shadows growing paler and paler. On the contrary, it can show them in full light, so that every event, every date becomes expressive and persists as an eternal reminder of human depravity and human greatness. Those who are alive receive a mandate from those who are silent forever. They can fulfill their duties only by trying to reconstruct precisely things as they were, and by wrestling the past from fictions and legends.[12]

It is by trying to reconstruct things as they were by *all* means— those that partake in scientific method, and those that display the

---

12   Czeslaw Milosz, *Nobel Lecture*, December 8, 1980 (Oslo, Norway: The Nobel Foundation, 1981).

method's limits—that we fulfill our historic duties and, at the same time, fulfill our quintessentially human desire to know with nourishment worthy of it.

7 Witchcraft and Racecraft: Invisible Ontology in Its Sensible Manifestations

The right-minded teaching that "race has nothing to do with biology, but is merely a social construction," is true but misleading. For one thing, there is nothing "mere" about a social construct. From the days of Thomas Jefferson, what Americans believe in as biological race has always been, at the same time, embodied and disembodied, visible and invisible. For another, discovering the independence from biology of what Americans call race opens the way to investigating social construction itself, as thought and as action. By identifying the properties of witch beliefs, the great anthropologist E. E. Evans-Pritchard set theoretical questions about rationality that busied British philosophers for a generation. Inspired by his work, and the extended debate it catalyzed, this chapter explores rationale and rationality in American race beliefs.[1]

By [1959] I could see that the visible and invisible differences between living races could be explained only in terms of history.

Carlton S. Coon, *The Origin of Races*

---

1 Originally published as "Witchcraft and Racecraft: Invisible Ontology in Its Sensible Manifestations," in George C. Bond and Diane M. Ciekawy, eds., *Witchcraft Dialogs: Anthropological and Philosophical Exchanges* (Athens, OH: Ohio University Press, 2001), 283–315. With thanks to the director, staff, and fellow researchers of the Maison des Sciences de l'Homme d'Aquitaine, Université de Bordeaux III, and in memory of Mlle. Anne-Marie Pasquet.

I propose to consider together topics that are usually considered separately. My research has pressed me to explore both witchcraft (with the invisible ontology it presupposes) and what I will call racecraft (with the invisible ontology that it, too, presupposes), but I have attended to them one after the other, in the African and the Afro-American sides of my work. Moreover, while attending to them separately, I have weighed them differently. Following the well-established practice of most Africanists in this country, I have been granting the rationality of witchcraft, but not that of race-craft. That practice now seems to me troublesome, logically and ethically. If we judge by the dependence of both on presuppositions that are demonstrably false according to modern science, then both sets of traditional beliefs should go down together as irrational. But if we discount their falsity by that standard, then they should rise together as rational. Under our usual practice, they do neither. It is as though they were as different as cabbages and kings—a mistake, it seems to me. Still, I will not argue that they are both cabbages or both kings, but that study of their traits in common can increase the power of the intellectual tools with which we try to understand both.

By now, E. E. Evans-Pritchard's path-breaking study, *Witchcraft, Oracles and Magic Among the Azande*,[2] has shown over two generations of researchers how Africa's traditional beliefs about an invisible ontology of spirits can be rationally held, even if false— and even if held onto in the presence of countervailing evidence. On the one hand, by accepting his analysis, we have come to regard the falsity of those beliefs as their most apparent yet least important trait. On the other hand, our equally well-established practice in regard to race beliefs accents the falsity of those beliefs in a quite un-Pritchardian way. Thus, although traditional race beliefs (like traditional spirit beliefs) have resisted the better part of a century's worth of disconfirming scientific demonstrations, we do not give

---

2   E. E. Evans-Pritchard, *Witchcraft, Oracles and Magic Among the Azande* (Oxford: Clarendon Press, 1937).

them their own Pritchardian hoist into the realm of rationality. We approach witchcraft and racecraft as if they belonged to two different orders of phenomena: as if one were compelling belief and the other, a bad choice in matters of belief; one, truth of a different order and the other, false beliefs destructible through the propagation of truth; one, an element of human diversity and the other, an ugly reaction to that diversity.

This disjunction in our practice is of long standing, and I have begun to suspect a short-circuit deep in the intellectual apparatus that Evans-Pritchard bequeathed to us. I propose, therefore, to query this different treatment and to locate the short-circuit. My suggestion is that witchcraft and racecraft are so like one another that, by not comparing them, we conceptualize neither as sharply as we might and, besides, stumble continually into paradox. Here, then, are some not yet fully linked or elaborated thoughts that arise from my current ethnographic work in progress about racecraft in an American community. The new work is informed by my past analyses of witchcraft in several African communities.³ As a first step, let me make three disclosures that will situate, and perhaps clarify, what I have to say.

The Half-Light of Evans-Pritchard's Legacy

RATIONALITY OF WITCHCRAFT, IRRATIONALITY OF RACECRAFT

First, my reading of *In My Father's House* by the Ghanaian philosopher K. Anthony Appiah throws the logical and ethical conundrums just indicated into sharp relief.⁴ In the chapter titled

---

3   Karen E. Fields, "Charismatic Religion as Popular Protest: The Ordinary and the Extraordinary in Social Movements," *Theory and Society* 2:3 (June 1982); "Political Contingencies of Witchcraft in Colonial Central Africa: Culture and the State in Marxist Theory," *Canadian Journal of African Studies* 16:3 (December 1982); and *Revival and Rebellion in Colonial Central Africa* (Princeton: Princeton University Press, 1986).

4   K. Anthony Appiah, *In My Father's House: Africa in the Philosophy of Culture* (New York: Oxford University Press, 1992).

"Old Gods, New Worlds," Appiah defends the rationality of spirit beliefs by applying and imaginatively extending the interpretive strategies that Evans-Pritchard pioneered. But in a separate chapter on race beliefs, he applies different strategies that, relying on modern science, cannot serve such a defense. The inevitable results are disclosed by the chapter's title: "*Illusions* of Race" (emphasis mine). There, Appiah logically, but paradoxically, concludes that, owing to his failure to transcend those illusions, the great antiracist W. E. B. Du Bois was both a lifelong opponent of racism and a lifelong racist. The subject throughout is Du Bois' tragic enmirement in false, irrational belief, and consequent moral error. Meanwhile, at the other end of the book, Appiah's discussion of the invisible ontology of spirits climbs (after Robin Horton[5]) from ethnography into philosophy of science and suspension of moral judgment. Observation from that vantage point reveals African theoretical thought to be, not unlike its European scientific cousin, "underdetermined by observation."[6] A thought-provoking mouthful, that, so let us stop and think: What sort of intellectual strategy is it that permits us both to dismiss race beliefs as illusions and at the same time to insulate spirit beliefs from the same dismissal? Without our professional habit of thinking about them separately (even, as in this case, between the covers of a single book), Africanists would assign both the fate of the outlaws in the German proverb "Caught together, hung together."

RATIONALITY OF RACECRAFT, IRRATIONALITY OF WITCHCRAFT

Evans-Pritchard's classic implicitly assigned them separate fates. After all, his work disputed a postulate of racecraft, namely, the inferior intellect of African "primitives," as allegedly proved by their holding onto traditional spirit beliefs in the teeth of countervailing

---

5   Robin Horton, "African Traditional Thought and Western Science," in Bryan R. Wilson, ed., *Rationality* (New York: Harper and Row, 1970).

6   Appiah, *In My Father's House*, 119.

evidence. Evans-Pritchard was writing at a time when the old arguments from craniology had imploded but, hydra-like, were rapidly being replaced. In other words, a racecraft demonstrably able to resist evidence against it stood at his very elbow as he devised still more evidence against it—*but* evidence of precisely the kind that, by his own demonstration, would not have prevailed against Zande beliefs and mental habits. Therefore, deployed against the postulate of Africans' intellectual difference, his demonstration implied a commitment to one or both forms of the following assumption: Either his European readers were in fact intellectually unlike his African subjects, or Africa's witchcraft and Europe's racecraft were different orders of phenomena, which (both being artifacts of the mind) boils down to the same thing. Either form imperils the position from which he began, that humankind is intellectually one.[7]

Witchcraft, Oracles and Magic is a powerful book of interpretation, but it is not a work of recognition. In it a gifted observer hands his readers keys to something remote and strange, but stops at an equivocal, paradoxical, and ultimately illogical halfway house on the way to human oneness. As a work of interpretation only, the book could not go further. But it was also a practical work and, in some sense, did not need to. In his preface, Evans-Pritchard addressed the book to colonial administrators, missionaries, and medical professionals—Europeans at work among the Azande, yet as far from the Azande as Europe's secular, scientific rationality placed them. So Evans-Pritchard's comparing that secular, scientific mode to the Zande mode was an amazing tour de force, but at the end of the day it nonetheless provided equivocal, paradoxical, and illogical evidence about the intellectual oneness of humankind. My dissatisfaction with it brings me to my second observation.

---

7   However, note his extremely complicated and subtle defense of Lucien Lévy-Bruhl, who is taken by many to have been arguing the opposite. See E. E. Evans-Pritchard, *A History of Anthropological Thought*, André Singer, ed., with an Introduction by Ernest Gellner (New York: Basic Books, 1981), 119–31.

Meanwhile, beliefs and habits that are Zande-like, so to speak, thrived close to Evans-Pritchard's home—and they still do, close to our own. He had Europe's secular, scientific rationality in mind, not the differently constituted, common-sense rationality of everyday life; but modern science did not, and could not, extinguish its longer-established and more prolific relative, which both energizes and bedevils science itself.

SHARED IRRATIONAL FEATURES OF WITCHCRAFT AND RACECRAFT

In my work on racecraft, I have been struck over and over again by such intellectual commonalities with witchcraft as circular reasoning, prevalence of confirming rituals, barriers to disconfirming factual evidence, self-fulfilling prophecies, multiple and inconsistent causal ideas, and colorfully inventive folk genetics. And to these must be added varieties of more or less legitimized collective action such as gossip, exclusion, scapegoating, and so on, up to and including various forms of coercion (which is to say that the logical and methodological byways of racecraft, like those of witchcraft, are rife with dangers to body as well as to mind). Taken together, such traits constitute a social world whose inhabitants experience (and act on) a marrow-deep certainty that racial differences are real and consequential, whether scientifically demonstrable or not. Obviousness is the hallmark of such a world. The evidence is everywhere, populating the banalities and the showstoppers of life. So the results of telling any inhabitant of such a world that races do not exist are like those I used to read from colonial district commissioners' reports of informing villagers that witches do not exist.[8] Those results amount to a What's-up-with-you? incredulity.

---

8 See, for example, various discussions of the Witchcraft Ordinance enacted in British African colonies, as summarized and analyzed in Karen E. Fields, *Revival and Rebellion in Colonial Central Africa*, Classics in African Studies (Portsmouth, NH: Heinemann, 1997), Chapter 2.

What is more, there seems to be little difference between the mental makeshifts of the proverbial person-in-the-street and the accentuated rationality of academic life. I regularly get What's-up-with-you? reactions in college classes; and I once got them at a panel on race by University of Rochester biologists, whose professional engagement with modern population genetics did not, in their view, undermine the folk classification. The question that issued from my almost-solitary black face—Why not?—earned me the kind of withering certitude that is but a step removed from anger. I take it as characteristic that the rational software of racecraft, like that of witchcraft, accommodates disconfirming evidence in additive, rather than transformative, fashion.

SHARED RATIONAL FEATURES OF WITCHCRAFT AND RACECRAFT

I did not say the irrational software of either, and that brings me to my third disclosure. Since the irrationality of racecraft is part and parcel of our ethical stand against it, my setting that irrationality aside, even for the sake of argument, may seem perverse. But in my work of retranslating Emile Durkheim's masterpiece *The Elementary Forms of Religious Life*, I came to a realization that sobered me. If he is right, the roots of racecraft are not unreason but its dignified human opposite, reason. One of Durkheim's core arguments is that reason is born in social life, but that society can exist only by being collectively imagined—that is, by constituting a real world that acquires its reality by transcending fact as available to the senses operating on their own. That aspect of reason cannot possibly be secular—open to choice—or provisional—temporary and open to disconfirming evidence.

In one among many harrowing examples, Durkheim tells us the response of an Australian member of the Kangaroo clan to being shown a photograph of himself. The Kangaroo points to the photo and affirms to the ethnographers that he and the kangaroo are the same.[9] He could not have been telling the truth unless the invisible ontology of totemic essences (not to mention the folk genetics) made it so. But—and here is the thing—neither could he have been truthfully stating his matrilineal descent, which he shared with others of the Kangaroo clan. The study of totemic clans interested Durkheim because, as he says on the first page, it would yield "a fundamental and permanent aspect of humanity." Unlike *Witchcraft, Oracles and Magic*, the argument of *Forms* was not a "they" argument, with interpretational keys to open doors abroad but not those at home.

DURKHEIM'S LEGACY

Our grasp of the sobering intensity of this argument tightens when we recall that Durkheim was working toward *Forms* in the midst of European imaginings about national identity. It was a time when imagining French-ness kept throwing off volatile rituals of intra-European racecraft—incandescent ones in the street demonstrations of the *antidreyfusards*. And so it was also a time for imagining rebarbative ritual antidotes. For example, Rabbi Armand Bloch sought to imagine a French nationality with Jews, rather than without, by showing his congregation how a statue of Jeanne d'Arc could be suffered in their sanctuary (was she not in a sense like Queen Esther?).[10] It is as a witness to this hot-button blood politics, though also as an accused, that Durkheim studied the phenomena through the ethnographer's strategy of remote imagining.

He found that this collective imagining (at home or elsewhere)—this adding to whatever could possibly be real in the physical sense—is at the fount of reason, not its opposite. Such

---

9   Emile Durkheim, *The Elementary Forms of Religious Life*, translated and with an Introduction by Karen E. Fields (New York: Free Press, 1995), 134.

10   See Ivan Strenski, *Durkheim and the Jews of France* (Chicago: University of Chicago Press, 1997), 46.

figments are reason's raw material. To borrow now from Appiah, they contain theories "that contribute to forming our experience and give meaning to the language we use for reporting it."[11] If figments have that function, they come to us, and must come to us, as certainties ubiquitously evidenced. Doubt is not obviously sensible.[12] But neither, on Durkheim's showing, is reason itself.

Invisibility and Reason

To claim there is heuristic value in examining witchcraft and racecraft together is not to claim that they are alike in all respects or, despite their geographical separation, are one and the same thing. Nor, on the other hand, is it to claim that the trait I think they share—presupposing an invisible ontology—is the sole basis for comparison. In point of fact, by selecting the term *witchcraft* I have foreshortened Evans-Pritchard's three-part title and the three distinct arguments that correspond to it: (1) witchcraft accusations displace structurally inbuilt social tensions onto available victims; (2) oracles work within an idiom of thought that seems bizarre but nonetheless has markedly logical and systematic features; and (3) professional specialists in magic know how to obtain (within their own logic) both true and tricked results. Potentially at least, all are distillable into illuminating comparisons and might promote broader generalizations: of what we know about scapegoating; of what we have been discovering about the social world of scientific work; and of the (witting and, more interesting, the unwitting) tricknology that has kept race science spicy and popular in America. Likewise, different (and not necessarily parallel) arguments could be developed from the definition of racecraft that I

---

11   Appiah, *In My Father's House*, 119.
12   Here is another important point to take from Durkheim. Doubt is always possible. And so it is rituals repeated periodically, and symbolic reminders in their interims, that serve to keep the evidence ubiquitous. As he says over and over, rituals express and create observations, create and express realities.

will presently offer. It is easy to think up more or less apt analo-gies between particular physical traits and their supposed effects. Nonetheless, those are traits that come to the analysis ready-made, as it were, and with their clothes on. The interesting moments are those Durkheim recounts when, in the midst of human doing, soul becomes visible—for example, as blood. Then, as he says, the soul itself can be seen "from outside."[13]

Invisibility is part and parcel of whatever other traits we may notice: Neither witchcraft nor racecraft can exist without it. Therefore, how people cope with that fact links the difficulties of unmasking a witch with those that motivate the continuing search for a way to match up physical and nonphysical race. The inhabit-ants of the West once experienced in their own sensible world an invisible ontology rather like the one Appiah describes. According to Durkheim, that realm was downgraded to the designation "supernatural" only after modern science had created "awareness that there is a natural order of things."[14] In making the arguments he does about reason's additions to the real, thereby making possi-ble a human real world, Durkheim, the empirical scientist, devoted a long chapter of *Forms* (Book II, Chapter 8) to the concept of soul—of all things. He sets out to reconstruct soul on the terrain of real things done. Once shorn of confounding reference to the supernatural, invisibility turns out to have properties that can be explored empirically.

I can go ahead if the following conceptions of witchcraft and racecraft pass muster, at least provisionally. First witchcraft: Setting aside the various issues posed by different terms in differ-ent languages, the English word *witchcraft* can be defined this way: one among a complex system of beliefs, with combined moral and cognitive content, that presuppose invisible, spiritual (i.e., nonma-terial) entities underlying, and continually acting upon, the visible, material realm of beings and events. Now *racecraft*: one among a

---

13   Durkheim, *Elementary Forms*, 246.
14   Ibid., 24.

complex system of beliefs, also with combined moral and cognitive content, that presuppose invisible, spiritual qualities underlying, and continually acting upon, the material realm of beings and events. I assign the English suffix -*craft* to both in the same right, for we need the component of socially ratified *making* or *doing* and its companion, the socially ratified *belief* that travels before and after it, as input and as output. Marking the terms linguistically with -*craft* announces that the workings of those phenomena are not open to objective or experimental demonstration, that is to say, by anyone, anywhere, and independent of doing or believing. We all can be more certain that witchcraft exists than that witches do. The same holds for racecraft and races.[15]

THE UBIQUITY AND MISCELLANY OF THE INVISIBLE

That said, let us notice first the invisible realm of witchcraft. Therein spirits are ubiquitous and continually at work in the big events and small happenstances of everyday life. Moreover, they are at work miscellaneously: There is always room alongside their invisible, mystical influences for what Westerners would call natural causes, as well as for explicit (and true) technical ideas about how things work. Their miscellaneousness means that judgments of which is which, when, do not flow neatly from rubrics and categories under which events can be subsumed in advance, and without overlaps or remainders. In short, as the saying goes, "Circumstances alter cases." That miscellaneousness goes with invisibility as a crucial trait of spirit beliefs and, again, with ubiquity. We are not in the presence of "Now you see it, now you don't." You never see it, yet you can always see it. Real-world evidence is ever at hand. By its nature, though, such evidence is miscellaneous. Not fixed or even

---

15 It is true, of course, that some race researchers settle for the folk categories while anticipating their future experimental vindication; but this commitment independent of demonstration seems to me as remarkable as a similar posture in relation to witches would be. See p. 24, note 71.

fixable in any list of possible occurrences, that list is irremediably ad hoc. It stands ever open to addition as well as to change in the spiritual, logical, and even technological particulars of the items on it. Addition is one thing; subtraction or upending by incompatible evidence is quite another.

THE OBVIOUSNESS OF THE INVISIBLE

The existence of spirits is obvious in certain settings. Belief in them is "uncontroversial" and taken to be "obviously true" in Ashanti, Appiah tells us. In daily practice, they stand no more in need of rational defense than the planets' movement around the sun would in Europe.[16] According to Appiah, however, that obviousness does not arise because people use examined or consistent ideas about what spirits are or how they work, but because, despite the invisibility of crucial operations, people regularly encounter their sensible outputs. As Appiah puts it, "The evidence that spirits exist is obvious: priests go into trance, people get better after the application of spiritual remedies, people die regularly from the action of inimical spirits."[17] In short, confirming rituals seem regularly to be reconfirmed by nature itself. Thus, reason turns in a circle of its own making, towing the senses with it. Accordingly, in applying the term *sensible* to such evidence, I want to keep its two meanings in view: available to the senses and reasonable.

EVIDENCE THROUGH DOING

Furthermore, Appiah goes on, "The re-interpretation of this evidence, in terms of medical-scientific theories or of psychology, requires that people have some reason to believe in them;

---

16   Appiah, *In My Father's House*, 113. I take it that Appiah is referring, elliptically, to our un-experimental acceptance of this experimental finding, which was colossal in its day.

17   Ibid., 117–18.

but again and again, and especially in areas of mental and social life, the traditional view is likely to be confirmed."[18] Besides, he says (after Evans-Pritchard), this evidence is not only likely to be confirmed, but also, and just as important, it cannot easily be contradicted by experience: Spirit workings transcend experience; and the corresponding human practices presuppose a coherent system of mutually supporting beliefs. *Witchcraft, Oracles and Magic* is, above all, a book about doing. If we follow Durkheim, there is more to say. At the same time that practices presuppose a system of belief, they confirm it as well. They make beliefs available to the senses through real-world doing. Confirming rituals can be ceremonious and occasional, or they can be deeds that fit into the profane comings and goings of everyday life. Combining both in early modern Europe, learned Continental investigators used judicial torture in investigations of witchcraft, extracting confessions of invisible (and sometimes impossible) deeds. As St. Paul said of cheerier convictions, some things we believe by hearing and not by sight.

EVIDENCE THROUGH INFERENCE

Some of Evans-Pritchard's examples bring out another sort of evidence, in which folk biology and genetics make invisible deeds of witchcraft visible. Among the Azande, witchcraft perpetrated by living people was discoverable through oracular trial, but since theory held witchcraft to be a physical substance located in the entrails of a witch (or of his or her close male kin), the verdict could be checked by autopsy. As he did frequently throughout the book, Evans-Pritchard stopped in the full midst of this strange thicket of invisible improbabilities with a reminder to his readers: Nonetheless, the Azande were not so very different from Englishmen: "the Zande mind is logical and inquiring within the framework of its culture and insists on the coherence of its own

---

18 Ibid.

idiom." Evidence was important to them, and invisible deeds left biological signatures. Thus: "If witchcraft is an organic substance its presence can be ascertained by postmortem search. If it is hereditary it can be discovered in the belly of close male kinsmen, as in the witch's."[19] He drove his point home by citing a case of a convicted witch's vindication through autopsy of a juvenile nephew who died; the child's undistinguished innards retrieved the reputation of the man and his kin.

EVIDENCE AS PHYSICAL INDICES OF NONPHYSICAL THINGS

Taking to the next level Evans-Pritchard's emphasis on the rational incorporation of physical and genetic evidence, C. G. Seligman observed in his foreword that Evans-Pritchard remained vague throughout about what the postmortem evidence consisted of. Presumably, though, this lapse occurred because his informants were equally vague in what they could tell him.[20] After all, anything found could not possibly be more than a visible index of still-invisible deeds. Since those autopsies did not spring from interests like those Western pathologists have when they open cadavers, the informants may have been uninterested in that sort of question, but courteously responsive to the curious outlander, who kept asking. The important point, it seems to me, is not what that substance was or exactly where it might be found, but that Zande theory postulated one. Invisible ontologies require—and therefore acquire—anchors in sensible experience, including quasi-biological anchors. By their nature, they must be propped up and helped along, one way or another. An innovation that made carriers of the substance readily recognizable at fifty yards would shift the problem of invisibility, but not necessarily solve it.

19 Evans-Pritchard, *Witchcraft, Oracles and Magic*, 42.
20 On the assumption that sincere belief ruled out the fudging and tricking of results, Evans-Pritchard went to great lengths to deny that the Azande resorted to such practice in their various procedures of discovery.

Even so, visible physical difference is an unparalleled prop for invisible things. At first glance, the invisible aspect of racecraft is less immediately apparent than that of witchcraft. Race, it would seem, is eminently visible. But if it were, no one in America could possibly have understood Martin Luther King, Jr.'s *I Have a Dream* speech. The invisible aspect of race becomes apparent, however, as soon as we reflect that the focus of racecraft is not the outward, visible color of a person's skin (hair type, bone structure, etc.) but the presumed inward, invisible content of that person's character. It is always black *and*, yellow *but*, white *therefore*, and so on, and is rarely a matter of appearance standing by itself.[21] As a limiting case, take the example of Louis Agassiz, the Swiss naturalist and expert on fossil fish teeth, who immigrated to America and to Harvard. His case has further interest because, as Stephen Jay Gould wrote in his masterly study of American race science, "No man did more to establish and enhance the prestige of American biology during the nineteenth century."[22]

In 1846, having encountered black serving men at his Philadelphia hotel, Agassiz wrote to his mother: "In seeing their black faces with their thick lips and grimacing teeth, their elongated hands, their large curved nails, and especially the livid color of their hands, I could not take my eyes off their face in order to tell them to stay far away." In motion, the hands took on hyperphysical significance: "And when they advanced that hand in order to serve me, I wished I were able to depart in order to eat a piece of bread elsewhere, rather than dine with such service."[23] Shocked by that first encounter, Agassiz began to doubt "all our ideas about the confraternity of humankind [*genre humain*] and the single [*unique*]

21 Apparently, however, there exists a psychoanalyst (whose writing I want eventually to retrieve, to pillory it) who speculates that hostility to African skin tones is associated with primitive infantile responses to feces—not to chocolate or, say, the expensive leather couch that stands in the living room.

22 Stephen Jay Gould, *The Mismeasure of Man* (New York: Norton, 1996), 43.

23 Ibid., 47.

origin of our species"—and presently converted to polygenesis, America's distinguishing contribution to the biology of the day.[24]

Perhaps Agassiz calmed down when he became a distinguished visitor in wealthy Charleston milieux, where the owners of black servants made intimate domestic use of them. But even if he did not, it is important to notice that the slave owners operated with different perceptual conventions, and so the physical features of black slaves did not speak for themselves. Or, if they did, there was no easy predicting of what they might say. Like any other visible traits that might have been chosen, the visible conformations of the servants' hands served merely as an index for an invisible reality that was independent of them. Before long, Agassiz's idiosyncratic physicality yielded to the more general mental habit of "black *and*." By 1850, the empirical scientist was, like his new compatriots, riveted on invisible features: "The indomitable, courageous, proud Indian—in how different a light he stands by the side of the submissive, obsequious, imitative negro, or by the side of the tricky, cunning, and cowardly Mongolian!"[25] For the Swiss biologist to make such a connection, evidence was needed. But given the nature of the invisible things to be evidenced, theoretical thought ("underdetermined by observation") was needed as well, just as it was in the case of the Zande pathologists, who linked invisible deeds with visible particularities of the gut. In his demand for specifics about these particularities, Seligman was trapped in vulgar empiricism.

There we must momentarily end the analogy with Zande pathologists, however, because no ethnographer to nineteenth-century race scientists would have found them uninterested in specific details of their evidence. Mountains of detail accompanied

---

24   Ibid., 42–72. Since, as Gould tells us, Agassiz's original letters were censored by Mme. Agassiz, we are indebted to him for having retrieved and translated them. I have slightly altered Gould's renderings of *genre humain* and *unique*.

25   Ibid., 47.

those researchers down a convoluted path, starting from a physical "here" (presumed to be systematically demonstrable) and headed to a nonphysical "there" (known in advance of demonstration). Even the "here" proved recalcitrant to systematization, since no trait or set of traits permitted the establishment of internally unified and mutually exclusive categories. Until today, the physical evidence has spoken like the storied villager who stops and starts in giving directions and finally gives up, saying, "You can't get there from here."

VISIBLE AND INVISIBLE PROPS FOR INVISIBLE THINGS

What is interesting about invisible ontologies is precisely that they are held up and helped along by props, without which they are unavailable to sense; but they are not the creatures of those props and, therefore, not dependent on any particular one. The usable props are analogous to the oddments with which Lévi-Strauss defined *bricolage* in contrast to the specific-purpose material of engineering.[26] Once the existence of an invisible this or that is obvious, and everydayness makes rational defense irrelevant, evidence is everywhere at hand, available for miscellaneous, ad hoc use. Thus, in a witchcraft-cleansing episode, Bemba villagers—given the specific practical purposes at hand—ignored their exact knowledge of the difference between the skulls of chimpanzees and humans.[27] The

---

26   Claude Lévi-Strauss, *The Savage Mind*, trans. John Weightman and Doreen Weightman (Chicago: University of Chicago Press, 1966), 22ff. Hence, also, the rational properties of myth in contrast to science. I find his notions hard to apply to the present case for two reasons. First, they give us nothing about the relationship of doing to the thinking with which Lévi-Strauss is concerned. Second, myth adds to that relationship a third term, art; and I find his mode of sketching that relationship elegant but unpersuasive. It reminds me of the complicated care with which Durkheim argued his decision to exclude myth from the central arguments of *Elementary Forms*.

27   Audrey I. Richards, "A Modern Movement of Witchfinders," *Africa* 8 (1935), 435.

difference did not matter: Cleaning was cleaning. In racecraft, what matters fundamentally is not the physical particular but what follows the *and* in "black *and*," "white *and*," "yellow *and*."

Racecraft can even do without the physical descriptor altogether, giving theoretical consistency full sway. Homer Plessy of the US Supreme Court's Plessy v. Ferguson decision, which created the doctrine of separate but equal, appeared white until he announced his "colored" essence. The brief written by his white liberal counsel, Albion Tourgée, stated that Plessy had "one-eighth African blood, with no discernible black features, and [was] thus entitled to the legal privileges of a white man."[28] It was Plessy's invisible traits that got him moved on his Louisiana train, in the same right as Agassiz's black, long-handed "negro" would have been, and as Booker T. Washington actually was—that tan, gray-eyed son of a white man and a slave who quietly engineered Plessy's suit. Invisible ontologies require, and therefore acquire, visible props. But those props no more need be vulgarly empirical than do the substances extracted from Evans-Pritchard's Zande witches. Hence, the Nazis did indeed rely on their visual conception of Jews, but not so slavishly as to deny themselves help from badges and armbands.

Let me open some parentheses. Durkheim makes this point unforgettably in presenting an Australian world with human members of the Kangaroo, Cockatoo, Lizard, and Louse clans. The clansmen are born with a shared essence (of kangaroo, say), but with neither mutual resemblance to one another nor mutual difference from the members of other clans. Conventional emblems easily rectify both their inborn failure to resemble their respective totems, and their even more consequential failure to resemble one another. With the observation that all human Kangaroos can look alike only through social contrivance—that is, through craft—I close the parentheses.

28   Kevin R. Gaines, *Uplifting the Race: Black Leadership, Politics, and the Culture of the Twentieth Century* (Chapel Hill, NC: University of North Carolina Press, 1996), 29. On this point I am indebted to my colleague Jesse Moore.

In racecraft, physical features function merely as a visible index of an invisible essence that is separate and different from them. Racial essences belong to racecraft's invisible ontology even though the visible manifestations of those essences are usually available to most Americans, from fifty yards or more, as race.

But they need not be. Providing a vivid example of action by invisible entities in the sensible realm, the sociologist E. Franklin Frazier wrote about the house cleaning a Southern woman undertook after discovering that the seemingly white patron of "colored people" she had just received in her parlor actually was not white, but "colored." On what happened next, let me quote Frazier: "she chopped up the chair in which he had sat and, after pouring gasoline over the pieces, made a bonfire of them."[29] If the real-world results were less tragic, the migration from one failed physical criterion to the next in nineteenth- and twentieth-century race science would be just as comical as that lady's frenzied house cleaning. The empirical project of giving the prescientific races an empirical basis in visible traits had failed by the 1930s. Even so, Harvard University, into the 1960s, had on its faculty a polygenist, Carlton S. Coon, a fossil representative of the (by then) long-abandoned theory that the world's (he says five) races had evolved in separate lines and in different epochs. What often follows the "and" in racecraft clung to the discoveries Coon published in *The Origin of Races*, in which we read about "the bulbous forehead, protruding eyes, and other infantile features characteristic of living Negroes."[30]

What is more, in America, those setbacks to scientific classification turn out not to have blocked allegedly scientific study of nonphysical characteristics, such as propensity to violence, intelligence, morality, and even exotic matters that arise haphazardly in the comings and goings of life. Back in the 1980s, Tom Brokaw presided over a television program about racial differences in

29   E. Franklin Frazier, "The Pathology of Prejudice," *Forum* 77 (June 1927), 862.

30   Carlton S. Coon, *The Origin of Races* (New York: Knopf, 1962), 655.

sport. His guest was an Israeli researcher who had devised a special machine, set up near a hoop that measured jumps by black and white basketball players. The numbers he collected, as evidence of racial differences in the jump, revealed to him that black people are fast muscle-twitch athletes. (Apparently, none of the dramatis personae could recognize that if one started with people defined as black and white, they could not escape circular argument in arriving at their conclusions.) A Labor Department sociologist I knew (a black woman) used to tell about the assignment she once got, to investigate the disproportionate wintertime use of Vaseline by black prison inmates, in comparison with their white peers. (Since no one was prepared to credit her with having an answer from down home sans research, she did the research and then told them: People used to use it for chapped skin.)

Invisible Ontologies, Real Worlds

Now, if I have shown, at least provisionally, that the notion of invisible ontology applies equally well to witchcraft and racecraft, let me return to the logical conundrum. Those who know Appiah's remarkable book will notice that I have cribbed the phrase "invisible ontology" from the chapter "Old Gods, New Worlds," where spirit beliefs are defended. Now, consider two similarly constructed statements. First: "The truth is that there are no spirits: There is nothing in the world that can do all human beings ask spirits to do for them."[31] Second: "The truth is that there are no races: There is nothing in the world that can do all we ask race to do for us."[32] Appiah's readers will notice that I cribbed again, taking the second statement, word for word, from the chapter "Illusions of Race." If we hold both positions—defending the rationality of spirit beliefs, attacking the rationality of race beliefs—we arrive at this: Spirits

---

31   The statement could be rephrased, replacing *spirits* with *witches, demons,* or other terms denoting invisible entities—in English or in other languages.

32   Appiah, *In My Father's House*, 45.

do not exist, but belief in them is rational. Races do not exist, but belief in them is irrational. What distinction could we be making, and what might warrant it?

We may well observe, as Appiah correctly does, that spirit beliefs are acquired in the course of African rearing, and, furthermore (to quote him again), "The evidence that spirits exist is obvious: priests go into trance, people get better after the application of spiritual remedies."[33] But we may equally well observe that race beliefs, too, are acquired in the course of rearing and, furthermore, that the evidence that races exist is obvious. "Racial" incidents are frequent, criminals and medical patients are counted by race, statistical studies reveal racial differences in everything from death from prostate cancer to rates of decline in the incidence of teenage pregnancy. Since race is ubiquitous, that list is open to indefinite extension. One could add to it everything from blood pressure to consumer preferences, athletic prowess, propensity to welfare dependence (or to allegedly unfair claims to jobs), likelihood to be transporting illegal drugs on the nation's streets and roads (or, lately, through its airports), and much else. In our race-conscious world, virtually anything that can be counted will eventually be sorted, classified, and published by someone according to "racial" differences—which, as such lists demonstrate, are everywhere and have inner mechanisms that, it is assumed, science will eventually vindicate.

Appiah also proposes that, as a vocabulary that organizes experience, Africa's invisible ontology organizes the world in one among many possible ways. It conceptualizes relations between spirits and persons as relations between persons. This is a powerful point that Evans-Pritchard made about the Zande idiom of thought. Such a conceptualization does indeed seem to preempt the space that impersonal causes occupy in Western science. And Appiah is quite right to say that there is little reason for medical-scientific or psychological evidence to win out over traditional evidence,

33   Ibid., 117–18.

especially in the realms of mental and social life. What is more, as he points out, the spirit evidence suits those realms, not least because they are home territory for controlling and judging the doings of people, not of things: "Azande assume that the world is in some kind of evaluative balance—in short on the sort of assumption that leads monotheistic religions to develop theodicies."[34] To progress in understanding the How? of things that happen, scientific rationality had to get out of the business of accounting for good and bad fortune—in short, to abandon to religion teleological questions of Why? Africa's invisible ontology accommodates such questions.

Let me offer as example a recent phone conversation I had about a geologist (with a French doctorate) who has spent several years unemployed in France. His wife was telling me that he had been *bloqué*. It transpired in conversation that she did not mean "blocked" by French-born competitors faced with an African-born black man who merely held French nationality, but, instead, by jealous kin in his home village. It would have been irrelevant and impertinent for me to rebut her assessment or, for that matter, even to ask questions about her logically and methodologically expanded conception of traditional notions about causing action at a distance. My friend was pointing to a truth about important relationships back home, and to terms of human connectedness in a home community that are in reality determinative for her husband's life. They are his kin. Besides, as we both knew, twenty years earlier those same jealous kin had engineered a disabling psychotic episode. Thereafter, until a reputable spiritual doctor intervened, they had effectively blocked his passing the French-imported monster exam that stood between neo-colonials and bachelor's degrees.

But just as we can say that Africa's ontology of spirits underpins personal modes of conceptualization, we can also say, comparably, that America's does similar work. That invisible ontology underpins a conceptualization of relations between persons as relations

34 Ibid., 134.

between races. And it, too, has provided a highly flexible yet deeply authoritative vocabulary in which to conceptualize good and evil, hence also the distribution of good and bad fortune. I have often been struck by the campus contrast between middle-class white students, who arrive inertially at college from their suburbs, and less well-off black students who, by finishing high school *and* going to college, represent a minority within a minority. The tough individualists belong to the latter group, but no amount of argument can shake the perception and conception of them, from fifty yards, as undeserving beneficiaries of handouts—at best, and at worst, as dangerous people. A white student of mine suddenly remembered, during a classroom discussion, that, as he sat studying in the library late one night the previous week, campus police had limited their card check to a table where a group of black students sat studying.

That anti-individualism, so strange in America, connects the dots between doings as separate from one another as higher punishments for the same crimes and lower pay for the same skills. The pop statement of the theodicy problem—Why do bad things happen to good people?—has a pop answer of ancient pedigree: People to whom bad things happen cannot be all good. Max Weber stated long ago that, for most of human history, suffering indexed moral depravity and odiousness in the eyes of the gods, and acquired a "plus sign" only as the ingenious invention of Judaism and then of Christianity. For the general rule is this: "The fortunate man is seldom satisfied with the fact of being fortunate. Beyond this, he needs to know that he has a right to his good fortune. He wants to be convinced that he 'deserves' it, and above all, that he deserves it in comparison with others ... Good fortune thus wants to be 'legitimate' fortune."[35] Appiah's insight

---

35   Max Weber, "The Social Psychology of the World Religions," in Hans Gerth and C. Wright Mills, eds., *From Max Weber* (New York: Oxford University Press, 1946), 271; and "The Religion of Non-Privileged Strata," in Guenther Roth and Claus Wittich, eds., *Economy and Society: An Outline of Interpretive Sociology* (Berkeley: University of California Press, 1978), 49.

that invisible ontologies are especially well suited for imagining the world's "evaluative balance" is something to retain. Once again, however, the obviousness of such ontologies is an achievement of craft, never simply given.

That is why my black colleague recently arrived from overseas, the late Sam Nolutshungu, marveled at the attention given to the O. J. Simpson case—he dismissed it early on as a "sordid domestic murder." It is also why, crossing in the hall after Simpson's acquittal, a usually courteous (and garrulous) white colleague in the same building passed me in silence, gaze averted, face in a rictus of rage, white as a ghost. Although a black South African with profound knowledge of apartheid, Nolutshungu seems nevertheless to have had a different apparatus for perceiving and conceiving race than we. That difference gave him the luxury of looking on like an ethnographer, with nothing personal at stake. As a black American, I carried around a deforming apparatus similar to my white American colleague's. For Nolutshungu, by contrast, nothing inflated the import of the private tragedy or extended its scope. He had not acquired in childhood the conventional perceptions and affects that make this exception to American individualism powerful. Linguists study the acquisition of language. A fruitful line of fresh inquiry into both witchcraft and racecraft would involve watching how the acquisition of racecraft occurs in childhood, gradually overcoming the child's not-yet-socialized capacity to "see" from within its horizon.

Put in terms of spiritual realities, the to-be-socialized capacity to "see" takes something like the insider-outsider form of a collective representation,[36] as proposed by Lévy-Bruhl: "Not a being,

36 By the way, Evans-Pritchard explains this term, with whose irritations to English speakers Durkheim has been saddled, by saying that French sociologists seemed to have translated it from the German term *Vorstellung*: "It suggests something very abstruse," Evans-Pritchard tells us, "whereas [Lévy-Bruhl] meant by it little more than what we would call an idea or a notion, or a belief; and when he says that a representation is collective, he means no more than that it is common to all, or most, members of a society." See E. E.

not an object, not a natural phenomenon in their collective representation is what appears to us. Almost all *we* see in it escapes *them*, or *they* are indifferent to it. On the other hand, *they* see in it many things which *we* do not even suspect."[37] To young children, from that standpoint, adults are surely a *they*. Let me offer a commonplace instance that arose in conversation not long ago. A close friend told me of what she called a racial encounter, in which her four-year-old daughter, Abby, walked up to a swearing, shouting, hyperventilating street altercation between two heavyset women. Before a nearby security guard stepped between her and them, the little girl had walked up close and sternly warned them (as her nursery school teacher does), "You are not practicing peaceful community." In America, this story does not have its full meaning without the colors, so let me supply them—the white child, her white mother, the black women, the black guard. "Abby didn't see colors," her mother told me. But this is America, the grown-ups did see colors, and Abby soon will. Some version of America's race belief eventually will seem no more worth querying to Abigail than the existence of spirits does to children in Appiah's Ashanti.

Let me note once again, however, that, once acquired, this seeing serves miscellaneously. To say that it plays a role in the social discernment of good and evil and of good and bad fortune is one thing. To think of it as causing particular events or judgments and then hitch it simplistically to them would be another—and would be wrong. It provides not a detailed constitution equipped with authoritative and self-activating rules for every possible case, but simply a kind of raw material. Once acquired, that seeing becomes open-endedly applicable to specific contingencies of life, as they come up, or at least until the theorizing impulse hardens them into fixed forms. Thus, the victim of the lynching in D. W. Griffith's 1915 American classic *Birth of a Nation* became black by being lynched;

Evans-Pritchard, *A History of Anthropological Thought* (Oxford: Clarendon Press, 1981), 24.

37 Ibid., 125 (emphasis mine).

8 *Racecraft*

he was not lynched because already black. Again, that film's half-black, half-white Reconstruction politician became half-black and not half-white through the same process, but need not have done elsewhere or under different circumstances. Meanwhile, in the real world depicted by the film, those two kinds of drama were at the hot core of new politics destined to shape public discourse about who gets what, and why. The late C. Vann Woodward's great biography of Tom Watson recounts the life of a man who began as a populist advocate of poor farmers' interests, black and white, but evolved into a virulent and violent racist.[38]

I think of witchcraft in a similar way. It is adaptable to all kinds of contingencies, so long as it moves in step with the human doing and thinking that together confirm its reality—in other words, by keeping its invisible underpinnings sensible. If either were only a museum specimen of human reason, to be gazed upon more or less elegantly, it would not matter whether our intellectual machinery enabled us to grasp them adequately. But getting that right matters, for both are active in the world. They are active not only as resources for making sense of evil but also as sources of evil in their own right. To gain the edge for Jesse Helms in his closely contested last Senate race, all it took was for the senator's TV admen to show a white hand receiving a pink slip and a black one receiving a pay stub. Analogously, the health crisis that has followed Africa's economic crisis has allowed anti-witchcraft practitioners to gain fresh prominence and, in some cases, to do terrible harm. Propagating the scientific truth of human likeness until doomsday, as President Clinton did in his 1998 State of the Union Speech, cannot undo the power of racecraft, any more than propagation of the truth that there are no witches has undone the power of witchcraft. Perhaps some other method can, if we set out to study the sort of rationality they share, purposely and with a sense of something important at stake.

---

38 C. Vann Woodward, *Tom Watson: Agrarian Rebel* (New York: Oxford University Press, 1987; orig. ed. 1938).

The Half-Dark of Evans-Pritchard's Legacy

AN ETHICAL DILEMMA

I am one of those who have resisted as ethnocentric, if not directly racist, the conclusion that spirit beliefs bespeak African peculiarities or deficiencies of rational thought, even when those beliefs are put into hideous action in the killing of witches. I therefore used Evans-Pritchard's methods in my demonstration that seemingly irrational spirit beliefs powered rational strategies against British colonial rule—even though, in one such episode, the Mwana Lesa episode of 1925, many Africans accused of witchcraft lost their lives.[39] But I myself am subject to the illogic I have criticized insofar as I resist the conclusion that if those beliefs pass the test of rationality, so should America's race beliefs—those beliefs, too, are sometimes put into hideous action. Therefore, once again, unless so different that I err in treating them as comparable, both sets of traditional beliefs should be regarded in the same way: as extremely resilient falsities that lead to moral error and human suffering; or as extremely complicated truths that reflect the capacity of reason, our most human holding, to uplift and degrade our humanity as it will. We do not treat both sets of traditional beliefs as comparable, I think, because we (myself included) tend not to juxtapose the conclusions we reach in those different realms. We experience some version of the intellectual compartmentalization that, according to Evans-Pritchard, protected Zande beliefs in general, and that specifically protected certain foundational intellectual investments attached to them—the axiomatic inviolability of their king's oracle, for instance.

As inheritors of the Enlightenment, we have foundational intellectual investments not in traditional authority but in rationality. We turn to rationality in both cognitive and moral reflection. In rough and ready fashion, therefore, we require a certain consistency

---

39 Fields, *Revival and Rebellion in Colonial Central Africa* (Princeton, NJ: Princeton University Press, 1986), Chapter 5.

between them. But even if the comings and goings of life or of thought do not yield that consistency, we do not feel obligated to abandon that investment. In this way, I think, Western scholars learned, professionally at least, to suspend moral judgment on spirit beliefs and witchcraft (even in their bloody manifestations) by learning to grasp their rationality—all the while believing the beliefs to be false. But because we expect consistency, the consequence of treating racecraft as rational (or even reasonable), would be to blunt the intellectual tools with which we most readily condemn it as immoral: It is false, and once one has seen evidence of its falsity, continuing to act on the basis of it moves one from a cognitive problem to a moral one.[40] The same strategies that allow us to deny the rationality of racecraft should allow us to deny that of witchcraft and condemn it accordingly. Instead, they give us racecraft as (objectively) false and witchcraft as true (in its own fashion), but not witchcraft as (objectively) false and racecraft as true (in its own fashion).

THE SHORT-CIRCUIT IN EVANS-PRITCHARD'S MACHINERY

The problem is not only the moral and ethical dilemmas we confront as a result. There is also a short-circuit in our intellectual machinery that lessens its power. If racecraft is unlike witchcraft, then lifting from us what Appiah calls its "burdensome legacy" becomes easy lifting. All that is needed is propagation of the truth. Repetition of the scientific statement "There are no races" will suffice. But if racecraft is like witchcraft, then repetition can do no more than transmute the scientific statement into the ritual drone of a mantra. By the time we get to the end of Evans-Pritchard's monumental work, the original wiring that connected racecraft with his problem has been cut—and therewith his own access to a far closer cognate than Western science. For his comparison he connected Zande modes of thought not with English modes of

---

40 Appiah, *In My Father's House*, 14.

thought that have similar properties, but with scientific modes. As a result, we no longer have a climactically intense problem of how disconfirming evidence breaks across ships of false belief without sinking them, indeed in wave after seen-but-unnoticed wave.

MAKING THE STRANGE FAMILIAR...

To examine more closely how Evans-Pritchard moved intellectually beyond the obvious (to the ethnographer) falsity of witchcraft, let me return once again to his masterpiece. It is appropriate to remind ourselves that Evans-Pritchard set out to apply in the field notions about the sociology of knowledge, as suggested by Durkheim in *The Elementary Forms of Religious Life* and, differently, by Lucien Lévy-Bruhl in *Les Fonctions mentales dans les sociétés inférieures*. From his standpoint in the twentieth-century West, Evans-Pritchard posed a fundamental question about witchcraft, which can be paraphrased in this way: "How can one account for its appearing to a normally constituted, rational person as something whose reality cannot readily be doubted?" His answer used the strategy of remote imagining that ethnographers sometimes call "making the strange familiar." His mistake was to apply that strategy while assuming, implicitly, that his own world, secular and scientific, possessed nothing like it. He correctly argued that, if properly situated in their socially determined intellectual context, witchcraft beliefs would make sense not only to his ethnographic subjects but also to anyone who took up intellectual residence there, including himself. They constituted a coherent idiom of thought, with particular traits. For example, Azande were not satisfied with knowing that a person died from the physical results of a poisonous snake bite, but required to know why—why the snake slithered where the victim passed, how the victim happened to take that unfortunate path, and so on. What struck the Azande as a culturally satisfying answer was couched in terms of personal agency, not simply of impersonal qualities of poisons acting on a human

body. In other words, start from the Zande assumptions about the
correct question to ask and the nature of a correct answer, assume
the existence of spirits and their activation through witchcraft, and,
voilà, even a native from Oxbridge like Evans-Pritchard can appreciate why spirits could appear to a normally constituted person as
something whose reality cannot readily be doubted.

...WHILE NOT MAKING THE FAMILIAR STRANGE

Though the gains are clear and have led to much fruitful research,
nonetheless it seems to me that an ethical problem has traveled with
those gains as a barnacle does with a ship. Since Evans-Pritchard's
own doubt—and his readers'—remains as strong at the end of
Witchcraft, Oracles and Magic as at its beginning, that very doubt
set up a fundamental inequality. An elitism of getting it right raises
the ethnographer and his readers above the Azande, who, for the
reasons carefully laid out, could not help getting it wrong. The
truth remained that there are no spirits and that there is nothing in
the world that can do what the Azande expected spirits to do. So the
problem became one of working out how those false beliefs come
into being and how they could be part of what held a community
together, cognitively and morally. To complete that analysis, he
needed something that was as hard for a European to doubt as the
existence of spirits was for a Zande.

Without it, we get the elitism of doubt just referred to: doubt
easily come by for Evans-Pritchard and for his European readers,
but not for the Azande. Evans-Pritchard was keen enough to
open the question of indigenous doubt, which he answered with
several notions. One such notion was "the secondary elaboration
of belief,"[41] a rubric for various ways in which failures of doing
and inconsistencies of thought come to be shrouded from view.
Another notion is "idiom of thought." Thus, spirit beliefs are the
very texture of a Zande's thought, and he cannot think that his

---

41   Evans-Pritchard, *Witchcraft, Oracles and Magic*, 320.

thought is wrong. As I said earlier, then, we displace but do not get rid of particularized notions about African thinking. For the original problem to be kept a general one about humanity and about human thinking, Evans-Pritchard's strategy of making the strange familiar was not enough. The capacity for doubt of Evans-Pritchard, the ethnographer, was an intellectual holding a tad too easily come by, because it rested merely on outsiderhood. Anyone can identify what seems odd or false in the mental habits of an alien "somewhere." But if something is the very texture of any insider's thought, anywhere, it is the work of genius, not of ordinary men and women, to think that one's thought is wrong. That is why I suggest that it is important to complement, and establish checks within, Evans-Pritchard's strategy of making the strange familiar, with the opposite one of making the familiar strange.

It seems to me that, right through the twentieth century, American race beliefs continued to offer us an invisible ontology whose reality cannot readily be doubted by normally constituted, rational American men and women. It provides an idiom of thought, is protected by secondary elaboration of belief, is acquired as obvious and uncontroversial, and so forth. Setting that invisible ontology alongside other people's is one way of keeping ourselves honest, and modest. If we say, "The truth is there are no races," and in any way blink, then racecraft can provide a useful complement to Evans-Pritchard's strategy of remote imagining. When twentieth-century Africans went on making their visible world of beings and events collectively comprehensible, by underpinning it with an invisible ontology, they did not exhibit a problem that humans anywhere can avoid and remain fully human.

In America, it is neither here nor there to affirm the truth that there are no races. Like witchcraft in its African contexts, racecraft points to truth about important relationships here, and to terms of human connectedness in our home community that are in reality determinative for all our lives. In those circumstances, talk of color-blindness resonates either as the visionary message of King's

I Have a Dream speech or as a kind of peekaboo dishonesty on the part of self-interested racecraft. In like fashion, African villagers suspected that their self-appointed "civilizers" were dishonest, self-interested autocrats from afar, or, at best, well-intentioned but naive deniers of reality. We can think of King's dream as his own kind of civilizing mission in his own land, the natives of which have a choice to make. That choice is every bit as haunting as the one Appiah sets forth at the end of "Old Gods, New Worlds": "If modernization is conceived of, in part, as the acceptance of science, we have to decide whether the evidence obliges us to give up the invisible ontology."[42] America is modern, has accepted science, and has yet to decide whether the evidence obliges us to give up the invisible ontology.

I have tried to suggest that Appiah refers to a predicament that is not restricted to African contexts but shared by all human beings. That being the case, our studies on witchcraft require general formulations that can apply beyond our immediate geographical sphere of work. My contention that examining witchcraft and racecraft together can illuminate both is one means to that end. My extending, and I hope not distorting, Appiah's notion of invisible ontology is another, so long as we can keep our footing along its slippery limits. I have shown that, in our different approaches to spirits and races, we have been traveling those slippery limits logically and ethically.

---

42 Appiah, *In My Father's House*, 135.

8 Individuality and the Intellectuals: An Imaginary Conversation Between Emile Durkheim and W. E. B. Du Bois

The American reviewer of a recent travel book about France marveled at the author's account of a despised people called the Cagots. The rituals that set them apart conjure up the American South during much of the twentieth century: forbidden to marry outside their group; restricted to designated entrances and seating at church (where the communion Host was delivered from the end of a stick); required to announce their presence by an identifying badge (which might be a goose foot pinned to the tunic), and so on. According to the reviewer, the "mystery of the Cagots is that they had no distinguishing features at all."[1] As the following essay illustrates, different appearance is by no means essential to the deployment of a double standard based on ancestry. The essay juxtaposes America's turn-of-the-twentieth-century "Negro Problem" with France's "Jewish Question" of the same epoch. It imagines two great founders of sociology, Emile Durkheim and W. E. B. Du Bois, examining together the prospect of universal human rights.[2]

---

1 Ruth Scurr, on Graham Robb's *The Discovery of France: A Historical Geography from the Revolution to the First World War* (New York: Norton, 2007), in *The Nation*, December 10, 2007.

2 Originally published as "Individuality and the Intellectuals: An Imaginary Conversation between Emile Durkheim and W. E. B. Du Bois," in Christian Lerat and Nicole Ollier, eds., *Expansions/Expansionismes dans le monde translatlantique*, *Actes du colloque international*, Bordeaux, janvier 25–27, 2001 (Bordeaux: Maison des sciences de l'homme d'Aquitaine, 2001), and in a slightly different version, *Theory and Society* 31: 4 (October 2002), 435–62. I thank the

Religion is first and foremost a system of ideas by means of which individuals imagine the society of which they are members and the obscure yet intimate relations they have with it.

Emile Durkheim, *The Elementary Forms of Religious Life*[3]

W. E. B. Du Bois found few promising interlocutors among American social scientists when he wrote in 1903, "The problem of the twentieth century is the problem of the color line—the relation of the darker to the lighter races of men in Asia, in Africa, in America, and the islands of the sea."[4] While everyone recognized the color line, not everyone considered it a problem. For some, indeed, the color line was the solution. Economically, its benefits were obvious, whether in America or in Europe's far-flung colonies. Morally, the "darker" races counted for less than the "lighter" ones. For scientists, the theoretically interesting problem was not the color line itself, but the biological basis of differences and different treatment that were held to be self-evident.[5] To see the color line itself as a puzzle or a problem required an ability to look skeptically at the evidence of one's own eyes. For that subject, white American researchers, like white Americans in general, had little space on their mental templates. But in France,[6] where races

National Endowment for the Humanities and TIDE/CNRS at the Maison des Sciences de l'Homme d'Aquitaine for supporting the extended research project on which this article has drawn—the first, by granting me a Fellowship for Independent Study, and the second, by inviting me to join an *équipe* as a visiting scholar. I thank Michael O. West, Nahum Chandler, and Barbara J. Fields for reading various drafts closely and for sharing their erudition with me.

3   Emile Durkheim, *The Elementary Forms of Religious Life*, translated and with an Introduction by Karen E. Fields (New York: Free Press, 1995), 227.

4   W. E. B. Du Bois, *The Souls of Black Folk*, in *Three Negro Classics* (New York: Avon, 1965 [1903], 221.

5   As the late Stephen Jay Gould showed, with great elegance, they kept turning their theory inside out to prevent empirical data from appearing to contradict the self-evident inferiority of the inferior. See *The Mismeasure of Man* (New York: Norton, 1981).

6   This distinguishing trait of the Republic did not, however, preclude the

and colors figured in a different way, Du Bois would have found a promising interlocutor: Emile Durkheim. Durkheim found questions of theoretical interest and import, not self-evidence, in Europe's racial identifications—though all Europeans were what Americans would designate as "white."

Pursuing fundamental questions about religion and reason, Durkheim began the studies in the late 1890s that culminated in his 1912 masterpiece, *The Elementary Forms of Religious Life*. Durkheim pursued those questions through sustained analysis of aboriginal Australia's racial identifications—though all were "black" by American standards. In the process, he exposed the raw materials of mind and devices of social life by which social groups fashion a collective understanding of themselves. However, usual readings of *Forms* generally do not keep those various levels in view. In today's studies of race, for example, bits and pieces from *Forms* travel separately from it, reduced to glib formulas about the "social construction" of "collective identities."[7] As a result, we lose sight of the living subjects and active verbs by which Durkheim arrived at the hard-won discoveries of *Forms*. We also overlook the historical context in which he won those discoveries: that of the Dreyfus Affair. This huge storm exposed a racist undertow in the politics of France's Third Republic that arrested Durkheim's attention—and that of W. E. B. Du Bois. Imagining them in conversation, therefore, is one way to draw fresh lessons from the sharp wit, spiritual heat, and abiding theoretical preoccupations of Durkheim's astonishing book.

However, to draw those fresh lessons from *Forms*, it is necessary to retrieve two facts, often forgotten or ignored: first, that they

---

institution of the color line in the colonies.

7   To keep in full view the objective facticity of the identifications that are the focus of *Forms*, I use the term "identification" throughout, not "identity." The confusions and ambiguities of the latter have been usefully combed apart by Rogers Brubaker and Frederick C. Cooper, "Beyond 'Identity'," *Theory and Society* 29:1 (2000), 1–47.

were contemporaries—Durkheim was born in 1858 and Du Bois in 1868; second, that in their own lives and scientific work, they grappled with comparable predicaments when racist politics took center stage in their respective societies. The "Durkheim and Du Bois" section below explores their comparable predicaments. The next section lays out possible topics of conversation between them. A fragment of one such imagined conversation then follows.

Academics traditionally imagine conversations in order to work out lines of intellectual descent (relating Durkheim to Comte or to Marx, for example), thereby sharpening our reflection on enduring problems. We also use them to explore intellectual contemporaneity, and sometimes do so with a vividness that registers the ongoing life of classical problems—for example, a recent collection that applies the term "misunderstandings"[8] to markedly different positions that Durkheim and his contemporary Max Weber *held without regard to one another.* Here, an imagined conversation between Durkheim and another contemporary he never met will, among other things, suggest new answers to longstanding questions about his shift in the late 1890s toward the study of religion. Given that purpose, I range freely over other writings without necessarily stopping to revisit traditional debates with other purposes. Prepare, now, to encounter these profoundly engaged men of science on terms they could have set, if they had looked out over the social world together when their science was new and promising.

They meet on a Paris afternoon in 1916. The human costs of the war have been staggering. They ponder what is to be done if, as both hope, the Allies win. They of course do not know, as we do, that Nazism lies over the horizon of that victory. They begin on intellectual common ground. They agree that in *Forms* Durkheim uncovered fundamental truths about humankind—and most centrally, the diverse corollaries of his sobering conclusion that

---

8   See Monique Hirschorn and Jacques Coena, eds., *Durkheim, Weber: vers la fin des malentendus* (Paris: Harmattan, 1994).

unreasonable divisions of humankind seem to be born from reason itself, not from its opposite. But what should be done in light of those truths? In that regard, each is disconcerted by writings of the other: Du Bois by Durkheim's 1898 article, "Individualism and the Intellectuals"; and Durkheim by Du Bois' 1903 book, *The Souls of Black Folk*. Although both believe that upholding the value of humanity as such is the central problem of their time, each reproaches the other for having taken it up at the wrong end. Durkheim finds in "the Negro" of *Souls* an unwarranted particularism. Du Bois finds in the *qualité d'homme* of "Individualism" an unwarrantable generality. Now, as then, that disagreement does not stand open to facile choice between their positions, either conceptually or in the realm of politics. I have borrowed from the ancient form of the dialogue, because it suits questions that can be answered coherently in at least two different ways. Durkheim died in 1917, but Du Bois lived on until 1963 and repeatedly revised his answers. In America and in France, the questions and arguments are with us still.

Durkheim and Du Bois: The Predicament of Individuality in the 1890s

COMMON GROUND IN THE PREOCCUPATIONS OF *FORMS*

I offered above an unhabitual reading of *Forms* as if it were obvious and in no need of justification. Since neither is the case, let me begin again by briefly summarizing the book's rather particular theory of "religion," which I consider to be inseparable from its account of collective social identifications. The scaffolding of its main argument is an extended study of collective identifications imagined in the same way as races: the totemic clans of aboriginal Australia. Unlike the Europeans' racial identifications, however, those of the Australian Aborigines cannot possibly be construed as natural; their claims of common traits and common descent implicate animals, plants, and sometimes physical objects, as well as other human beings.[9] Durkheim's general question is this: How is it that humans come to hold on to beliefs about cosmic nature that cannot possibly be true—and that, besides, cosmic nature unceasingly contradicts?[10] He finds the answer in their social being, which is also the source of the most fundamental human capacity: reason itself.[11] Australia's totemic clans, Durkheim argues, permit study of that social being, and reason itself, in "elementary form"—elementary meaning basic and, in consequence, universal, not meaning inferior or a peculiarity of designated peoples.[12] But that answer raises another question of equivalent import. How is it that humans come to embrace beliefs about themselves that cannot possibly be true—and that, besides, their human nature contradicts? In that second inquiry, fundamental to the first, Durkheim studies the collective alchemy by which *reason* converts bald-faced inventions into external and constraining facts of nature, capable of resisting individual doubt.

To see this point concretely, let us turn to a stark example given by the real Durkheim that would have arrested the attention of my

---

9   I take this conception from *Suicide*: "Recently race has been understood to mean an aggregation of individuals with clearly common traits, but traits furthermore due to their derivation from a common stock." Emile Durkheim, *Suicide: A Study in Sociology*, trans. John A. Spaulding and George Simpson, ed., George Simpson (New York: Free Press, 1966 [1897]), 83.

10   I borrow from the tidy, though misapplied, formulation of Raymond Boudon, who attaches it to a theory of magic that he claims can be gleaned from (unspecified) footnotes in *Forms*. In fact, his formulation suits religion—and specifically not magic—for reasons integral to strong positions of Durkheim's: in particular that, unlike the ends of religion, those of magic are technical, utilitarian, and individualistic, and that, furthermore, the relationships on which magic depends are "accidental and transient" rather than enduring. See Raymond Boudon, in Hirschorn and Coenen-Hutter, *Durkheim, Weber*, 104–12; and Durkheim, *Forms*, 39–42, 42 n16.

11   It was Durkheim's ambition to solve sociologically the problem of knowledge as set by Kant.

12   See Karen E. Fields, "Religion as an Eminently Social Thing," translator's Introduction to Durkheim, *Elementary Forms*, xxxviii–xl, lix–lxi.

imaginary Du Bois. A Kangaroo, shown a photograph of himself by anthropological investigators, uses his relationship to his own photograph to illustrate for them his relationship to the kangaroo: "Look who is exactly the same thing as I," he tells them. "Well! It is the same with the kangaroo." Durkheim adds that "the Kangaroo was his totem," which is to say that he traced his descent through membership in a clan with the name "Kangaroo" and was as much like his fellow clansmen as he was like the kangaroo. Such statements must not be taken, Durkheim warns, in their "everyday empirical" sense.[13] The Kangaroos do not resemble the kangaroo; nor do they necessarily resemble one another. Moreover, they do not resemble one another (or differ from White Cockatoos, for instance) in ways that would give both groups internally unifying and mutually exclusive common traits. What makes them alike is the abstract notion of common essence (kangaroo-ness). Bearing the same name logically presupposes it.[14] Special affinities and moral obligations of various kinds derive from it. And so, too, for Durkheim, does the human capacity to form concepts.[15] Any imaginable name-essence can express the overthrow of perception by conception: White Cockatoo, Black Cockatoo, Emu, Lizard, even Louse.[16] Through periodically repeated ritual, and through symbolic reminders between times, the name-essence is experienced as palpably real. In that way, it gains an objectivity that makes individual dreams of repudiating the shared identification not so much undreamable as irrelevant. Such shared identifications are not negotiable contracts.

13 Durkheim, *Elementary Forms*, 191.
14 Ibid., 134.
15 Ibid., 239–41.
16 Notice that from one point of view, this diversity is merely a diversity of collective identifications (a system of the form A, B, C, etc.). From another, however, it boils down to designating who is a member and who is not (a system of the form A/not-A). For an incisive discussion of the mistakes that follow inattention to this distinction, see Barbara J. Fields, "Whiteness, Racism, and Identity," *International Labor and Working-Class History* 60 (2001), 48–56.

In vivid set-pieces, Durkheim depicts these shared identifications as becoming immediately real to the participants in frenzied rites, which he calls *effervescences collectives*. My imaginary Du Bois would thus have given full attention when Durkheim wrote, on the very first page of *Forms*, that he was not studying Australia's rites for their own sake, but because they promised access to something "fundamental and permanent" about "present-day man," since there is "no other that we have a greater interest in knowing well." Durkheim made this point even more prominent in the first English translation (1915) by dropping his French subtitle, "Le Système totémique en Australie."

LA QUESTION JUIVE, THE NEGRO PROBLEM

Even so, at first glance, nothing would seem more distant or different from Australia's totemic clans than the racial designations of Europe. They might seem less distant, however, if one imagined the France of the 1890s while reading Durkheim's vivid and, it seems to me, troubling descriptions of the *effervescences collectives* that enabled Australians simultaneously to create and experience their exotically contrary-to-nature collective identifications. Durkheim the scientist, if still alive in the 1930s, would have seen that point demonstrated in the rites of the Nazis.

I suspect that Durkheim's intuition may have begun with *effervescences collectives* that he had seen operating in France in precisely the same way. As a Jewish child growing up in Alsace, he surely heard about and may have witnessed the anti-Semitic demonstrations to reaffirm and re-arm French-ness that came in the wake of France's traumatic defeat by Prussia in 1870, making Alsace-Lorraine German. In 1894 there was the court-martial for treason of Captain Alfred Dreyfus. Dreyfus, the first Jew to rise to the General Staff of France's army, was falsely accused and convicted of passing secrets to the German government, and saw that conviction reaffirmed even after the real culprit had become known. In the wake of his trial—or rather, anti-Semitic railroading—came ugly street demonstrations and a nationally divisive struggle for justice that went on for twelve years.[17] During those years, Durkheim the sociologist became Durkheim the activist, and a co-founder of the League for the Defense of the Rights of Man and Citizen.[18]

Du Bois reports having watched the Dreyfus Affair closely.[19] Perhaps he drew a parallel between the frenzied French crowds and the American ones that sometimes seized prisoners and lynched them. Lynchings had wide enough acceptance for a *New York Times* headline in 1900 to read: "Negro Murders a Citizen: Posse are looking for him and he will be lynched."[20] Perhaps he saw a parallel with another defining court case of the same era, Plessy v. Ferguson, in 1896. In that case, the Supreme Court of the United States found the segregation laws being enacted in the South to be consistent with equal treatment under law as supposedly guaranteed by the Fourteenth Amendment of the Constitution, adopted in the wake of the Civil War.[21] That case and the political

17   The only incriminating evidence was proved to be a forgery. The real culprit, Commandant Walsin-Esterhazy, was unmasked in 1897 but acquitted the following year, to widespread celebration. Emile Zola exposed the outrage in his famous open letter, "J'accuse," charging the army's general staff with the scandal of having condemned an innocent individual, and was himself tried and convicted of defamation. Rioting and anti-Semitic demonstrations followed. A review by the Conseil de France again found Dreyfus guilty, but pardoned him. In 1906, a third trial finally exonerated Dreyfus, and thereafter he was reintegrated into the army.

18   Melvin Richter, "Durkheim's Politics and Political Theory," in Kurt H. Wolff, ed., *Emile Durkheim, 1858–1917: A Collection of Essays, with Translations and a Bibliography* (Columbus, OH: Ohio University Press, 1960), 172.

19   W. E. B. Du Bois, *The Autobiography of W. E. B. Du Bois: A Soliloquy on Viewing My Life From the Last Decade of Its First Century* (New York: International Publishers, 1968), 122, 177, 184.

20   Julius Lester, ed., *The Seventh Son: The Thought and Writings of W. E. B. Du Bois* (New York: Random House, 1971), 29, quoting from Rayford W. Logan, *The Betrayal of the Negro: From Rutherford B. Hayes to Woodrow Wilson* (New York: Collier, 1965).

21   Specifically, the case concerned segregated seating on intrastate carriers. It began when Homer Plessy, who appeared to be white, revealed his

developments it epitomized announced the twentieth-century world in which Du Bois the sociologist was shortly to become Du Bois the activist and a founder of the National Association for the Advancement of Colored People (NAACP).

From the same vantage point in time, however, and faced with what seem to me analogous outrages, Durkheim wrote in a quite different spirit from Du Bois' about the line between Jews and Christians in Europe. If he imagined the possibility of a coming crisis along that line, he did not say so. What he said instead, together with the spiritual heat of *Forms*, provided my point of departure. In "Individualism and the Intellectuals," he wrote in defense of the agitation to free Dreyfus, and specifically in response to Ferdinand Brunetière, an ardent *antidreyfusard* who had recently blasted "individualism" as anti-social, anti-patriotic, anti-French. For the *antidreyfusards* in groups such as the *Ligue de la Patrie française*, the honor of the army—hence, that of the nation—was the fundamental value at stake.

Durkheim's article is passionate, a masterpiece of concise argument, justly famous, and yet, on the surface, rather strange. It is a response to the judicial railroading of Captain Dreyfus and to resurgent anti-Semitism in France; but it never mentions Dreyfus or Jews. Indeed, Durkheim says, "Let us forget the affair itself and the sad spectacles of which we have been the witnesses."[22] Given the "sad spectacles" to be seen in America, therefore, I imagine Du Bois in rather sharp discussion with Durkheim about what he chose to say, and not to say, in that article. But since Du Bois would also have understood Durkheim's position, it seems to me they would have had much to say to one another about the complexities

---

Negro-ness after having been seated in the "whites-only" section of a train in Louisiana. Thereupon, he was ejected from the train. Plessy then sued the Pullman Company. The Plessy case coincided with a violent campaign of disfranchisement and repression across the South.

22   Emile Durkheim, "L'Individualisme et les intellectuels," in the Paris publication *Revue politique et litteraire: revue bleue* 10 (1899), 7 (my translation).

and the perplexities of living out one's own creative intellectual life amid the constraints of having not one but two pregnant identifications: in Durkheim's case, French and Jew; in Du Bois', American and Afro-American.

The common historical context of these two great social scientists was a time when "the Negro problem" in America and "the Jewish question" in France imposed themselves on the working lives of talented individuals, thereby forging and shaping their individuality. In *Forms*, Durkheim repeatedly argued—correctly, I believe—that individuality takes shape within collectivity. Nevertheless, let me underline the term "individuality." While my task is to set both men's work in the social context of a certain time, I do not mean to reduce those men of genius, or their work, to just that particular social context. To avoid crudely causal metaphors that dissolve individuality in collective identification and reduce complex thought to single themes, I propose an un-crudely causal metaphor, that of irritating sand in a pearl-producing oyster. Without the irritation, there is no pearl; but the form of a pearl cannot be predicted, explained, or even adequately described in terms of the sensation and the suffering that produce it.[23]

DURKHEIM AND DU BOIS AS CONTEMPORARIES

Since we so consistently think of Du Bois and Durkheim separately, let me now add other dimensions in which it is instructive to think of them together. First, if Du Bois' academic career was possible only in the context of his people's emancipation, so, too,

---

23 Let me add that the historical and contextual issues about race that I have brought out here should open up *Forms*, not narrow it to suit well-worn academic slots. Some of Durkheim's passages, like the one about the human Kangaroo, invite new sorts of conversations among colleagues in the separate disciplines that study "mind," "brain," and the observable deployment of each in social life. If he is right, then we should abandon the proto-scientific notion that still has free reign in scientific milieux: racism as a response to the perception of physical difference.

was Durkheim's. Both men were inheritors of great emancipations following great democratic revolutions. That of French Jews came through a series of decrees beginning in 1790, which released them from various restrictions.[24] That of most African Americans came seventy-five years later, as an outcome of the Civil War, which Du Bois sometimes spoke of as "the Revolution of 1865"—although some, among them Du Bois' grandfather, were emancipated at the time of the American Revolution.[25] In addition, both men thought, taught, and wrote with passion about what democracy required amid the social and above all economic turbulence of the late-nineteenth-century world. Also, because they were committed democrats, they were committed universalists. For the same reason, I think, they read and listened to the socialists with attention—although neither rushed to embrace socialist politics, for different yet perhaps related reasons.[26]

24 Paula Hyman, *From Dreyfus to Vichy: The Remaking of French Jewry, 1906–1939* (New York: Columbia University Press, 1979), 4. These restrictions applied in France's New World colonies. Thus, in 1777, through the provisions of Article I of the *Code Noir* (promulgated in 1685), a Jewish merchant in Bordeaux who received a plantation in St. Domingue, for payment of a debt, was able to secure possession of it only after obtaining a royal patent two years later. See Hélène Sarrazin, *Bordeaux: La Traite des Noirs* (Bordeaux: CMD, 1999), 45.

25 H. Digby Baltzell, "Introduction," W. E. B. Du Bois, *The Philadelphia Negro* (New York: Schocken, 1967 [1899]), xi.

26 Du Bois upbraided American socialists for their shuttling between outrage when white workers were oppressed and silence when it came to black workers. It is commonly said, in relation to Durkheim's position, that the socialists' crude economic determinism and doctrines of class struggle, plus his own native conservatism, made him keep his distance from socialism (for example, Steven Lukes, *Emile Durkheim, His Life and Work: A Historical and Critical Study* [New York: Harper, 1972], 323–30). But it is also the case that, within socialism, anti-Semitic currents rushed alongside universalistic ones. See again Lukes, ibid., as well as Robert F. Byrnes, *Antisemitism in Modern France, I: Prelude to the Dreyfus Affair* (New Brunswick, NJ: Rutgers University Press, 1950), 156–78, and Kenneth Thompson, *Emile Durkheim* (New York: Tavistock, 1982), 44. Adolph Reed, *W. E. B. Du Bois and American Political Thought: Fabianism and the Color Line* (New York: Oxford, 1997), has much of interest

Second, as pioneers in sociology, they opposed biological (or quasi-biological) understandings of the new discipline. Each lived on a racially defined edge of his society. In consequence, I submit, each was in a position to experience the social intuitively as a realm fundamentally distinct from the realm of nature. Du Bois' 1899 study *The Philadelphia Negro* argued against the racist theorizing that was common in American social science. He deployed empirical evidence to show that the causes of the pathology to be found in Philadelphia's Seventh Ward were social in character, not emanations from the inner essence of black people. He attacked racist arguments by providing detailed evidence of normality and advancement, to which he also assigned social causes. It followed that the racial theorists' quasi-biological causation could not accommodate those two opposite effects. Du Bois' American colleagues would already have seen Durkheim use that same strategy in *Suicide* (1897). There, for instance, he set up and then picked apart statistics about European races that could have been used to allege that Germans carried in their blood a "sad primacy" in killing themselves.[27]

Third, although both men were witnesses to the terrifying racist and proto-fascist developments of the 1890s in their respective democracies, neither was prompted to embrace emigrationist strategies in response as propounded, for example, by Bishop Henry M. Turner in America and by Theodor Herzl in Europe. Both argued in word and deed not only that reform in the land of his birth was possible, but also that the scientific investigation of social life provided the would-be reformer of that land with tools.[28] Because some of the necessary tools were to be had in Germany, each

---

to say about Du Bois' own conservatism and equivocal relationship to socialist politics in the early twentieth century.

27 Durkheim, *Suicide*, 85–93.

28 However, six decades later and in his nineties, Du Bois decided to expatriate to Ghana. For good measure, perhaps, and certainly with high humor, he took out a membership in the Communist Party of the United States of America, just as he was leaving.

traveled there early in his career—Durkheim in 1885–86 with a government fellowship, just after his *agrégation*, and Du Bois in 1892–94 with philanthropic support, just before his Harvard doctorate.[29]

SOCIETY AS SEEN FROM OUTSIDE

In ways that, like their situations, are different yet comparable, Durkheim and Du Bois picked up the tools of social science from a particular position that combined a designated racial outsider-hood with an actual cultural insider-hood. Both men were inheritors of comparatively recent and still incomplete emancipations; neither was fully free or fully armed as a citizen. The everyday weight of those realities must have been epitomized in both men's minds by the two court cases of the 1890s that I mentioned earlier: Dreyfus in France and Plessy in America. I think of Du Bois as an outside insider and Durkheim as an inside outsider. In terms of his Protestant values, Harvard education, and general culture, Du Bois was far more like than unlike the mainline elite of white American academics in his day. He was excluded from its upper sancta only because racist practice foreclosed his becoming, to use his phrase, a "co-worker in the kingdom of culture."[30] Although he published important scholarly works in important places, his individuality had to be extruded through the narrow apertures of America's system of Jim Crow, in both the North and the South. One result, I think, is the high spiritual temperature of all his work, together with qualities of both topic and rhetorical mode that I think of as its "outsider imagination." Those qualities, I submit, he shared with the Durkheim of *Forms*.

In terms of education and general culture, Durkheim, too, was also more like than unlike the main line of French academics in

29   Lukes, *Emile Durkheim*, 86–95, and David Levering Lewis, *W. E. B. Du Bois: Biography of a Race, 1868–1919* (New York: Holt, 1993), 117–76.

30   Du Bois, *Souls of Black Folk*, 215.

his day. But he was included in their upper sancta and integrated as a DuBoisian "co-worker." The ideology of Republican France was, as Americans would say today, "color-blind." Careers were open to talent, or so it must have seemed—until the Dreyfus Affair. Nevertheless, Durkheim was free to implement his vision of sociology from the pinnacle of French higher education: first at Bordeaux, where he began building *L'Année sociologique* with a team of colleagues and pupils; and then at the Sorbonne, where he continued and, in addition, became a powerful university administrator and politician.[31] What is more, Durkheim had the task of helping to reform education throughout France, in accordance with the secularizing agenda of the Third Republic.[32] His chair at the University of Bordeaux bore the two-fold title "pédagogie et sciences sociales." There came a time when his courses in the sociology of education were required for all French students who aspired to teaching careers in the humanities and social sciences.[33] It is said that his graduates working in little villages would wave away ignorant, meddling priests and ex-schoolmasters with sheaves of their lecture notes.[34] Du Bois had no such Archimedean point in the American academy. To suggest, then, that Durkheim's predicament and Du Bois' were comparable is not to minimize the differences. Those can be sketched in a rough-and-ready way by a historical What if? What if, in 1897, Harvard had created a chair in sociology and appointed Du Bois to it?

Notwithstanding such differences, here are two individuals who must have shared a marrow-deep intuition that the external and constraining social fact of bearing a collective racial identification

31 Lukes, *Emile Durkheim*, 372.

32 For a gripping biographical account of the portentous issues, described from the standpoint of a major participant, see Gabriel Merle, *Emile Combes* (Paris: Fayard, 1995), 237ff.

33 Lukes, *Emile Durkheim*, 372.

34 Ibid., 13. As late as the 1940s at least, the "Durkheimian sociology" with which teachers were equipped had an aroma of subversiveness. Interview with Hélène Sarrazin, May 22, 2002.

is the source and resource of human individuality, including that of creative genius. Even if Durkheim's days were not necessarily shaped by the aspersions of those who called his work "Talmudic sociology,"[35] with anti-Semitic intent, he lived in the atmosphere created by the propaganda that spread through print and caricature in the 1880s and 1890s. For example, the two-volume book of the journalist and newspaper editor Edouard Drumont, *La France juive: essai d'histoire contemporaine* (1886) was an enormous bestseller.[36] According to one analyst, Drumont was the first to set up an explicitly racial opposition between "Semite" and "Aryan."[37] Then came the accusation of Dreyfus, who had risen as a talented, hardworking individual, and, above all as a loyal Frenchman, but found himself accused and hated in his collective racial manifestation as a Jew. At the very least, Durkheim must have lived in a state of continual irritation—hence my image of the sand and the pearl. I submit that, if we read *Forms* against the background whose importance I have been sketching, we find therein traces of that irritation.

Forms is not only audacious, but also obnoxious and heated, in ways that he and Du Bois will notice below. What is audacious and obnoxious about *Forms* is not only that, in it, Durkheim seemed to divinize society. That was bad enough at a time when some of the French were struggling to resuscitate a dying traditional God, from whom Durkheim had withdrawn his allegiance.[38] It is also that his argument entailed the social invention of precisely that French-ness which some of the French were embracing as a matter of common

---

35   Robert A. Nisbet, *The Sociology of Emile Durkheim* (New York: Oxford University Press, 1974), 10.

36   Byrnes, *Antisemitism in Modern France*, 137–55, 320–40.

37   Pierre Birnbaum, "Drumont contre la France juive," *Le Monde: dossiers et documents* 310 [January 19, 1987] (June 2002), 3.

38   God, as earlier deployed by French kings, as deployed by militant Catholics in *fin-de-siècle* France, and God, period—Durkheim had decided against revealed religion as a matter of personal belief.

descent to which he had no access.[39] Furthermore, there is a caustic and ironic display of paradox in the dead-serious, yet at one level hilarious, accounts presented in *Forms*. There, dark-skinned men paint physical resemblance (for example, to white cockatoos) onto their bodies, and then, looking at the resemblance they themselves have just painted, affirm that they have shared it with those birds and with one another from time immemorial. According to his showings in *Forms*, anything at all could serve this purpose, without in any way disturbing anyone's assumptions about real resemblance.[40] I do imagine Durkheim laughed to himself as he kept making that point with different examples, in the process showing that three distinct species of lice had been called into service to designate three distinct kinds of human beings. I think of those moves —*Forms* is full of them—as eruptions from his outsider imagination. A related element of that outsider imagination was his taste for paradox. And I mean "paradox" literally: not as "strangeness," but rather as "against received teaching." Recall how the vignette of the man-kangaroo informed him about the workings of reason, not the supposed unreason of "primitives."[41] Early on, his preface

---

39   The matter of racial designation is a story whose complexities are indicated, if not fully explicated, by Michael R. Marrus, *The Politics of Assimilation: A Study of the French Jewish Community at the Time of the Dreyfus Affair* (New York: Oxford, 1971), 1–27.

40   In this way, it was not contradictory for the Nazis to hold that the physical distinctiveness of Jews was obvious to anyone's naked eye, though not so slavishly as to do without badges and armbands.

41   Here is an example of Durkheim's humor in deriding, *en passant*, one of the more preposterous ethnographic claims made about the Australians. The text starts this way: "Strehlow, like Spencer and Gillen, declares that, for the Arunta, sexual intercourse is by no means the sufficient condition of procreation..." A dry footnote continues: "Strehlow goes so far as to say that sexual relations are not even considered a necessary condition, a sort of preparation for conception. True, a few lines further on, he adds that the old men knew perfectly well the relationship between physical intercourse and procreation—and that, so far as animals are concerned, children know." He concludes: "This is bound to dilute somewhat the import of the first statement." *Forms*, 253 and 253 n55.

to *The Rules of Sociological Method* (1894) feistily declared: "If the search for paradox is the mark of the sophist, to flee from it when the facts demand it is the act of a mind that possesses neither courage nor faith in science."[42]

It may be that the qualities I have just noted are the same ones noted in the perennial charge among Durkheim's commentators that both his conception of society as a reality *sui generis* and his rhetoric are extreme. For example, at the start of his masterful intellectual biography of Durkheim, Steven Lukes says that "Durkheim's style often tends to caricature his thought: he often expressed his ideas in an extreme or figurative manner, which distorted his meaning and concealed their significance."[43] But I believe Durkheim was fully in charge of his prose. Therefore, if that prose seems hotter than seems called for by his subject, then a review of our own understanding of his subject may be called for—it certainly is more than "religion" as conventionally understood. I say the same about the disparagement of his rhetorical mode as "manifesto-like,"[44] a trait that would put him in "infamous and suspect company"—people like the Dadaists and the surrealists, to come, or the Marxists, who for some were suspect already.[45] Durkheim's tendency toward stark, even shocking, formulation is sometimes explained (not mistakenly, I think, so long as it is not explained away) as a scientist's zeal in various debates over the object, structure, scope, and methods of sociology. But, important as that point is (and I would not dream of diminishing it), I suggest that, even

---

42   Patricia McCormack brings this statement front and center in her instructive article about *The Rules of Sociological Method*. See "The Paradox of Durkheim's Manifesto: Reconsidering the Rules of Sociological Method," *Theory and Society* 25:1 (1996), 85.

43   Lukes, *Emile Durkheim*, 4.

44   Thompson, *Emile Durkheim*, 39, 92–3. Thompson approvingly quotes the statement by Ginsberg that "in general, *la société* had an intoxicating effect on his mind," from Morris Ginsberg, *On the Diversity of Morals* (London: Heinemann, 1956), 51.

45   McCormack, "Paradox of Durkheim's Manifesto," 88.

if his sociology could be separated from his rhetorical mode (and I doubt this can easily be done[46]), much more than that is at stake. After all, a scientist's zeal does not lead a life separate from its human source.

Spiritual intensity and rhetorical excess in the work of Du Bois have, so far as I know, puzzled no one. Those qualities are routinely recognized in his work; he termed them double-consciousness and wrote about the experience. "Of Our Spiritual Strivings," an essay published in *The Souls of Black Folk*, gives us an imaginary conversation with a white compatriot who asks him, "How does it feel to be a problem?" For Du Bois, double-consciousness meant an irreducibly complex awareness of himself as his own self, an unsettled and always evolving subject, and at the same time as a despised object, fixed in caricatures, braced for the daily ritual insults of outsider-hood, enduring in all ways what Adolph Reed calls "the ascriptive lot of a racial collectivity."[47] But outsider-hood also carried with it an ability to stand on the edge of that very world to which he could not fully belong, and, from that vantage point, to see beyond its seemingly self-evident givens. He called that capacity "second sight." Here is the way he put those claims:

> After the Egyptian and Indian, the Greek and Roman, the Teuton and Mongolian, the Negro is a sort of seventh son, born with a veil, and gifted with second sight in this American world—a world which yields him no true self-consciousness, but only lets him see himself through the revelation of the other world. It is a peculiar sensation, this double-consciousness, this sense of always looking at one's self through the eyes of others, of measuring one's soul by the tape of a world that looks on in amused contempt and pity.

---

46 McCormack insists (ibid., 86–7), correctly I think, that no such separation can (or, indeed, should) be made.

47 Reed, *W. E. B. Du Bois and American Political Thought*, 105, in the context of a nice examination (91–125) of the various uses and abuses to which "double-consciousness" has been subject.

One ever feels his two-ness—an American, a Negro; two souls, two thoughts, two unreconciled strivings; two warring ideals in one dark body, whose dogged strength alone keeps it from being torn asunder.[48]

Du Bois waged battles to re-educate America's collective consciousness, partly to prevent the apparent justification of outrages of all kinds, and partly because this consciousness served as a mirror whose reflections were one source of a tormented double-consciousness among black Americans. He sought to disrupt the social processes that invented "the Negro" as the object that he called a *tertium quid*: more than an animal, less than a human being. Turn to Durkheim, however, and the corresponding battles become indirect and convoluted.

In an 1899 article, he conceded that certain failings of "the Jewish race" could be invoked to justify anti-Semitism, but insisted that those failings were counter-balanced by virtues.[49] Besides, he wrote, "The Jews are losing their ethnic character with an extreme rapidity. In two generations the process will be complete."[50] If he and Du Bois had spoken in that year, Du Bois might have told him that, in the last analysis, cultural similarity or difference was not the heart of the matter. His exemplary study of Philadelphia's Seventh Ward did not earn him a post at the University of Pennsylvania. This insult was tendered to "the Negro" he was, not to the cultured New England Calvinist he also was, with ancestral roots in America going back to before the American Revolution.[51]

Durkheim, however, embraced the France of the *Declaration*

---

48 Du Bois, *Souls of Black Folk*, 215.

49 Lukes, *Emile Durkheim*, 345. The phrase "the Jewish race" is Lukes's. It appears, however, that in the France of Durkheim's day, Jews and non-Jews used the language of race. See Marrus, *Politics of Assimilation*, 10.

50 Lukes, *Emile Durkheim*, 346.

51 Du Bois reflects at length on his genealogy in his 1940 autobiography *Dusk of Dawn*, a subjective, individualist genre that nonetheless bears the subtitle *The Autobiography of a Race Concept*.

of the Rights of Man, that is, not the France of Gobineau but the "color-blind" Republic. Unlike Theodor Herzl, who considered French racism vis-à-vis Jews to be an authentically native product, Durkheim regarded it as a German import, amounting to no more than "a consequence and the superficial symptom of a state of social malaise."[52] It was true, he conceded, that in France certain right-wing Catholic ambitions had started to batten on that malaise. But he reasoned that if anti-Semitism had indeed been the rank flower of Catholicism in the 1890s, its fresh flowers would have been in full bloom twenty years earlier, when religious sentiment was, if anything, stronger. Yet this was not true, he claimed; and so it was more likely that anti-Semitism was not intrinsic to Catholicism but an epiphenomenon of social disorder and economic distress. His solutions were to seek justice, to mend the social fabric, and to educate the French differently. I do not minimize either his analysis or his solutions; every aspect of the problem is complex.[53] I simply point out that he advanced nothing like the DuBoisian agenda of doing battle forthwith, and very directly, to take the *tertium quid* out of play and to replace it with a full-scale human being. Hence this from Durkheim:

When society undergoes suffering, it feels the need to find someone whom it can hold responsible for its sickness, on whom it can avenge its misfortunes: and those against whom public opinion already discriminates are naturally designated for this role. These are the pariahs who serve as expiatory victims. What confirms me in this interpretation is the way in which the result of Dreyfus's trial was greeted in 1894. There was a surge of joy on the boulevards.

---

52   Lukes, *Emile Durkheim*, 354.
53   The complexity of the question, even for Germany, is brought out in voting research that found that the Nazis never won the electoral support of Catholics in rural Germany. See the analysis and summary of voting patterns by Richard Wolin, "Between Fact and Interpretation: On the Social Misconstruction of Reality," *Theory and Society* 27:5 (1998), esp. 717.

People celebrated as a triumph what should have been a cause for public mourning. At last they knew whom to blame for the economic troubles and social distress in which they lived. The trouble came from the Jews. The charge had been officially proved. By this very fact alone, things already seemed to be getting better and people felt consoled.[54]

In other words, whoever or whatever cannot lay claim to "fellow-feeling" is available for designation as society's "It"—Du Bois' *tertium quid*—at whose expense that fellow-feeling is affirmed. Durkheim does not stop to examine how the *tertium quid* is created. Looking back years later, though, he placed in the late 1890s his revelation as to the importance of religion. I suspect that those observations about the Dreyfus Affair let us glimpse one intuitional source of *Forms*.[55]

What can be known for certain is that Durkheim reproduced this formulation almost exactly in the last chapter of Book III, on rites of mourning, which famously demonstrates the independence of such rites from the subjective states of individuals.[56] There again, however, he does not stop to examine how the expiatory victim and its fate come into being:

---

54 Lukes, *Emile Durkheim*, 345. Lukes drew this from comments Durkheim made in 1899 to a journalistic inquiry into anti-Semitism.

55 It is unimaginable that a work as complex as *Forms* would have only one such source. See Fields, "Religion as an Eminently Social Thing," xxvi–xxxi, which explores his religious upbringing.

56 In addition, that chapter examines in detail William Robertson Smith's *Lectures on the Religion of the Semites* (1894), to which Durkheim acknowledged a large intellectual debt in regard to the priority of rites over beliefs. It is also worth considering that the prevalence of anti-Semitism at the time would have set discussion of Smith's book afloat on complicated and sometimes troubling currents of opinion. See the flawed, yet instructive, analysis of Ivan Strenski, *Durkheim and the Jews of France* (Chicago: University of Chicago Press, 1996), and a review of it by Karen E. Fields, in the *Journal of Religion* 79:1 (1999).

If every death is imputed to some magical spell and if, for that reason, it is believed that the dead person must be avenged, the reason is a felt need to find a victim at all costs on whom the collective sorrow and anger can be discharged. The victim will naturally be sought outside, for an outsider is a subject less able to resist; since he is not protected by the fellow-feeling that attaches to a relative or neighbor, nothing about him blocks and neutralizes the bad and destructive feelings aroused by the death.[57]

POSSIBLE TOPICS OF CONVERSATION

If Durkheim and Du Bois had had a talk in 1899 that made explicit the common features of their different predicaments, Du Bois might have upheld his own public actions against "the Negro" as America's *tertium quid* by relating both of those passages to Durkheim's famous relativistic definition of crime in *The Rules of Sociological Method*. Following his own principle of relating social facts to other social facts, Durkheim there defined crime as that which is repressed in any given society, thus permitting the *conscience collective* to affirm itself. That analysis holds the criminal character of an act not to be intrinsic to it or valid for all societies. But if *Rules* was right in its claim that crime and repression of crime have the positive function of providing the means and the occasion for reaffirmation of the *conscience collective*, then, it would seem, pariah-hood would work analogously: Periodic affirmations of pariah-hood would then have the function in social life of permitting the periodic affirmation of insider-hood.

Looking ahead now to *Forms*: If Durkheim was right there, then in both instances, public opprobrium, ritually enacted, would

---

57 Durkheim, *Forms*, 404. What comes next is also interesting, in that its own "social construction" could have been applied to women's status, but had to await other minds. Durkheim simply writes: "Probably for the same reason, a woman serves more often than a man as the passive object of the most cruel mourning rites. Because she has lower social significance, she is more readily singled out to fill the function of a scapegoat."

simultaneously create and express what it will thereafter be alleged merely to have expressed. In addition to all the other achievements of mourning rites that Durkheim sets forth, they also define the boundaries outside which stands the victim. In Dreyfus's fate, crime and pariah-hood came together. As a citizen found guilty of treason, he was sentenced to deportation for life to France's steaming prison colony in Guyana. As a member of the army elite found guilty of disloyalty, he was subjected to a solemn degradation ceremony on the parade ground of the École Militaire as part of his sentence: the defacement of his uniform; the breaking of his sword; and the shouted insults of his brother officers, while a crowd added their voices from outside in the street. An artist's rendering of that huge ceremony in the courtyard of the École Militaire appeared in *Le Monde Illustré*.[58]

A different talk in 1899 might have exchanged programmatic statements that both Du Bois and Durkheim had made about the agendas each had for the properly sociological posing of social problems—Durkheim in *The Division of Labor in Society* (1893) and *The Rules of Sociological Method*, Du Bois in *The Philadelphia Negro* and in "Sociology Hesitant," an extended critique of American sociology that, for various reasons, he never published.[59] A talk in 1901 would have revealed Durkheim's invitation to leave Bordeaux for a post at the Sorbonne, there to keep building his *équipe* and its research journal. In addition, one aspect of his work at the Sorbonne would be to lay a scientific basis for secular public education in France. Durkheim would have learned that Du Bois had been dreaming analogous dreams in 1897, when he went to Atlanta University, there to busy himself with plans to build his own laboratory, his own team, and a series of publications. Du

58   Larousse, *La Grande Encylopédie* (Paris: Editions Larousse, 1973), 3979.

59   Lewis (*W. E. B. Du Bois*, 202) reports his belief that "Sociology Hesitant" is no longer extant, but dates its completion as some time after 1900 and characterizes it as a robust critique of regnant forms of grand theory that, at best, minuetted with observable facts.

Bois' grand proposal was to document the working-out of democratic ideals, central to the West for the previous hundred years, by conducting a broad-gauged, longitudinal study of emancipation in America—his *Atlanta Studies*. That talk about the successor regimes to slave-trading and slavery might, in turn, have led them to discuss the imperial élan of republican France, just then consolidating exploitative interests "in Asia, in Africa, and in the islands of the sea"—and, as two recent analysts put it, inserting "a ring in the nose of the republic."[60]

They could actually have met in person in 1900, since both traveled to Paris for the Exposition Universelle. Du Bois had major responsibility for an exhibit, which won a gold medal, on Negro achievement since Emancipation.[61] Durkheim was there lecturing at the Congrès Intérnationale de l'Education Sociale, an event that was part of France's contribution to the exposition.[62] Or they might have come to know one another by reputation through the *American Journal of Sociology*, for which Durkheim was an advisory editor from 1895 until the war,[63] and in which a response by Du Bois to a scurrilous paper titled "Is Race Friction in the United States Growing and Inevitable?" appeared in 1904.[64]

If the two had met in 1916, they could have discussed their respective patriotic writings in the service of war against Germany—with Du Bois making it clear that America's involvement was inevitable, as well as desirable. Let me mention these writings, but for now characterize only briefly certain differences between them.

---

60   Nicolas Bancel and Pascal Blanchard, "Le Colonialisme: un anneau dans le nez de la république," in a special issue titled "L'Héritage colonial: un trou de mémoire," in *Hommes et migrations* 1228 (November/December 2000), 80.

61   Lewis, *W. E. B. Du Bois*, 247.

62   Lukes, *Emile Durkheim*, 350.

63   Lewis, *W. E. B. Du Bois*, 247.

64   Ibid., 372. Lewis reports, in addition, that a brief commendation of Du Bois' *Atlanta Studies* appeared there in 1903. By the way, I do not assume that Du Bois was unaware of Durkheim's work. But since his papers have long been difficult of access, knowing about that must await future study.

Durkheim was writing government-commissioned pamphlets and open letters to the French, and so he was able to speak, as it were, in major key. By contrast, Du Bois wrote his wartime exhortations for *The Crisis*, the magazine of the NAACP, and in minor key. He insisted that black Americans must prepare to fight enthusiastically "over there" on their own behalf, as Americans of long lineage, while knowing full well that it was vital to prevent their enemies at home from adding disloyalty to the already long indictment of the race.[65] Both men looked forward to improvement after the war. Durkheim was enthusiastic about an "enriched vitality" and a heightened "moral enthusiasm," that could be husbanded once peace was re-established. Then, he thought, it would be possible to "revive the sense of community, to render it more active and make the citizens more accustomed to combining their efforts and subordinate their interests to those of society..."[66] Like Durkheim, Du Bois saw over the horizon of Allied victory and looked forward to renewed fervor—but the fervor he welcomed was specifically that of black Americans. Writing, as usual, in the minor key of double-consciousness, Du Bois felt certain, nonetheless, that victory by the Allies would help spread "new ideas of the essential equality of all men."[67]

In 1916, the two men might also have discussed each other's contributions to wartime documents of a different sort. As editor-in-chief of *The Crisis*, Du Bois not only continued to display Afro-Americans' achievements but also began publishing evidence

65   W. E. B. Du Bois, "World War and the Color Line," *The Crisis* 9:1 (1914), reprinted in Lester, *The Seventh Son, Vol. I.* In 1916, Du Bois campaigned for the training of Negro officers, even under the conditions of a separate, segregated training camp, and he detailed the exploits of Maj. Charles Young in Mexico and in Haiti, hoping (along with many Afro-Americans) that Young would be projected into leadership when America entered the war (Lewis, *W. E. B. Du Bois*, 517). Although its spirit is present earlier, Du Bois' famous (to some, infamous) piece titled "Close Ranks" did not appear until 1918.

66   Lukes, *Emile Durkheim*, 553–4.

67   Du Bois, "World War and the Color Line," 67.

of their patriotism and willingness to die for their country. Those displays were meant as Exhibit A against the gathering racist onslaught, and were produced in an extended report after the war.[68] Along with double-consciousness went what can be called "double death"—dying once for America and once for Afro-America. Dead or as surviving veterans, African Americans had to be counted as black dead or black survivors, else their sacrifices on America's behalf would not be recognized as such.[69] If Du Bois had been watching his colleague closely, however, he would have seen that Durkheim faced the same predicament—in his capacity as president of the Research Committee for Documents of the Société des Études Juives. By 1916, anti-Semitic attacks were on the rise, often taking the form of slurs against the loyalty of Jews, who were said to be German agents. Durkheim himself was publicly slurred by name at least twice during that year, notwithstanding the loss of his son to the slaughter.[70] In that climate, the Research Committee of the Société began collecting and verifying the names of Jewish soldiers killed, wounded, decorated, or promoted during the war. According to the Committee, "the love which they bear for their country does not command them to deny their Jewishness … It is not without interest to know how Frenchmen of Jewish origin, who have not embraced another religion, conducted themselves in the war."[71] Among France's fallen heroes, too, the outsiders had

---

68 Lewis, *W. E. B. Du Bois*, 501–34.

69 I note, however, that the African colonial non-citizens who defended France in World War I, as *Tirailleurs sénégalais*, gained a memorial near the main training camp, at Cazeau, only in 1967, and that their inclusion in Armistice Day ceremonies began only in November 1998, under the impetus of the Union des Travailleurs sénégalais. Interview with UTS members, Bordeaux, November 2000.

70 Lukes, *Emile Durkheim*, 557.

71 The results were published under the title *Les Israélites dans l'armée française*, in 1920 and 1921 by Albert Manuel, treasurer of the Committee and secretary-general of the Paris Consistory. See Hyman, *From Dreyfus to Vichy*, 57.

to die twice, once to defend the country against external enemies and a second time to defend themselves against internal ones. Wide publicity was accordingly given to the exploit of Rabbi Abraham Bloch, who was killed while delivering a crucifix to a mortally wounded Catholic soldier.[72]

"Individualism and the Intellectuals": A Fragment of Conversation

Therefore, a conversation in 1916 could have moved from the sad spectacle of double death to Durkheim's instruction at the start of "Individualism and the Intellectuals": "Let us forget the affair itself and the sad spectacles of which we have been witnesses." It would move from there to the fact that this remarkable piece does not mention Dreyfus, Jews, or anti-Semitism. The article does not so much attack the attackers as defend the defenders—and proclaims the central issues of the Affair to be the preservation and expansion of Individualism and Reason. Those, he claims, go "infinitely beyond the actual incidents and should be separated from them."[73] One need not claim otherwise to observe, nonetheless, that "Individualism and the Intellectuals" seems an abstract response to a blood-and-guts issue.

In that article, we learn from Durkheim that the individualism of the French utilitarians (also of Spencer and the economists) is rightly attacked as incompatible with social existence. But there is another "individualism," which he calls its "opposite," that was formulated in *The Declaration of the Rights of Man and Citizen* and is the very basis of social existence. This individualism makes the human person the touchstone of morality. It is individualist "because man is its object, and man is individual by definition."[74] The individualism of the Rights of Man takes on the character of

---

72 Ibid., 12.
73 Durkheim, "L'Individualisme," 7.
74 Ibid., 10.

a religion in which man is the believer and the God. Therefore, an attack on life, liberty, or honor is like profaning an idol. No *raison d'état* can supersede this individualism, contrary to Brunetière's claim, because it is prior to the state. This individualism has left its ivory tower company of Kant and Rousseau, and has so deeply penetrated institutions and mores that to remove it would mean reforging everything, top to bottom. Furthermore, such is the social diversity of the modern world that the only thing held in common is human-ness (*la qualité d'homme*). There is nothing to love and honor collectively, if not man himself. Far from being the source of anarchy, then, individualism is the only system of belief capable of ensuring the moral unity of the country. To defend it is therefore nothing less than to defend the very patrimony of the nation.

Durkheim goes on to describe the "religion of humanity, which has all it takes to speak just as authoritatively as the religions it replaces." This religion does not flatter the instincts, but does violence to them (a point about religion he makes repeatedly in *Forms*), for the sacredness of the individual does not arise from individual characteristics and individual characteristics do indeed work against solidarity. "This cult, of which the individual is agent and object, is not addressed to who the person is and has his name, but to the human person wherever met with and in whatever form incarnated ... It glorifies the individual in general."[75]

"But who is that 'individual in general?'" Du Bois might have asked Durkheim—as a prelude to recounting an enigmatic story about individual identity and collective identification, as he had experienced them during his travels through Europe between 1892 and 1894:

> My dark face elicited none of the curiosity which it had in blond Germany, for there were too many dark Gypsies and other brunettes. I saw poverty and despair. I was several times mistaken for a Jew. Arriving one night in a town of north Slovenia, the driver

75 Ibid., 11.

of a rickety cab whispered in my ear, "Unter die Juden?" [Among Jews?]. I stared and then said yes. I stayed in a little Jewish inn. I was a little frightened as in the gathering twilight I traversed the foothills of the dark Tatras alone and on foot.[76]

Du Bois: I know your "Individualism and the Intellectuals." When I wrote *The Souls of Black Folk*, everything within me pushed "How does it feel to be a problem?" onto the page. But, even if someone held a pistol to your head, I don't think you could write, "How does it feel to be a question?" It's as though everything within you pushed it off your page. You rest your case on a certain *qualité d'homme* that you suppose joins us all amid the diversity of the modern world. I think you've rested your case on shifting sand.

Durkheim: Ah, perhaps. But it is the only place I have to rest it. If in France we can just proceed with a scientific understanding of the kind of society France is, we can realize the promise of 1789. As I wrote in that article, "With social diversification, the growth of individuality reaches a point where the only thing held in common is human-ness [*la qualité d'homme*]. There is nothing to love and honor in common if not man himself. This is why man is a god to himself and can no longer make other gods for himself."[77] [Both savor this turn on the Ten Commandments.]

Du Bois: No doubt, my dear M. Durkheim, that elevated sentiment greatly calmed the very Catholic M. Brunetière. [Wicked chuckles from both.] I, too, know how to plant mines on my pages. But, you know, it's not the religious mines that blow the most shrapnel in America. It's, say, my comparing illiterate Negro peasants with illiterate Austrian clodhoppers, showing the published illegitimacy rates among the Negroes to be no higher. I need not be

---

76   Du Bois, *Autobiography*, 174–5.
77   Durkheim, "L'Individualisme," 11.

close enough to have a "cigar and a cup of tea" with a white Jim Crow Southerner to know his likely reaction to my transgressing the color line's etiquette, even with statistics. [Laughs.] Seriously, though, I am convinced you are right about the kind of morality we need. I myself wrote that one stream of modern thinking is "swollen from the larger world … [and that] the multiplying of human wants in culture-lands calls for the world-wide cooperation of men in satisfying them. Hence arises a new human unity, pulling the ends of earth nearer, and all men, black, yellow, and white."[78] But to leap from that useful unity to a shared moral humanity poses a question, not an answer, and it is the question for any "religion of humanity." You see, I went on to say this: Behind that stream of "thought lurk[ed] the afterthought of force and dominion—the making of brown men to delve when the temptation of beads and calico cloys."[79] So, in the end, who is *l'homme* that *l'homme* should take account of him? [They laugh, recalling the 8th Psalm.]

Durkheim: I know what you mean. How *l'homme* comes to recognize *l'homme* morally is the most important question our discipline can help us answer.

Du Bois: But you seem to assume, rather than demonstrate, that *l'homme* can possibly recognize *l'homme* in the abstract. I thought you showed precisely the opposite in *Forms*, that a man can become convinced he is as different from another man as a kangaroo is from a tree louse, when actually they all look as much like one another as you French do—or, as they say, you of "the Latin race." [Eyes twinkling.]

Durkheim: Quite so. You caught that one, did you? Vulgar empiricism will no more give you physical resemblance between a man

---

78 Du Bois, *Souls of Black Folk*, 271.
79 Ibid.

and a tree louse than it will the resemblance between two members
of the Tree Louse clan—or, yes, two members of our "Latin race."
That is that, for the vaunted races of Europe, and, besides, for your
different races in America. Human mentality is flexible enough to
accommodate the most disconcerting designations, *n'est-ce pas?*
The whole *raison d'être* of my work in education is that human mentality can also accommodate other designations that are, to Reason,
rather less *déconcertantes*. But we must inculcate the young with
them, and we must see that they are enacted periodically. *Forms* is
about a human world. That world exists through human doing and
is therefore our own ethical responsibility.

Du Bois: That is true. But even so, again I ask, "What constitutes
l'homme?" Let's suppose it means having a soul. If it's having a
soul, a spark of divinity from that divinized social unity of yours
in *Forms*,[80] then think about that unseemly outburst of mine, *The
Souls of Black Folk*. It was my Exhibit A for *la qualité d'homme*. In it,
I set my soul—our souls in colored America—against something
else: namely "the sincere and passionate belief that somewhere
between men and cattle, God created a *tertium quid* and called
it a Negro…"[81] All my words about "double-consciousness,"
and about how it feels to be a problem, finally led some people
at long last to suspect my—our—humanity, in other words, the
humanity of that *tertium quid*. Rev. Washington Gladden, gallant
warrior for social justice, went so far as to tell his congregation
that reading *Souls* would "give [them] a deeper insight into the real
human elements of the race problem than anything that [had] yet
been written."[82] The "*human* elements," notice. What on earth did
they imagine before? But if I had ever doubted what claiming those
"human" elements meant to some of my compatriots, the *New York
Times* reviewer dispelled all doubt: According to the *Times*, *Souls*

---

80   Durkheim, *Forms*, 265.
81   Du Bois, *Souls of Black Folk*, 271.
82   Lewis, *W. E. B. Du Bois*, 294 (my emphasis).

boiled down to something very simple. Du Bois' hidden personal agenda was "to smoke a cigar and drink a cup of tea with the white man in the South."[83]

Durkheim: So it is that way in America. Then again, perhaps I do know what you are talking about. A century and a half ago, Moses Mendelssohn was—how did you say it?—he was an "Exhibit A." Most people still doubted that Jews had *la qualité d'homme*. Some thought Jews might have it (those were the open-minded ones). And so, never having met *la qualité d'homme* in a Jewish body, they invented it as a purely theoretical possibility to debate over.[84] Enter Mendelssohn. His task was to try to prove, in the flesh, that "a Jew could be philosopher, aesthete, even Prussian patriot ... and most of all that ... a Jew could be virtuous."[85]

Du Bois: I think I understand, and that's not so very long ago. But look what happened next. If he was human, for them it followed that he ought to embrace Christianity. No, my dear M. Durkheim, I am unconvinced that it's enough to talk now only about shared universal humanity, your lovely *qualité d'homme*. I came to believe long ago that each group has its special gift and brings that to common humanity, a place where we can then agree—maybe—to be "co-workers in the kingdom of culture."[86] Even now, I maintain my position that peoples have to battle their way into common humanity, tribe by tribe.

Durkheim: What did William James say about your book? Since the 1890s, we've been reading with great interest his provocative

83   Ibid., 293.
84   Michael A. Meyer, *The Origins of the Modern Jew: Jewish Identity and European Culture in Germany, 1794–1824* (Detroit, MI: Wayne State University Press, 1974), 15.
85   Ibid., 18.
86   Du Bois, *Souls of Black Folk*, 215.

work in psychology and his philosophical arguments about the nature of truth. Was James not your teacher?[87]

Du Bois: Oh, yes. He thought *The Souls of Black Folk* was a "decidedly moving book," and he sent off a copy to his brother Henry, noting that it was written by a "mulatto ex-student of his."[88]

Durkheim: [Pauses] *Ah, oui.* I think I comprehend your predicament.

Du Bois: Let's come back to our *qualité d'homme* in this war.

Durkheim: It is true, my dear M. Du Bois. Your predicament and mine in this dreadful war is to record second deaths of our own people. It has not been enough simply to count the corpses—*hélas*. We cannot count and mourn everyone together in their *qualité d'homme*. Still, if we just take hold of the present vitality in this land, and guide it, we can complete the great work of our grandfathers. *Malgré tout*, I still believe as I did in 1898: If we build that religion of humanity as we should, there will be strong opposition to all that threatens our common faith. "If every enterprise directed against the rights of an individual revolts [us], it is not only by sympathy with the victim, neither is it for fear of having to suffer like injustices [ourselves]. It is that such attacks cannot go on with impunity without compromising the nation's existence."[89] I think sociology can enable us to bring that about. With it, we can uncover the profound dynamics of social life that make the social world we see before our eyes.

---

87   For a searching examination of what, if any, influences can be found of James's notions of double or multiple consciousness on Du Bois's, see Reed, *W. E. B. Du Bois and American Political Thought*, 100–5.

88   Lewis, *W. E. B. Du Bois*, 294.

89   Durkheim, "L'Individualisme," 11–12.

Du Bois: I read that article. You went on and on about Individualism and Reason. You got more and more heated as you went on. Such attacks can't be made, you thought, "without arousing the sentiments that were violated." Those were the "only sentiments that [could] bind the nation," so they couldn't weaken without disrupting the cohesion of the society. Otherwise there would be *un veritable suicide moral*—a veritable moral suicide. Without Individualism and Reason, there is moral suicide! Hellfire preaching, that, M. Durkheim! Still, you had the sinners dead to rights: men of impoverished conviction, you called them; they weren't apostles overflowing with anger or enthusiasm, you said; they weren't savants bringing forth products of research and reflection, you insisted. They were men of letters seduced by an interesting theme and playing games of dilettantes. So you thought it impossible that those games of dilettantes would manage to hold the masses for very long—if we knew how to act, you said. Your "we" was whoever, in democratic France, embraced humanity as the reason and the goal of morality.

Durkheim: I did say all that. I deeply believe all that. Yet I am, like you, reconciled to gathering invidious memorials of double death. For now, it cannot be helped.

At the time W. E. B. Du Bois began his work on the problem of the color line, Emile Durkheim had set for himself the problem of religion—in particular, religion's characteristic freight of false statements about nature and humankind, with their singular capacity to survive disproof. If he had not underlined his interest in "present-day" man, his itinerary might not have crossed Du Bois' in the ways I have suggested, and we might well hold that his study of Australian totemic cults has little to teach us about his social world, or our own. But for me, at least, *Forms* invites new sorts of conversation about collective identifications, formulated so as to link sociologists with colleagues who approach the study of human intellect with the different tool kits of disciplines such as economics, philosophy, and brain science.[90] If Durkheim is right, obvious physical difference is the wrong place to start, but so, too, is reason conceptualized with individualistic models.

Again, if Durkheim had conceived religion differently—for example, as the subjective experience of individuals—his intellectual itinerary might not have converged with Du Bois'. But those itineraries did indeed cross, because Durkheim located religion in human groups—in the social and intellectual processes that designate groups, their boundaries, their members, and the place of all the foregoing in the larger cosmos. Conceived that way, religion met race, not only in the rarefied world of philosophy and scientific theorizing but also in the real world of ethical choices and practical politics. I think this is why nowadays Durkheimian ideas find themselves on DuBoisian terrain: In studies of race, the notion of double-consciousness jostles that of collective identifications produced in social life. Even so, the two men's different approaches to the practical questions have not resolved into one. What is to be done is no more obvious now than it was on my invented Paris afternoon in 1916. I cannot say what difference it would have made if they had met. What I can say is that the stakes were high, as the unfolding of the twentieth century proved.

---

90 See, for example, recent work by an economist who stretches his discipline's methodological individualism toward its limits: Glenn C. Loury, *The Anatomy of Racial Inequality* (Cambridge, MA: Harvard University Press, 2001).

Conclusion:
Racecraft and Inequality

In the preceding essay, Emile Durkheim and W. E. B. Du Bois grapple with the racism that usurped democratic politics in France and the United States at the turn of the twentieth century. Our viewing them together stands as a reminder that what Americans designate by the shorthand "race" does not depend on physical difference, can do without visible markers, and owes nothing at all to nature. As the social alchemy of racecraft transforms racism into race, disguising collective social practice as inborn individual traits, so it entrenches racism in a category to itself, setting it apart from inequality in other guises. Racism and those other forms of inequality are rarely tackled together because they rarely come into view together. Indeed, the most consequential of the illusions racecraft underwrites is concealing the affiliation between racism and inequality in general. Separate though they may appear to be, they work together and share a central nervous system.

Does the election of Barack Obama add anything to the old story? When we proposed the present collection to a publisher during the spring of 2008, everyone agreed that we ought to mention the coming presidential election. No matter what the outcome, the nomination of a candidate of African descent by a major party seemed a significant moment. It was not self-evident, however, exactly how and why the moment was significant. If anything, it has become less evident since.

The significance of that moment is certainly not that racism has ended. A piece of gallows humor indulged in by a powerful Afro-American member of Congress, even as we pondered our conclusions, delivered a telling comment on the notion that the election signaled a "post-racial" era in American history. As was mentioned in Chapter 1, in late May 2009 an Afro-American police officer pursuing a car thief in the East Harlem neighborhood of New York City was shot dead by a white New York City police officer, who mistook him for an armed criminal. At a public event two days later, a reporter asked Representative Charles B. Rangel what President Barack Obama should do during a brief visit to the city that he and his wife planned for later that day. "Make certain he doesn't run around in East Harlem without identification," was Rangel's off-the-cuff response. Predictably, the remark drew clucks of disapproval from the mayor and parts of the press, and Representative Rangel soon apologized.[1] But what made the remark sting was its tasteless exposure of an undeniable truth. Although the president, surrounded by his Secret Service detail, is safe from any such mischance, other black men, even black police officers, are not.

It is true that racism is no longer, as in the past, the nuclear weapon of American politics, guaranteed to obliterate an opponent. From the Jim Crow era to Richard Nixon's "Southern Strategy" to the Willie Horton ads during Bush Sr.'s campaign against Michael Dukakis in 1988, an appeal to racism could not fail, even if, since the end of World War II, the fallout has often contaminated politicians who wielded it. (Orval Faubus and George Wallace spent the last years of their lives trying to dissociate themselves from the grandstanding segregationism of their political prime, and Lee Atwater, mastermind of the Willie Horton ads, was widely reviled up to his death and since.) Nowadays, public invocation of racism no longer

---

1 Nina Bernstein, "Rangel's Quip About Obama Provokes Critical Reactions," *New York Times*, June 1, 2009, A18; No byline, "Rangel Apologizes for Remark About Obama Visiting Harlem," *New York Times*, June 2, 2009, A20.

guarantees success. To the contrary, a racist insult directed light-heartedly at an American of South Asian origin helped to sink a candidate for reelection to the Senate in Virginia in 2006. And in April 2010, the governor of Virginia had to amend a proclamation of Confederate History Month that omitted any mention of slavery.[2]

Awareness that old-school racism is losing its potency stokes the rage of the die-hards. Thus have arisen such laughable antics as priming six- and seven-year-old children to chant "Assassinate Obama, Assassinate Obama" while riding a school bus in Rexburg, Idaho, the day after the election, and agitating to prevent the president from speaking to public school children about the need to study. (A talk-show host in Kansas City implied that the president could not be trusted around children. "I wouldn't let my next-door neighbor talk to my kid alone; I'm sure as hell not letting Barack Obama talk to him alone," he declared.)[3] Thus, too, have arisen less laughable antics: the circulation of shooting-range targets bearing the president's photograph, websites advocating assassination, and the carrying of loaded firearms to presidential events.[4] Though

2 Kate Zernike, "Macaca," *New York Times*, December 24, 2006, Week in Review, 4; Anita Kumar, "McDonnell Admits a Major Omission; Confederate History Month Declaration in Va. Altered to Add Slavery," *Washington Post*, April 8, 2010, A1. A self-identified "evangelical Christian who generally votes Republican" expressed dismay both at the failure to mention slavery in the proclamation and at the assumption the proclamation with its omission was meant to appeal to conservatives like her. Carolyn Keehan, Letters, *Washington Post*, April 9, 2010, A20.

3 Timothy Egan, "Hunting Wolves, and Men," *New York Times*, September 2, 2009, A23; James C. McKinley Jr. and Sam Dillon, "Obama Plan for Talk to Students Ignites Revolt," *New York Times*, September 4, 2009, A16. Agitation to prevent the simultaneous broadcast of the president's speech to other classrooms provoked counter-agitation in many districts and reversals in some. Dan Frosch, "District Relents on Obama Talk," *New York Times*, September 11, 2009, A16.

4 An attendee received applause at a town hall meeting in northern California in August 2009 for proclaiming himself "a proud right-wing terrorist." A candidate for governor of Idaho dismissed as "politically correct"

politically ineffectual, such activities are not harmless, given the ease with which homicidal zealots (like Timothy McVeigh, the Oklahoma City bomber) may acquire firearms, explosives, and lethal chemicals.

Even if troglodyte racism no longer plies the surface of American life, it still hides out in subterranean fastnesses, to emerge now and again in episodes ranging from the trivial (segregated senior proms in Southern public schools)[5] to the serious (the exclusion of Afro-Americans from jury service in several Southern states)[6] to the deadly (the murder of an Afro-American security guard by a white supremacist at the Holocaust Memorial Museum in Washington, DC).[7] Nor are persons of African descent alone in discovering that troglodyte racism remains just below the surface, Obama or no. In the spring of 2009, an all-white jury in Pottsville, Pennsylvania, found a Mexican immigrant as much to blame for his own death as the drunken white cowards who kicked and punched him to death in a six-against-one street assault. Many local white residents agreed with that verdict.[8]

While troglodyte racism breaks the surface only now and again, workaday racism remains a workaday reality. Obama or no, the

the widespread revulsion that followed his "joke" about "Obama tags" during a discussion of tags issued to would-be wolf hunters. He made the comment about Obama tags after someone mentioned assassinating the president. Timothy Egan, "Hunting Wolves, and Men," *New York Times*, September 2, 2009, A23.

5 Sarah Corbett and Gillian Laub, "A Prom Divided," *The New York Times Magazine*, May 24, 2009, 24–9.

6 Report by the Equal Justice Initiative, "Illegal Racial Discrimination in Jury Selection: A Continuing Legacy," June 1, 2010, 17–21, http://eji.org/eji.

7 David Stout, "Security Guard is Killed in Shooting at Holocaust Museum in Washington," *New York Times*, June 11, 2009, A16; Michael E. Ruane, Paul Duggan, and Clarence Williams, "At a Monument of Sorrow, A Burst of Deadly Violence," *Washington Post*, June 11, 2009, A1.

8 David Montgomery, "Melting Point; A Small Immigrant Town Simmers in the Wake of a Brutal Murder," *Washington Post*, September 2, 2008, Met 2 Ed.; Michael Rubinkam, "Immigrant's Beating Death Not a Hate Crime, Pa. Jury Decides," *Boston Globe*, May 3, 2009, 10.

poverty rate among black children is approaching 50 percent. Unemployment among Afro-Americans stands at twice the national average, and the rate for Afro-Americans with college degrees is twice that of white people with college degrees. At the end of 2009, an estimated 563,500 black men and 28,000 black women were in state or federal prisons, a rate of 3,119 per 100,000 US residents for men and 142 per 100,000 for black women.[9] While Afro-Americans accounted for 14 percent of drug users in the United States in 2006, they accounted for 35 percent of those arrested for drug offenses, 53 percent of those convicted, and 45 percent of those in prison for drug offenses as of 2004.[10] The penal disparity begins early. The case of a six-year-old Afro-American girl arrested by police officers and taken away in handcuffs for throwing a tantrum in her kindergarten class is extreme only because of the child's age.[11] Nationally, zero-tolerance discipline falls disproportionately on poor Afro-American children, who are suspended from school for minor infractions at a rate three times that of white children for similar conduct.[12]

Residential segregation, the outcome of deliberate government policy as well as individual actions, provides the material

9 Bob Herbert, "Far From Over," *New York Times*, May 9, 2009, op-ed; Dan Rodricks, "Jim Crow Alive and Well in U.S. Prison System," *Baltimore Sun*, April 8, 2010; Patrick McGeehan and Mathew R. Warren, "Black-White Gap in Jobless Rate Widens in City," *New York Times*, July 13, 2009, A1; Michael Luo, "In Job Hunt, Even a College Degree Can't Close the Racial Gap," *New York Times*, December 1, 2009, A1; US Department of Justice, Office of Justice Programs, Bureau of Justice Statistics, Bulletin, "Prisoners in 2009," December 2010, NCJ 231675, Appendix Table 15, 28.

10 The Sentencing Project, "Reducing Racial Disparity in the Criminal Justice System: A Manual for Practitioners and Policymakers," www.sentencingproject.org.

11 Bob Herbert, "Innocence Is No Defense," *New York Times*, August 4, 2009, op-ed.

12 Erik Eckholm, "School Suspensions Lead to Questions and Legal Challenge," *New York Times*, March 19, 2010, A14.

underpinning for many forms of everyday inequality based on racism.[13] The provision of unequal resources to public education in black urban and suburban neighborhoods depends on it. The purging of black voters from registration lists, using formulas based on zip code, depends on it.[14] The provision of inferior public goods and services in redlined neighborhoods (transportation, post offices, banks, street cleaning and lighting, trash disposal, policing, zoning) depends on it. So does the disproportionate placing of environmental hazards (sewage treatment plants, toxic waste dumps, manure lagoons, and highways) in or near such neighborhoods. The stranding of New Orleans residents during Hurricane Katrina demonstrated the lethal cumulative outcome of such inertial racism. Segregated in neighborhoods peculiarly vulnerable to a storm surge, they were further isolated by their reliance on public transportation in an automobile-centered society. Few onlookers praised them, however, for having green credentials. Instead, their car-lessness registered as fecklessness. If they did not load family and belongings into an SUV and drive to a motel when advised to evacuate, something must be wrong with them.

Racism and class inequality in the United States have always been part of the same phenomenon. Afro-Americans began their history in slavery, a class status so abnormal by the time of the American Revolution that it required an extraordinary

13   Ira Katznelson, *When Affirmative Action Was White: An Untold History of Racial Inequality in Twentieth-Century America* (New York: Norton, 2005), revisits the discriminatory administration and outcome of two warmly remembered legacies of the New Deal: the GI Bill and the Federal Housing Administration.

14   Recent attempts to purge voters of Latin American origin or descent have turned to more elaborate cross-matching of databases. See Robbie Brown, "Florida's Approach to Purging Voter Rolls of Noncitizens Prompts Federal Lawsuit," *New York Times*, June 13, 2012, A17; Lizette Alvarez, "Florida Defends Search for Ineligible Voters," *New York Times*, June 7, 2012, A17; Lizette Alvarez, "Legal Ruling in Florida on Purging Voter Rolls," *New York Times*, June 28, 2012, A14.

ideological rationale—which then and ever since has gone by the name *race*—to fit plausibly into supposedly republican institutions.[15] Emancipation discharged most of the former slaves into another status, that of a working class, that Americans, including the emancipated themselves, did not yet accept as a basis for citizenship. Like Jefferson, the former slaves regarded landownership as essential.[16] In the transition from slavery to freedom, anomalous class position defined Afro-Americans as a race. Once that definition became ingrained in social practice, improved class position might at any moment fall subject to a racist veto.

Even today, professional achievement can entrap a black person in the coils of a tacit sumptuary code. Thus, for example, an Afro-American former police chief dared not carry his weapon when off-duty in the predominantly white neighborhood where he lived. Having been stopped and questioned several times while out for a morning jog, he feared that carrying a weapon might turn an annoying encounter into a lethal one.[17] Nor is a black man's home necessarily his castle, as Shem Walker learned when he ordered a drug dealer (as he supposed) off his elderly mother's front stoop in Brooklyn, New York. The drug dealer turned out to be an undercover police officer conducting a buy and bust operation and, when Walker tried to shove him off the stoop, the officer or his partner shot him dead.[18] The whole incident—choosing private property for a potentially violent undercover operation in the first place

15 See above, Chapter 4.

16 "Committee of Freedmen on Edisto Island, South Carolina, to the Freedmen's Bureau Commissioner, and the Latter's Reply, doc. 108A," in Steven Hahn, Steven F. Miller, Susan E. O'Donovan, John C. Rodrigue, and Leslie S. Rowland, *Freedom: A Documentary History of Emancipation, 1861–1867*, series 3, vol. 1 (Chapel Hill, NC: University of North Carolina Press, 2008), 440.

17 New York State Task Force on Police-on-Police Shootings, *Reducing Inherent Danger: Report of the Task Force on Police-on-Police Shootings*, May 27, 2010, http://www.hks.harvard.edu (page 27).

18 Jim Dwyer, "A Fuller Measure of a Man Killed By a Police Bullet," *New York Times*, July 19, 2009, Metropolitan, 1.

and then deciding to shoot rather than leave when requested by the householder—would have been inconceivable at the home of a white person.

The initial designation of Afro-Americans as a race on the basis of their class position has colored all subsequent discussion of inequality, even among white persons. In racial disguise, inequality wears a surface camouflage that makes inequality in its most general form—the form that marks and distorts every aspect of our social and political life—hard to see, harder to discuss, and nearly impossible to tackle. The pattern began when slavery helped to mute class inequality by sheltering the white majority of the South from the cold winds of national and international markets.[19] Furthermore, the presence of slavery defined freedom, restricting the imaginative scope of democracy even for white people in the Northern states. Movements of working people ran into ideological headwinds when they claimed a birthright as Americans beyond the simple absence of slavery and formal equality before the law (for example, a ten-hour and, later, an eight-hour day).[20] During the Jim Crow era, many white voters in the South lost their right to vote under cover of the same laws that disfranchised black voters, while "good government" reform in the North often meant efforts to restrict the popular franchise.[21]

At the same time, however, the consolidation of Jim Crow set in motion a new dynamic of racecraft and inequality. With segregation and disfranchisement legal and explicit, complete with white-only primaries and a one-party system, a political bloc became entrenched in Congress that could define rights and entitlements for white Americans while making specific provision to exclude Afro-Americans. Allotments to the families of soldiers

---

19   See above, Chapter 4.

20   The classic account remains David Montgomery, *Beyond Equality: Labor and the Radical Republicans, 1862–1872* (New York: Knopf, 1967).

21   Alexander Keyssar, *The Right to Vote: The Contested History of Democracy in the United States* (New York: Basic Books, 2000).

during World War I, intended to preserve the absent soldier's position as breadwinner of his family, produced the unintended consequence of affording black soldiers' families the means of livelihood without signing on for domestic and agricultural labor for white employers. Thereafter, the Southern segregationist bloc dictated the exclusion of domestic and agricultural laborers from Social Security and other New Deal welfare legislation. Similarly, they designed the GI Bill to limit the bulk of its benefits to white veterans.[22]

The civil rights era inaugurated yet another dynamic of racecraft and inequality, by removing the legal basis for the exclusion of black Americans from both the body politic and the body social. When the long postwar economic expansion ended during the upheavals of the 1970s, white working people no longer enjoyed special white-only entitlements (such as GI loans and education); nor could space be cleared for them by explicit discrimination against Afro-Americans. Indeed, were every black job-seeker to be denied employment, there would still not be enough jobs for all white claimants, at a time when five people are vying for every job opening. (By the same token, as a wag once pointed out, if all the claims by white persons to have lost jobs because of preferences for black persons were valid, every black person would have to be holding down five jobs.) Today we live with a new version of the racecraft-inequality dynamic. With the economic deck now stacked against most working Americans and the white-only postwar bounty at an end, racecraft offers white Americans a plausible way to hold someone responsible, but not an effective way to seek redress.

Thus, for example, a white electrician in Martinsville, Ohio, held food-stamp users (visualized, no doubt, as Afro-American) in such contempt that he was ashamed to tell his parents that he himself needed government help to feed his family. His own family's need

---

22 Not until 1954 did these categories of workers become eligible for social security benefits. Katznelson, *When Affirmative Action Was White*, 42–4, 121–41.

did not soften that contempt when he "noticed crowds of midnight [food-stamp] shoppers once a month when benefits get renewed." Though a food-stamp user himself, out at midnight on legitimate business, he assumed that the people in the crowds were not on legitimate business. "Generally, if you're up at that hour and not working, what are you into?" he remarked.[23] Racism tagged the midnight shoppers as "into" something unsavory because they appeared to be out of work; racecraft concealed the truth that the electrician and the midnight shoppers suffer under the same regime of inequality.

Racism as readily prompts a suspicion that black Americans who hold jobs are "into" something unsavory, if they hold jobs from which discrimination previously excluded them. In 1990, Northern-based racecraft artists helped the late Senator Jesse Helms of North Carolina keep his Senate seat in a hard-fought campaign against an Afro-American opponent, Harvey Gantt. They devised an ad in which white hands crumple a job rejection notice while the voice-over says, "You needed that job. But they had to give it to a minority." So far from displaying a proper sense of shame, two campaign apparatchiks disputed authorship of the infamous advertisement.[24]

In truth, both black and white rural North Carolinians "needed that job." Unbeknownst to those taken in by the now-famous "white hands" ad, all would shortly face the departure en masse of manufacturing jobs, costing Robeson County, one of the hardest hit, an estimated $713 million in jobs, income, and business taxes.[25] The racecrafters contrived, via television, a collective hypnosis that stigmatized hardworking black people, while concealing the

23 Jason DeParle and Robert Gebeloff, "Food Stamp Use Soars Across U.S., and Stigma Fades," *New York Times*, November 29, 2009, 1, 26.

24 Eric Pooley, "Convention 96: Who is Dick Morris?" *Time*, September 2, 1996.

25 Leslie Hossfeld, Mac Legerton, and Gerald Keuster, "The Economic and Social Impact of Job Loss in Robeson County, North Carolina, 1993–2003," *Sociation Today* 2 (Fall 2004), http://www.ncsociology.org.

regime of inequality. Smoke from the fire of white workers' rage obscured the air-conditioned boardrooms where executives chose overseas destinations for North Carolina's manufacturing jobs, heedless of whether those left without work were white or black.[26] Racecraft operates on both sides of the screen, moreover. It provides a template for understanding inequality whose taken-for-granted rules are so pervasive that knock-off versions of them move down through the echelons. At a high school in a neighborhood where young black men had attacked Mexican immigrants, black students disparaged black classmates from backgrounds poorer than their own. In the same neighborhood, Mexican-Americans who had been born in the United States disparaged classmates born in Mexico. A black sophomore at a high school in the neighborhood apparently felt no stirring of either irony or historical memory when he pulled out of moth balls an old standard of segregationists: "I've got nothing against [Mexicans]. They work for my Moms. One even made me breakfast this morning."[27] Many a mistress from Jim Crow days distinguishing "her" Negroes from the general run might have said the same thing. The black and Mexican students could no more recognize their own circumstances in those of their classmates than the electrician could recognize his circumstances in those of fellow food-stamp recipients. In a manner of speaking, racecraft steps down the current of macro-economic inequality to suit the small appliances of everyday life and the limited purview of their hard-pressed users.

What happens when nothing is stepping down the current and inequality appears, full power, as what it is? Perhaps what happened during the fall of 2008, when a public outcry led the House of Representatives to vote against using the taxpayers' money to

---

26   In 2000, unemployment in Robeson County stood at 6 percent for white workers, 9 percent for Native American workers, 12.4 percent for Latino workers, and 16 percent for black workers.

27   Kirk Semple, "Young Residents on Staten Island Try to Make Sense of a Spate of Violence," *New York Times*, August 5, 2010, A23.

rescue failed bankers from the consequences of their own greed, incompetence, and folly. For a long moment, ordinary American taxpayers regardless of ancestry vented their outrage. "Tea Party" sentiments began to percolate, if not yet to crystallize or coalesce.[28] Fuming while bankers received what they considered their due and while CEOs landed in Washington, one-man-one-jet, to stake their claim for public assistance, working Americans of all backgrounds seemed to demand simultaneously: "Wait just a cotton-pickin minute." There stood the culprits, the outrageous embodiment of privilege in the midst of everyone else's loss. Their every gesture amplified Obama's call for Change.

At that moment, large numbers of people shouted a spontaneous "Hell, no," into the prevailing wind of politics as usual. But politics as usual won. The opposition party rescued a discredited president's plan to save the top 1 percent of the population, once again, at the expense of everybody else. Still, a fissure had opened through which one might glimpse, or at least imagine, a politics in which the mass at the bottom might stake a claim against the arrogant entitlement of the few at the top. The election of Obama held the potential, under those circumstances, to lift the taboo on public discussion of inequality. Racecraft being what it is, however, the chatter at the time fixed instead on the president's ancestry as the true significance of the moment. But what was truly significant was the election's taking place against a background of economic collapse that called in question thirty years' worth of apologetics in favor of inequality.

Inequality—of income, of wealth, of social prospects— supplied the raw material, the engine, the fuel, and the spark for disaster. Between 2002 and 2007, the income of the top 1 percent of American families grew at an annual rate of 10.1 percent, while that of the bottom 99 percent stagnated at a rate of 1.3 percent a year. In 2007, the top 1 percent of families received 23.5 percent of

28   Pat Dixon, "Libertarian Take on the Tea Party Movement," *Baltimore Sun*, March 31, 2010, http://weblog.baltimoresun.com.

total income.[29] No wonder real-estate prices rose above the decaying economy like a helium-filled balloon and no wonder financial instruments designed for speculation based on the balloon appeared and multiplied like maggots. The devil makes work for idle wealth, as well as idle hands. Meanwhile, modest salary-and-wage-earners survived by taking on ever-increasing debt. But metastasizing indebtedness could not overcome the consequences of inequality. CEOs earning 500 times the salary of their firm's average employee could not spend 500 times as much on items of ordinary consumption, no matter how self-indulgent or acquisitive they might be. Investment bankers surfeited with designer clothing, diamond-encrusted watches, fancy cars, yachts, aircraft, and extra houses still could not replace the aggregate demand for goods and services of persons whose income scarcely rose during the expansive years from 2003 to 2007. While those at the top were busy devising exotic ways to spend, invest, and shield from taxation previously unheard-of amounts of wealth, the bulk of American wage earners kept up their contribution to aggregate demand by borrowing, chiefly on houses and credit cards, to meet everyday needs.[30]

The ensuing collapse cost more than 2 million Americans their homes, depleted pensions, and wiped out savings for retirement and education.[31] Even discounting for the notorious understate-

---

29   Emmanuel Saez, "Striking it Richer: The Evolution of Top Incomes in the United States (Update with 2007 Estimates)," University of California, Berkeley, Department of Economics, Table 1, http://elsa.berkeley.edu; Lawrence Mishel and Jared Bernstein, "Economy's Gains Fail to Reach Most Workers' Paychecks," Economic Policy Institute Briefing paper #195, September 3, 2007, http://www.epi.org. As Joseph E. Stiglitz demonstrates in his recent book, which appeared while the present work was in page proofs, inequality of wealth and income increased in the wake of the crash of 2008. See *The Price of Inequality: How Today's Divided Society Endangers Our Future* (New York: Norton, 2012), 2–27.

30   Joseph E. Stiglitz, *Freefall: America, Free Markets, and the Sinking of the World Economy* (New York: Norton, 2010), 2–3, 312n.

31   Ibid., xi, 79.

ment of official unemployment statistics (which ignore persons
who have given up looking for work), the figure of 14.6 million
unemployed as of summer 2010 fails to capture the sensation of the
ground sinking under the feet of working Americans. According to
a survey by the Pew Research Center, 55 percent of the adult work
force suffered either the loss of a job, a cut in pay, or a reduction in
paid working hours.[32] That does not take into account prevailing
conditions on what someone has dubbed Back Street (in contrast
to Wall Street and Main Street), where poverty predates the current
collapse by at least ten years, where urban hunting of squirrels, rac-
coons, and rabbits ekes out family meals, and where a family of five
may crowd into a single bedroom.[33]

Governments at all levels, local, state, and federal, have been
forced to retrench just when the need for services is greatest.
They are turning off street lights, ending trash pickups, laying
off police officers, closing firehouses, hospitals, schools, day-care
centers, and senior centers, reducing school years, trimming hours
at kindergartens, libraries, and museums, eliminating health programs for the poor and unemployed, cutting back mail delivery,
and reducing public transportation while raising its price (or, as
in Clayton County, Georgia, eliminating it altogether).[34] The lost
income of furloughed or fired government employees threatens

32 Mark Trumbull, "Eight Ways the Great Recession Has Changed
Americans," *Christian Science Monitor*, June 30, 2010; Steven Greenhouse,
"More Workers Face Pay Cuts, Not Furloughs," *New York Times*, August 5,
2010, A1.

33 Barbara Ehrenreich, "Too Poor to Make the News," *New York Times*,
August 14, 2009, Week in Review, 10. Death is no equalizer, either, as a report
on disparate life expectancies at the top and bottom of society makes clear.
Congressional Budget Office, "Growing Disparities in Life Expectancy,"
Economic and Budget Issue Brief, April 17, 2008, http://www.cbo.gov.

34 Michael Cooper, "Budget Ax Falls, and Schools and Streetlights Go
Dark," *New York Times*, August 7, 2010, A1; Kevin Sack, "Medicaid Cut Places
States in Budget Bind," *New York Times*, June 8, 2010, A1; Michael Cooper,
"Struggling Cities Shut Firehouses in Budget Crisis," *New York Times*, August
27, 2010, A14.

further losses or closure for small businesses that rely on those employees' patronage—businesses already driven to the edge by the credit squeeze and the loss of customers through unemployment in the private sector.[35] The disaster also landed the United States in the absurd position of fighting two simultaneous, interminable, and vaguely defined foreign wars, while relying on foreign governments and central banks to hold the IOUs of the world's number one debtor nation.

The honest accounting that the collapse called for soon veered off-track, however. In mass-media commentary, the up-to-the-eyeballs indebtedness of the average household became a moral failing of the borrowers (incidentally opening a portal for racecraft), rather than the consequence of a skewed economic setup. By a subtle shifting of the kaleidoscope, the excess ceased to be that of bankers celebrating a coup in the mortgage market with $3,000 bottles of wine at lunch and became, instead, that of Jane Doe, who fulfilled a modest dream of owning her own home, for a brief while. First-time homeownership, once deemed praiseworthy, became instead the object of scorn: Ms. Doe was consuming above her place. The shadow of racecraft reached beyond Americans of African descent to darken the horizon of a wide swath of working Americans regardless of ancestry.

Meanwhile, as the jobs of ordinary workers went up in smoke, those responsible for the disaster imagined themselves its victims, and the media amplified their voices. Thus, a vice president of the American International Group, a company bailed out by the taxpayers to the tune of $182 billion, whined at being denied his

---

35 Small businesses employ over half of all private sector employees, pay 44 percent of the country's total private payroll, and generated 64 percent of net new jobs over the period from 1993 to 2008. U.S. Small Business Administration Office of Advocacy, Frequently Asked Questions, www.sba.gov/advo. Even businesses in well-heeled communities may succumb. Thirteen businesses have closed in a four-block area of Larchmont, New York, whose median household income is $154,000. Joseph Berger, "Empty Spots in a Norman Rockwell Downtown," *New York Times*, July 31, 2010, A15.

contractual bonus; after all, neither he nor his division caused the losses.[36] (Neither did millions of the unemployed whose firms fell victim to the banking crash through no fault of the employees themselves or their erstwhile employers; and the taxpayers neither paid them bonuses nor saved their jobs.) Press accounts underlined the difficulty of living within a salary of a mere half-million dollars a year, for bankers accustomed to multi-million-dollar bonuses.[37] A new genre replaced "lifestyles of the rich and famous": hardships of the super-rich-demoted-to-the-ranks-of-the-merely-rich. For the founder of McAfee Associates, hardship meant the "dwindling" of his fortune from $100 million to $4 million and the sale of three of his "homes," one of them a complex that included a general store, a cafe, a movie theater, several aircraft hangars, two guest houses, a swimming pool, and a fleet of antique cars for the use of house guests.[38]

A perverse language of moralism eclipsed reality. According to much of the commentariat, the subprime fiasco occurred because too many people coveted houses they could not afford. The truth, of course, is that no subprime borrower (or prime borrower, either, for that matter) secured a loan by holding a gun to the head of a mortgage company officer. Unemployed persons and minimum-wage employees might equally have coveted yachts, helicopters, and corporate jets that they could not afford; but bankers and mortgage company officials did not fall over their feet making loans for such purposes or packaging and securitizing them for sale to investors. Instead, they climbed onto the subprime bandwagon, because sensational fees beckoned as the real-estate bubble inflated, seemingly without limit. They discovered a sudden enthusiasm for

36 Jake DeSantis, "Dear A.I.G., I Quit," *New York Times*, March 25, 2009, A29.

37 Allen Salkin, "You Try to Live on 500K in This Town," *New York Times*, February 8, 2009, Sunday Styles, 1.

38 Geraldine Fabrikant, "Software Entrepreneur's Property is Sold at Auction," *New York Times*, August 31, 2009, B3; Ehrenreich, "Too Poor to Make the News."

subprime loans in poor neighborhoods that they had previously
redlined, that is, declared off-limits for lending. (Redlining continued, nonetheless, in a different form: high-income black families
were nearly twice as likely as low-income white families to end
up with subprime loans, even if they qualified for prime loans and
offered a down payment.)[39] Spreading the contagion around the
world, investment houses bought up mortgage originators, or
created new ones, because the packaging and securitization of subprime loans generated higher fees than conventional loans made
on prudent grounds.[40] In such reckoning as has followed the disaster, the prime movers in the economic collapse have all escaped
imprisonment for their actions. The only person to go to prison
for mortgage fraud was a man of modest resources who took out
a so-called "liar loan" with the knowledge and encouragement of
his broker.[41]

Inequality never stands merely as fact, as the way things are or
the way things are done: it requires moral reinforcement in collective beliefs. What beliefs and of what sort depends on place
and history. In a society in which each person was presumed to
serve "in that station unto which it has pleased God to call me"
(as the Anglican catechism used to put it), inequality was justified

39 Barbara Ehrenreich and Dedrick Muhammad, "The Recession's Racial
Divide," *New York Times*, September 13, 2009, Week in Review, 17. Redlining
goes back to the New Deal, when it was the official policy of the Federal
Housing Authority (later Federal Housing Administration). Katznelson,
When Affirmative Action Was White, 163–4; Marc Seitles, "The Perpetuation of
Residential Racial Segregation in America: Historical Discrimination, Modern
Forms of Exclusion, and Inclusionary Remedies," *Journal of Land Use and
Environmental Law* 14:1 (Fall 1998).

40 Stiglitz, *Freefall*, 85–90. Contrary to the moralist argument, the evidence
is that rich people are more likely than modest wage-earners to default when
their mortgages go underwater. David Streitfeld, "Biggest Defaulters on
Mortgages Are the Rich," *New York Times*, July 9, 2010, A1.

41 Joe Nocera, "In Prison For Taking a Liar Loan," *New York Times*, March
26, 2011, B1. Nocera, "The Mortgage Fraud Fund," *New York Times*, June 2,
2012, A21.

because God ordained it. That standard teaching had gone into eclipse in what became the United States of America by the time Jefferson and the other founders revolted against George III. Eventually, other doctrines came to uphold inequality. Up to the day before yesterday, the orthodox catechism in America held that inequality is a good thing because it promotes economic growth that (ultimately) benefits everyone, even if the benefits accrue only modestly, if at all, to those on the bottom. According to the dogma, efforts to lessen inequality, through progressive taxation or redistributive public spending, infringe the liberty of the rich. Furthermore, the rich deserve their reward. Ostensibly buttressing that view were studies suggesting that inequality in wealth and income results from genetically programmed differences in IQ. Intelligence determines merit, and merit apportions rewards. The racist implications of the most celebrated declaration of that thesis deflected attention from its implications for working-class white people: that, like Afro-Americans, white people consigned to the lower reaches of society were there because of low intelligence.[42] Until the curtain tore in 2008, criticism of inequality thus remained beyond the pale of acceptable public discourse.

From the earliest days of the republic, racecraft has lurked in the background, when it was not surging to the front, of any contest over the purposes toward which Americans might turn their political institutions. It ties our tongues and plants mines in our language. To many white Americans today, the word *welfare* irresistibly conjures up lazy Afro-Americans and cheating immigrants, until they need it themselves, like the electrician in Ohio. And even then, its associations cause feelings of shame that would be inconceivable to their counterparts in France, Germany, Scandinavia, or the UK.[43] Franklin D. Roosevelt enshrined freedom from want

---

42   Richard J. Herrnstein and Charles Murray, *The Bell Curve: Intelligence and Class Structure in American Life* (New York: Simon & Schuster, 1996).

43   By a very different route, the economist Jeffrey Sachs approaches this conclusion in *Common Wealth: Economics for a Crowded Planet* (New York:

among the "four freedoms" that he hoped the United States would champion throughout the world. But, to appease his party's segregationist power base in the South, he agreed to exclude agricultural and domestic laborers from the provisions of the Social Security Act. What is more, thanks to slavery, *welfare* had become a suspect word long before it had anything to do with social benefits for individual Americans. Slaveholders carefully excised the word from the Confederate constitution: theirs, unlike the federal constitution, did not undertake "to promote the general Welfare"; nor was the Confederate Congress empowered, like the federal Congress, to "lay and collect Taxes ... to pay the Debts and provide for the common Defence and general Welfare." After all, a government empowered to promote the general welfare might one day construe that welfare to require forcing the states to abolish slavery.

And what now?

Even as commentators at the time of Obama's election claimed to discern the coming of a "post-racial" era, their very harping on Obama as a "black president" reprised an age-old feature of racecraft: the turning of one person of African descent into a synecdoche for all. The classic historical instance is Booker T. Washington, anointed by powerful white persons to speak on behalf of all Afro-Americans, because disfranchisement had robbed them of the democratic prerogative of choosing spokesmen for themselves. Designating one Afro-American as a proxy for the rest masked the abrogation of democracy.[44] The token replaced the proxy during the Civil Rights Movement, when Afro-Americans began to reclaim their rights as citizens: a handful of students admitted to a white school to stave off calls for thorough desegregation, one person's accomplishment advanced as an argument against demands by the rest. "If Ralph Bunche can be ambassador to the United Nations,

Penguin, 2008), 265.

44 Adolph Reed, *Class Notes: Posing as Politics and Other Thoughts on the American Scene* (New York: New Press, 2000), 79–80.

what more do Negroes want?" went a segregationist refrain during the 1950s and '60s.

That bewhiskered ideological ploy resurfaced in the aftermath of Obama's election. When the newly installed attorney general charged that Americans are too cowardly to tackle racism, a political columnist retorted: "Barack Obama's election was supposed to get us past that."[45] In similar vein, a legal scholar concluded that the election of Barack Obama ended the need for the Voting Rights Act.[46] Americans of a certain age may think to themselves: "This is where we came in." Stokeley Carmichael's rejoinder to those who held up Ralph Bunche to forestall further agitation, "I can't have Ralph Bunche for lunch," applies today as it did then. Afro-Americans cannot have Barack Obama for lunch, any more than white Americans had George Bush for lunch. Nor can Afro-Americans, or any other Americans, have Barack Obama for the county council, the school board, the zoning authority, or the road commission. But local areas are where people live, unless they belong to the well-heeled and borderless cosmopolitan elite. Local circumstances form the material of their everyday lives. Whether children must walk through mud to reach a school bus in the black section of a rural county does not depend on the president's ancestry, but on whether the children's parents can hold the county road commission accountable.[47]

---

45 Maureen Dowd, "Dark Dark Dark," *New York Times*, February 22, 2009, op-ed. In the February 18 speech, Holder remarked: "Though this nation has proudly thought of itself as an ethnic melting pot, in things racial we have always been and continue to be, in too many ways, essentially a nation of cowards. Though race related issues continue to occupy a significant portion of our political discussion … average Americans … do not talk enough with each other about race." Remarks as Prepared for Delivery by Attorney General Eric Holder at the Department of Justice African American History Month Program, February 18, 2009, http://www.usdoj.gov.

46 Quoted in Adam Liptak, "Review of Voting Rights Act Presents a Test of History v. Progress," *New York Times*, April 28, 2009, A16.

47 J. Morgan Kousser offers a poignant lesson on the importance to people's

The racecraft-inspired political synecdoche short-circuits the issue of accountability. As President of the United States, Obama does not, in fact, belong to Afro-Americans more than to any other group of Americans. Arguably, he belongs to them less. Having kept his distance while campaigning for the presidency, he has continued to do so in office. President Obama, a columnist observed, "would rather walk through fire" than mention racism.[48] Though prepared to brave public censure for a multi-billion-dollar payout to the bankers who wrecked the national economy, he shied from intervention to hasten modest and long-delayed compensation payments for Afro-American farmers, approaching the end of their lives, to whom the USDA denied loans freely available to white farmers.[49] And he kowtowed with unbecoming haste before a false charge of racism leveled at an Afro-American official by a white blog-bully well known for mendacity and dirty tricks.[50] Wariness of appearing to favor Afro-Americans sometimes drives Obama to cultivate the appearance, and at times the substance, of aloofness from their aspirations.

The racecraft synecdoche operates asymmetrically, since there is no parallel category of "white president" for Obama's predecessors in office. It went without saying in the past that presidents were free to act in the interests of white Americans, and against the

---

lives of voting rights at the local level. See "The New Postmodern Southern Political History," *Georgia Historical Quarterly* 87 (Fall and Winter 2003), 445–7.

48 Bob Herbert, "Anger Has its Place," *New York Times*, August 1, 2009, op-ed, A17.

49 Ashley Southall, "Black Farmers' Bias Payments Come Too Late for Some," *New York Times*, May 26, 2010, A14.

50 In the shame-faced backtracking that followed the forced resignation of the official, it became clear that a malicious blogger enjoyed greater access to the White House than Afro-American elected officials who knew the full history and circumstances. Sheryl Gay Stolberg, Shaila Dewan, and Brian Stelter, "For Fired Agriculture Official, Flurry of Apologies and Job Offer," *New York Times*, July 22, 2010, A15.

interests of black Americans, without paying a political price. The sword of racecraft thus dangles over Obama as it would not over a white president who favored white Americans, or who simply treated them fairly. Right-wing opponents of health-care reform could insinuate, without provoking a horse laugh, that the purpose of the proposal was to benefit Afro-Americans.[51] The maneuver worked, not because the claim rested on any evidence whatsoever, but because the synecdoche made the argument without any need for evidence. Adept at racecraft ritual, the opponents knew that identifying health-care reform with black people would frighten away many white people who might otherwise have supported it. A right-wing blogger even dared to refer to Obama as a "welfare thug." He probably did not expect anyone to take the epithet at face value, any more than did the talk-show host who opposed Obama's meeting with schoolchildren by implying that he might be a pedophile. Both were manipulating a familiar device of race-craft to telegraph that Obama is "the black president," not "the President of the United States."

Nevertheless, it is of moment for everyone, not just for Americans of African descent, that Obama registers as a "black president" even while steadfastly refusing to act as one. Precisely because racism shares a nervous system with inequality in general, the same inclination to shun identification with black Americans makes it impossible for him to identify with the modest wage and salary-earners, the unemployed, and the working and disabled poor of all ancestries; in short, the bottom 99 percent of American society. It is one of the perversities of American public language that it is hard even to evoke these people—a majority of Americans, after all—without appearing to single out Afro-Americans; without, in other words, becoming entangled in racecraft.

Even as racecraft casts Afro-Americans as the heavies, it plants self-doubt in the minds of the growing ranks of white Americans

---

51   Ehrenreich and Muhammad, "The Recession's Racial Divide."

who feel the ground sinking beneath their feet. Once racecraft has ingrained the idea of food stamps as the province of undeserving black people, even changing the name to Supplemental Nutrition Assistance Program and replacing paper coupons with a plastic debit card cannot ease the shame of white recipients. Once race-craft equates the mortgage collapse with black people living beyond their means, white families unable to meet the mortgage or with mortgages underwater find themselves similarly tarred. Racecraft makes democratic possibility hard to imagine for all Americans, not just those who are directly in the crosshairs of racism. Racecraft is a ready-made propaganda weapon for use against the aspirations of the great majority of working Americans. Sooner or later, tacitly or openly, any move to tackle inequality brings racecraft into play.

The crude and stunted language available to discuss inequality and to stake claims for our due as Americans illustrates the powerful ideological undertow that racecraft sets up. For example: "Discrimination" and "reverse discrimination" are the closest we have to terms in which to claim a right to a sustaining job. They are not very close. Such terms presuppose that jobs are a scarce good, to be fought over by those in need of them, rather than something Americans can claim as a matter of right. They presuppose, too, that the moving of jobs overseas or their destruction in a banking collapse is an act of God, rather than a matter of public policy in which all of us have a stake and in which all of us should therefore have a say.

The United States has no such thing as a jobs policy. No public priority attaches to providing jobs for persons eager to work. The result is, in effect, a jobs policy limited to those at the top. The tax-payers rescued the jobs, salaries, bonuses, and perks of the bankers who ran their firms (and the American economy along with them) into the ground. Meanwhile, people put out of work by the bankers' shenanigans are on their own, punished a second time by employers who refuse to consider applications from those who have lost their jobs, "regardless of the reason," according to one advertisement.[52] Government may even encourage businesses to lay the fault for layoffs at the door of laid-off workers. In Florida, the state House and Senate differed over whether to reduce the duration of benefits for the unemployed or make it easier for businesses to represent the loss of a job as the worker's fault, rendering him or her ineligible for benefits.[53] The country seems to be returning to what Franklin D. Roosevelt dismissed long ago as "the so-called normalcy of the 1920's."[54]

A million and a half Americans had become "99ers" by the summer of 2010: out of work for more than 99 weeks and therefore ineligible for further unemployment benefits (and, in the eyes of some employers, ineligible for further employment).[55] Opponents of extended unemployment benefits eerily reproduced the language employed against welfare benefits back when it was plausible (though, even then, inaccurate) to portray the recipients as exclusively black. Government benefits discourage people from getting married and looking for work, according to one version popular in think-tanks and on Capitol Hill.[56] Meanwhile, American businesses have turned the elimination of jobs into a source of profit, even

52   Jane M. Von Bergen, "Unemployed Facing New Obstacle; Some Do Not Want to Hire the Unemployed Fearing They Were Lousy Workers," *Philadelphia Inquirer*, March 20, 2011, City-C Edition, C1.

53   Michael C. Bender and Jeff Harrington, "Jobless Are In Crosshairs," *St. Petersburg Times*, March 11, 2011, 1A.

54   Franklin D. Roosevelt, "State of the Union Message to Congress," January 11, 1944, The American Presidency Project, www.presidency.uscb.edu.

55   Michael Luo, "99 Weeks Later, Jobless Have Only Desperation," *New York Times*, August 3, 2010, A1; Bob Herbert, "The Horror Show," *New York Times*, August 10, 2010, op-ed; Testimony of Christine L. Owens, Executive Director, National Employment Law Project, Before the Equal Employment Opportunity Commission Meeting on "Out of Work, Out of Luck? Denying Employment Opportunities to Unemployed Job Seekers," February 16, 2010, http://www.nelp.org.

56   DeParle and Gebeloff, "Food Stamp Use Soars Across U.S."

with sales down.[57] (After all, who has the money to buy what they produce?) Just as companies are showing a profit without selling, so banks are turning profits by not lending—except to the United States Treasury, which provides them the funds in the first place, at virtually zero interest.[58] "The lions are being fed without having to hunt," is the way one 99er put it.[59] Her language, at least, was not stunted; but that of the Treasury secretary, heralding a "recovery" well nigh invisible to the unemployed, certainly was. To the desperation of people without jobs and the worry of those afraid they might soon be, the best answer he could manage was: "Private job growth has returned ... at an earlier stage of this recovery than in the last two recoveries."[60]

What have we the right to claim as Americans? What are we free to imagine? A decent job, a solid education, health care, dignity in old age? Like all ideologies, the prevailing ideology of inequality presents both a prescription and a proscription, an action and an inhibition, the thinkable and the unthinkable. A case in point. The city and state of New York and the federal government together pay a registered family day-care provider to look after a woman's children while she works at a low-paying, dead-end job as a waitress at an all-night diner. (Her husband has lost his job.) The day-care provider costs more than the waitress receives, or is ever likely to receive, in wages. The mother sometimes has to rouse her children in the middle of the night when she collects them from the day-care provider at the end of a late 10-hour shift.[61] It would be hard for her to visit her children's school, oversee their homework,

---

57 Nelson D. Schwartz, "Industries Find Surging Profits in Deeper Cuts," *New York Times*, July 26, 2010, A1.

58 Stiglitz, *Freefall*, 136–8; William D. Cohan, "You're Welcome, Wall Street," *New York Times*, April 20, 2010, op-ed, A21.

59 Michele Yulo Tucker, *New York Times*, August 13, 2010, Letters, A22.

60 Timothy F. Geithner, "Welcome to the Recovery," *New York Times*, August 3, 2010, op-ed, A23.

61 Susan Dominus, "Paying for Child Care, Unless It's From a Parent," *New York Times*, August 4, 2010, A14.

or read to them. She may even have trouble managing appoint-
ments for the children's (and her own) dental and medical care.
The thinkable, within the terms of reference of the prevailing ideology of inequality, is that a low-paying, dead-end, menial job is
better than offering the mother a cash welfare payment, no matter
how unwholesome the outcome for the children's or the mother's
well-being. The inhumanity of that judgment can be readily made
to vanish in the smoke of racecraft.

Once racecraft takes over the imagination, it shrinks well-
founded criticism of inequality to fit crabbed moral limits, leaving
the social grievances of white Americans without a language in
which to frame them. A thoughtful commentator illustrates how
unobtrusively the shrinkage may occur. He draws attention to
admissions policies at "eight highly selective colleges and universities" that place white applicants in certain categories at a
disadvantage. While participation in extracurricular activities generally works in applicants' favor, he points out, that is not true of
participation in such activities as high school ROTC, 4-H clubs,
or Future Farmers of America, activities associated with white
people in conservative or red-state America. He then resorts to
the characteristic language of racecraft, identifying his own list of
"underrepresented groups," working-class and mainly Christian
white people from conservative states and regions, and even
borrows the language of "diversity": "There's more to diversity
than skin color."

By framing the issue as diversity, the commentator has conceded
the game. However admissions officials may tweak their policies,
admission to a handful of colleges and universities will reach only
a handful of families, leaving the basic structure of educational
inequality intact. Alongside that vital concession rides an even
more damaging one: that graduates of such institutions constitute
a meritocracy, indeed, "*the* American meritocracy," from which,
he laments, the white working class is alienated. By saying so, he
contradicts the implication of his own argument. If admission to

the ranks is skewed and manipulated, then its members are not a meritocracy in the first place; they are a self-perpetuating oligarchy, even if they imagine themselves the best and the brightest.[62]

A similar shrinkage of moral imagination under the hypnotic influence of racecraft limits the means of redressing something most Americans would probably consider unjust if applied to themselves: the refusal of employers to consider job applications from the unemployed, regardless of why they lost their jobs. The practice is legally actionable, it seems, only if it produces a "disparate impact" on "older workers, workers of color, women or other protected groups," according to the executive director of the National Employment Law Project. What about unemployed persons who fall into none of those groups: white young-adult men, for example? The practice is equally unfair when applied to them, but lacks a legal rubric to make it actionable. In the shadow of racecraft, "discrimination" shoves "unfairness" out of the vocabulary available for public debate.[63]

Racecraft is an illusion that requires constant re-imagining. Therefore, even as it shrinks our mental world to its own pusillanimous measure, it takes up mental energy that we need for better things. The comeback of bio-racism[64] at this juncture is an act of destructive re-imagination on which well-meaning persons are now wasting precious mental resources. It is not a random occurrence, either, but a return of ideas developed a century and more ago to discredit a wave of new immigrants, most of them white, in an atmosphere of social distress amid excess not unlike today's. The resurgence of bio-racism recalls, too, the tangle that ensnared those charged with enforcing the ceremonial rules of the Jim Crow South. A woman who scolded Obama for checking

---

62   Ross Douthat, "The Roots of White Anxiety," *New York Times*, July 19, 2010, op-ed, A21.

63   Testimony of Christine L. Owens Before the Equal Employment Opportunity Commission, February 16, 2010.

64   See above, Chapter 1.

Racecraft

"African-American" on his census form (rather than "white" or "some other race") brings to mind the hapless streetcar conductors in turn-of-the-century Charleston, South Carolina.[65] Young Afro-American girls toyed with such conductors by boarding the streetcar in pairs of differing physical type, one black, one indistinguishable from white. The pair would sit together in the empty middle rows of the streetcar, laughing and chatting, while white passengers stared and pressure built on the conductor to send them to separate sections. Finally, he would order them curtly to "sit the way you are supposed to!"—meaning that the apparent white girl should move to the white section in front and her companion to the black section in back. At that point, both would move to the back of the black section, adhering to the letter of the law while making a fool of the conductor.[66] The woman upset over Obama's failure to fill out his census form "accurately" harks back to those conductors, chiding him for sitting with the black passengers.

People marching under the banner of biracialism and multiracialism, demanding "recognition" of "biracial/multiracial" bone marrow and umbilical cord blood and official sanction for "biracial" and "multiracial" as categories of human beings, may not be aware of the malignant history to which they are signing on. Other destructive imaginers know exactly what they are doing. A blogger with an on again–off again connection to the Tea Party deliberately sought to yoke racism to anger at bank bailouts, intrusive government, out-of-control spending, and tax increases by portraying the NAACP as their source and black people as the beneficiaries. He drew criticism only because his resort to old-style racism—in a mock letter to Abraham Lincoln, a former slave personified by the president of the NAACP called slavery a "great gig"—proved

---

65   Elizabeth Chang, "Why Obama Should Not Have Checked 'Black' on His Census Form," *Washington Post*, April 29, 2010, A17.

66   Mamie Garvin Fields with Karen Fields, *Lemon Swamp and Other Places: A Carolina Memoir* (New York: Free Press, 1983), 64–5.

both too brazen and too incoherent for many in the movement.[67] The instinct was sound, however. Skillfully invoked, racecraft can discredit any public policy initiative, good or bad, whether or not designed with Afro-Americans in mind.

The destructive imagination that inflates the racecraft balloon sucks away oxygen from the constructive imagining that we urgently need, and does so to the disadvantage of all working Americans, not just black or white ones. For example, if the imagination expended in devices to restrict high-quality education to a privileged few—coaches, consultants, ghost writers for college application essays, even (God save the mark) test prep courses for a kindergarten entrance exam—were devoted instead to repairing our dilapidated system of public education, fifteen-year-olds in the United States might not rank fifteenth out of twenty-nine OECD countries in reading literacy, twenty-first out of thirty in scientific literary, and twenty-fifth out of thirty in mathematics literacy.[68] Private schools and public schools in segregated suburbs may seem to promise "better" education for those in a position to attain them; but "better" does not always mean good enough, as anyone who teaches the products of such schooling (as the authors do) knows full well. For example, international students for whom English is a second language often have a better grasp of English grammar, syntax, and spelling than American native speakers trained at elite secondary schools.

Racecraft operates like a railroad switch, diverting a train from one track to another. It is unlike a railroad switch, however, in that the switchman seldom controls where the train ends up. It may end up on a siding in the middle of nowhere, its passengers stranded. By crowding inequality off the public agenda, racecraft has stranded

---

67 Helen Kennedy, "Tea Party Bags Big-Mouthed Fool," *New York Daily News*, July 19, 2010, 10.

68 Alliance for Excellent Education, Fact Sheet, "How Does the United States Stack Up? International Comparisons of Academic Achievement," March 2008, http://www.all4ed.org.

this country again and again over its history. It may do so again, permitting an economic sickness that arose from inequality to be treated homeopathically by further doses of inequality, which may eventually provoke rage that will sweep away respect for democratic politics and for the rule of law. Forestalling that calamity is our duty. The first and fundamental step in that direction is to observe racecraft in action, study its moves, listen to its language, and root it out. Only after doing so will we be prepared for the still harder work of tackling inequality. Are we up to it?

Occupy Wall Street erupted on the scene after we had sent the manuscript of *Racecraft*, including the foregoing, to our publisher. Spreading from an encampment in lower Manhattan in New York City, it set off echoes across the country. Like the Tea Party, Occupy Wall Street caught the imagination of a broad public convinced that the economic system is rigged against them. Unlike the Tea Party, Occupy Wall Street broke the taboo against making an explicit issue of inequality. It is too soon to know whether the taboo has been broken for now, let alone broken for good, or whether raising the cry of "class warfare" in defense of the well-heeled few will prove effective in reinstating it. It seems unlikely that persons whose salaries, benefits, and retirement are under siege, whose mortgages are underwater, and who live in fear of being laid off (let alone the working poor and the long-term unemployed) will easily accept a portrait of high-flying financiers and overpaid CEOs as job creators or as creators of wealth for anyone other than themselves. But unlike arguments for the benefits of inequality, racecraft does not depend on plausibility for its effectiveness. A presidential candidate's equation of "redistribution" with "redistribution to black people" and the effort to discredit a generation of laws against racist discrimination suggest that defenders of inequality may yet find the old-time religion—racecraft—to be a very present help amid awkward questions.

Acknowledgments

This book has taken shape over many years and in exchanges, spoken and written, with many interlocutors, some now deceased: teachers, colleagues, students, family, and friends. Although the footnotes identify some of our creditors in those categories, we must acknowledge others without calling their names. Here, we especially wish to acknowledge debts, some incurred individually and others jointly, to persons who have contributed to *Racecraft* in its current form.

Barbara wishes to express appreciation to Elizabeth Blackmar, William Leach, and Leslie S. Rowland who, as colleagues and friends, have listened over the years to her ideas on these matters and shared their own; to former graduate students and now colleagues Monica Gisolfi, Sam Haselby, Reiko Hillyer, Junko I. Kato, Adrienne Petty Roberts, Adam Rothman, and Michael R. West, who have traded ideas and, in some cases, contributed items for her "Inequality" and "Race Nonsense" files; to Gregory Baggett who, as doctoral student and teaching assistant, has helped to refine her ideas; and to Rodman Williams, a former undergraduate student who brings dispatches from the trenches during his annual visits to hear the latest metamorphosis of the "Invention of Race" lecture in her undergraduate "History of the South" course.

Karen wishes to express appreciation to Moussa Bagate, George C. Bond, Arthur Burghardt, Nahum Chandler, Ayala Emmett,

Nargis Harris, Christian Lerat, Danielle Ménauge, Nicole Ollier, and Michael O. West, who listened or read or supplied critique when asked, and who worked and worried with her, without being asked. Grants from the National Endowment for the Humanities and the American Council of Learned Societies supported parts of the research. The Maison des sciences de l'homme d'Aquitaine (Bordeaux, France) provided intellectual community. Well-read, resourceful librarians at the Boatwright Library, University of Richmond, and at the Tuckahoe Branch of the Henrico County Public Library never failed to locate needed documents nor stopped suggesting new trails.

First among those to whom the authors have incurred a joint debt is Maïmouna F. Bagate, adjutant extraordinaire. In addition to lending technical help in preparing the manuscript, she pitched in as proofreader, copy-editor, and auxiliary editor. Proceeding above and beyond the call of duty, she also proposed topics and illustrative material for inclusion and shared her expertise in biological matters, saving us from several blunders. In the midst of work on his own book, Robin Blackburn responded to a request for comments with a reading more thorough and detailed than many referee reports for publishers, capping that performance by putting us in touch with our current publisher. For reading chapters or the entire manuscript (sometimes more than once) and offering suggestions and encouragement, we thank Ira Berlin, Peter Dimock, Joseph L. Graves, Charles Grench, Junko Kato, Ira Katznelson, the late Jack Temple Kirby, David Lowenthal, Jonathan Marx, Edward Mendelson, Stephan Palmié, Ramzi Rouighi, and the anonymous readers for Columbia and Chapel Hill presses. Although he did not see Racecraft while we were at work on it, Martin Kilson has animated our thinking on these matters, and offered encouragement, since our undergraduate days. We only recently became acquainted with Geri Thoma, now our agent, but quickly came to appreciate both her professional skill and her understanding of the political and moral questions that are at stake in *Racecraft*.

Index

creator of social facts 231; of
deference and dominance 25,
35–37, 82–84, 137, 139, 188–9
Roosevelt, Franklin D. 79, 278, 284
Roosevelt, Theodore 34, 39
Rosenwald Day program 85
Rules of Sociological Method, The
(Durkheim) 242, 247, 248

Santayana, George 63
scapegoating 198
Scudder, John 59–62
segregation 17, 25–26, 77–78, 117,
161–63, 233–34, 287–88; blood
60; individual experience 82–84,
84–86, 86–88; and inequality
265–66; prison 45
"separate but equal," doctrine of 210
separate versus together 77–78, 93
Shadow and Act (Ellison) 105
Shaler, Nathaniel Southgate 41
Sickle Cell Control Act (1972) 55
sickle-cell disease 53–56, 64–65
Simpson, Lewis 143n
Simpson, O. J. 216
"single race" 115–16
skin color 8, 26–27
slaves and slavery 75, 86, 111, 117,
161, 266, 268; abolition 136,
141; and the Afro-American
experience 96; breeding 112;
Constitution's three-fifths
clause 118; corruption of 99;
development of custom and law
124–28; emancipation 128, 154n,
266–67; escapees 79–81; growth
in trade 127; ideology 141,
143–45; Jefferson on corruption
of 99; Jefferson and race-
racism evasion 97–99; Jefferson

and racecraft 18; legal status
established 130; origins 122–23;
in perpetuity 125; rule of descent
130; slaveholdings 131–32;
subordination 137; in Tudor
England 123
Snyder, Jimmy "the Greek" 112–13,
114n
"social equality" 39–40
Social Security Act 278
social landscape, Old South 140,
140–45
"Sociology Hesitant" (Du Bois) 248
soul (Durkheim) 202
Souls of Black Folk, The (Du Bois)
243–44, 254, 256–58
"Southern Strategy" 47, 262
South, the: anti–Yankee solidarity
88–90; federal patronage 34;
Free Negroes 143n; herrenvolk
democracy 144n; homestead
exemption 133; non-slaveholders
133; racial ideology 143–45;
Spain 106
spirit beliefs 212–14, 219–20, 222–23
stereotypes 71–72, 147
sterilization, compulsory 42–43
storytelling (Walter Benjamin)
180–81
Strange Career of Jim Crow, The
(Woodward) 161
subordination 84, 137–38, 141, 145
subprime mortgage crisis 271–77
Suicide: A Study in Sociology
(Durkheim) 230n, 237
sumptuary rules 25, 33–40, 70,
85–86, 267
supernatural, the 97, 99, 202
superstition 19, 20, 23, 101, 112
Supplemental Nutrition Assistance

product of thought and language
22; shared features with racecraft
198–200, 224; trials 23; undoing
power of 218; *see also* cause and
effect
*Witchcraft, Oracles and Magic Among
the Azande* (Evans-Pritchard)
194–95, 196–98, 205, 205–6;
legacy 219–24
Woods, Tiger 109
Woodward, C. Vann 149–69, 218;
on Afro-Americans 165–67; and
capitalism 163; and difference
152–53; on disfranchisement
154–56; on integration 161n;
international comparisons
165; on Jim Crow 159–61,
169; and language 167–69; on

lynchings 163–65; method
150; and Redeemers 153–54;
on segregation 161–63; use of
secondary literature 166–67; on
white supremacy 160
workaday racism 264–65
World Turned Upside Down, The
(Hill) 187
World War I 249–52, 258, 268; and
casualties 251–52
World War II 10, 51, 58–59
yeomanry (white non-slaveholders)
131–36; ideology of 134; social
independence 133–34
Young Man Luther (Erikson) 20n

Zephyr (LBJ's cook) 26
Zola, Emile 233n

On the Typeface

Racecraft is set in Monotype Fournier, a typeface based on the designs of the eighteenth-century printer and typefounder Pierre Simon Fournier. He in turn was influenced by the constructed type designs of the Romain du Roi, commissioned by Louis XIV in 1692, which eschewed the calligraphic influence of prior typefaces in favor of scientific precision and adherence to a grid.

With its vertical axis, pronounced contrast, and unbracketed serifs, the Fournier face is an archetype of the "transitional" style in the evolution of Latin printing types—situated between the "old style" fonts such as Bembo and Garamond and the "modern" faces of Bodoni and Didot. Other distinguishing features include the proportionally low height of the capitals and the lowercase "f," with its tapered and declining crossbar.

The italics, which were designed independently, have an exaggerated slope with sharp terminals that retain the squared serifs in the descenders.

The Fournier design was commissioned as part of the Monotype Corporation's type revival program under the supervision of Stanley Morison in the 1920s. Two designs were cut based on the "St Augustin Ordinaire" design shown in Fournier's *Manuel Typographique*. In Morison's absence, the wrong design was approved, resulting in the typeface now known as Fournier.